T0322033

The Internet of
Mechanical Things

The Internet of Mechanical Things
The IoT Framework for Mechanical Engineers

Sami Salama Hussen Hajjaj and
Kisheen Rao Gsangaya
Centre for Advance Mechatronics and Robotics (CaMaRo),
Institute of Informatics and Computing in Energy (IICE),
College of Engineering, National Energy University
(Universiti Tenaga Nasional), Malaysia

CRC Press
Taylor & Francis Group
Boca Raton London New York

CRC Press is an imprint of the
Taylor & Francis Group, an **informa** business

MATLAB® is a trademark of The MathWorks, Inc. and is used with permission. The MathWorks does not warrant the accuracy of the text or exercises in this book. This book's use or discussion of MATLAB® software or related products does not constitute endorsement or sponsorship by The MathWorks of a particular pedagogical approach or particular use of the MATLAB® software

First edition published 2022
by CRC Press
6000 Broken Sound Parkway NW, Suite 300, Boca Raton, FL 33487-2742

and by CRC Press
2 Park Square, Milton Park, Abingdon, Oxon, OX14 4RN

CRC Press is an imprint of Taylor & Francis Group, LLC

ISBN: 9781032110950 (hbk)
ISBN: 9781032110974 (pbk)
ISBN: 9781003218395 (ebk)

DOI: 10.1201/9781003218395

Typeset in Times
by codeMantra

Sami Salama Hussen Hajjaj

I dedicate this work to the spirit of my two fathers who recently passed away: my father and teacher, Salama Hussen Hajjaj, and my father-in-law, Abd Karim Md Hashim. Both of these men played a role in making me who I am today, so I dedicate this book to their memories.

I also would like to dedicate this book to my wife, Ella Karim Hashim, and my two children, Faris and Nabeil Hajjaj. Their love and support helped me push through hard times, and I could not have completed this work without their love. Finally, I dedicate this book to my family, my in-laws, and my friends and colleagues. Thank you.

Kisheen Rao Gsangaya

I would like to express my sincere appreciation and dedicate this book to my beloved parents, Gsangaya Sannasi and Parameswary Appanan, for raising me to be the person I am today. I also dedicate this book to my siblings, Manoj Rao, Muhindra Rao, and Shasi Rao, for always standing by me through thick and thin.

Lastly, I would like to thank my best friend, Manisha Stella, who has always been a source of strength through testing times. The love and support of my family and friends will always be a major spiritual motivation in my life.

Endorsements

"An excellent effort, superbly written by fellow expert mechanical engineers with years of experience in the topic, *IoT for Mechanical Engineers* benefits all mechanical and industrial engineers, especially in the era of Industry 4.0 and Digitization. With a balance of theories, strategies and hands-on training, I would recommend this book to everyone within the engineering world."

Prof. Ir Ts Dr. Vinesh Thiruchelvam
Regional Chair – South East Asia Region
Vice Chair International Strategy Board (ISB)
Institute of Mechanical Engineers (IMechE-UK)

"*IoT for Mechanical Engineers* is a great learning tool for those interested to learn about the Internet of Things from the perspective of Mechatronics, Automation, and Robotics. Aside from the extensive coverage on IoT theory, strategies and hands-on systems development, the book also covers remotely monitored/operated autonomous systems, IoT Robotics, multi-agent systems, and more."

Assist. Prof. Dr. Mohamed Khan
Chairman
IEEE Robotics & Automation Society (IEEE/RAS)
Malaysia Chapter

Contents

PART I *Theory and Concepts*

PART II   Hands-On System Development

Preface

In early 2016, while working on my PhD, on the Robot Operating System (ROS), I enrolled in a training titled *IoT with Raspberry Pi*. I had heard about Internet of Things (IoT) and I always wanted to learn more about it.

In that training, I discovered that IoT employs many technologies, frameworks, and skillsets that I had already covered in my PhD and prior research experience, namely, *C++*, *Python*, *Java*, other languages, the Linux Operating System, Cloud Computing, Web and App Development, and Mechatronics. It was then, even before completing my PhD, that I decided to focus on IoT research. In the following years, I completed many projects on IoT in several sectors, including agriculture, education, infrastructure, industry, and, of course, Robotics and Automated Systems.

My unique background, a mechanical engineer working on non-mechanical topics (Software, Electrical & Electronics, and IT), gave me a unique perspective. I recognized the dilemma my fellow mechanical engineers faced when working on IoT or related topics. This was even clearer during my IoT training sessions, based on the feedback and reactions I received from mechanical engineering participants. I realized that mechanical engineers (or, in general, all engineers not from Software, E&E or IT) need a specialized guide into the IoT world, which motivated me to write this book.

I met Kisheen Rao when he enrolled in my Robotics course in 2017. Soon we realized we share similar interests. Despite being a mechanical engineering student, Kisheen excelled in electronics, software, and embedded systems (Arduino).

Through the years, we worked together on IoT research and development, training, and education. We completed several projects together, co-authored papers and patents, conducted training sessions together, and presented our works at international events together. So it is only natural that we work on this book together as well.

Finally, we sincerely hope that our humble effort could help make a difference in the world.

The authors.

MATLAB® is a registered trademark of The MathWorks, Inc. For product information, please contact:

The MathWorks, Inc.
3 Apple Hill Drive
Natick, MA 01760-2098 USA
Tel: 508-647-7000
Fax: 508-647-7001
E-mail: info@mathworks.com
Web: www.mathworks.com

Author Biographies

Sami Salama Hussen Hajjaj, PhD, PEng, CEng is an academic with more than 15 years of experience in engineering education, research, and administration. His areas of interest include Automation, Robotics, Robot Systems, the Internet of Things (IoT), Data Science (Machine Learning), Engineering Education, and impact of Technology on Society. His projects cover a wide range of fields, including Infrastructure, Renewable Energy, Industrial Robotics, Agriculture Automation, Robots for TV and Film, and Educational Robots, among others. He taught courses on related topics, published journal papers, conducted training in multiple countries, registered patents and other intellectual properties (on IoT and Robotics), and won several international and industry innovation awards on related topics. He is a Professional Engineer (PEng), a Chartered Engineer (CEng), a Senior Member of IEEE (SMIEEE), a Certified IoT Specialist (CIoTs), and a Certified Professional Trainer.

Kisheen Rao Gsangaya holds a Master's in mechanical engineering, and has been working on Internet of Things (IoT) projects since 2017. For his Master's, he focused on IoT and its applications in agriculture, energy, vehicle systems, and others. He has published several papers and patents on related fields and has won numerous awards at university, national, and international levels.

He is a member of the Centre for Advance Mechatronics and Robotics (CaMaRo), specializing in controller programming, artificial intelligence, machine learning, and embedded systems. He contributed in developing the IoT training manual targeted for undergraduate students, from the student perspective, and co-conducted many of these hands-on sessions, under the supervision of his mentor, Dr Hajjaj. Upon graduation with first-class honours, he founded *EzyChip Technologies*, an engineering solutions company specializing in robotics, autonomous systems, IoT solutions, and related technologies. He is also a registered Graduate Engineer with the Board of Engineers Malaysia.

About This Book

This book aims to cater to everyone interested in the Internet of Things (IoT); this includes *Decision makers* and *Practitioners*.

Decision makers are the industry leaders and policymakers who want to learn about IoT and its related strategies and decisions. This includes Directors, Managers, and Owners.

Practitioners are those who would be involved in IoT system development and related technologies, such as engineers, designers, developers, programmers, trainers, educators, and students. As such, the content of this book is organized as follows:

Part I: Theory and Concepts
    Chapter 1: The Internet of Things (IoT)
    Chapter 2: Foundation Topics: Concepts

Part II: Hands-On System Development
    Chapter 3: Foundation Topics: Programming
    Chapter 4: Arduino-Based IoT Systems
    Chapter 5: Raspberry Pi-Based IoT Systems

As seen in the list, Part I focuses on building a solid foundation in IoT theory and concepts and discusses IoT implementation and deployment strategies. In Part II, we focus on honing the technical skills needed to implement these strategies and effectively develop IoT systems.

So, for best results, we strongly recommend that you complete all the chapters in this book, theory and hands-on, as this would allow you to get fully immersed into the world of IoT. This choice, of course, depends on your learning needs and requirements.

Concepts Revisited

Some readers might skip some chapters of this book; perhaps some are interested in the concepts and strategies alone. Others might be already familiar with these concepts and could skip directly to Chapter 4 or 5. So, this book is designed to cater for everyone.

You will notice that some foundation topics mentioned in earlier chapters are revisited in later chapters, perhaps re-introduced or expanded on from earlier discussions. For example, we first introduce *Linux Commands* in Chapter 3 as a foundation skill. Later, we revisit the same topic in Chapter 5 as part of the discussion on the *Raspberry Pi Commands*.

We did this on purpose to cater for those who might begin with Chapter 5 directly. Still, the revisited discussion is not a simple repeat of the earlier points but rather an expansion. So, for example, when we discuss Linux commands in Chapter 3, we would talk about them in the context of Linux in general, but in Chapter 5, we discuss them in the context of Raspberry Pi operations, and so on.

Hands-On Work and Safety Precautions

In Chapters 4 and 5, we use hands-on projects and exercises to reinforce the learning experience. Indeed, we feel that *Learning by Doing* is ideal for gaining the experience needed to develop IoT systems. Nevertheless, there are few points we would like to highlight.

- **Software**: All projects and exercises were tested and verified with the latest operating systems, Arduino libraries, and packages at the time of writing, June 2021. Compatibility with newer or older systems cannot be guaranteed.
- **Hardware**: We recommend using the same hardware we implemented in this book, as detailed at the beginning of each project or exercise. Although the tasks can indeed be implemented using other hardware, we can only guarantee the hardware we tested.
- **Safety**: The electronic components used in the hands-on projects and exercises are fragile and sensitive. If you are careless, you could damage some of the electronic components or cause injury. Therefore, we strongly recommend that you follow the recommended safety precautions outlined at the beginning of Chapters 4 and 5.

DISCLAIMER

By purchasing this book, you agree to implement the relevant safety precaution procedures before performing the hands-on work of this book. You also agree that, since we have no control over your work environment (such as your lab, classroom, and workshop), we are not liable to any equipment damage or injury that might occur due to ignoring safety precautions.

The IoMT Training Kit

As discussed before, Chapters 4 and 5 of this book would include extensive hands-on work where you can *learn by doing*. To complete these tasks, you will need a set of electronics and hardware components, including boards, sensors, wires, and miscellaneous components.

Chapters 4 and 5 begin with detailed listings of these items, along with installation and setup instructions. You can indeed procure the items and set them up yourself; you can consider this task a project on its own and part of the learning experience.

Alternatively, you can purchase the *IoMT Training Kit* through us. The training kit is a box that contains all components needed for the hands-on work in this book, as listed in Table 0.1.

TABLE 0.1

The Current Contents of the *IoMT Training Kit*, Valid at the Time of Writing

No	Items – Boards and Modules
1	Arduino Uno Rev. 3+USB Cable
2	LoLin NodeMCU V3
3	ESP8266 Wi-Fi module
4	Raspberry Pi 3 Model B (or newer)
	Items – Sensors and Actuators
5	GL55 light intensity sensor
6	HC-SR04 ultrasonic sensor
7	DHT11 temperature and humidity sensor
8	Pushbutton module
9	Active piezoelectric buzzer
10	SG90 micro servo motor
11	5 mm LEDs (red, yellow, green, blue) @ 10 pcs each, or 40 total
	Items – Miscellaneous Components
12	Jumper cables (M-to-M, M-to-F, F-F) @ 40 pcs each, or 120 total
13	Resistors (1 kΩ, 10 kΩ) @ 10 pcs each, or 20 total
14	Solderless breadboard
15	Arduino Uno transparent case
16	Raspberry Pi transparent case
17	16 GB microSD memory card
18	5 V 2.5 A micro USB power supply adapter
	Items – Accessories
19	Organizer box
20	HDMI to VGA converter

All items are *plug-n-play*, meaning they can be used right of the box, with all needed software (operating systems, libraries, etc.) pre-installed and configured. Figure 0.1 shows an example of the IoMT Training Kit in action.

FIGURE 0.1   The IoMT Training Kit.

ORDERING THE IOMT TRAINING KIT

To order an IoMT Training Kit or a set of Kits, please send us an email at IoMTBook@samihajjaj.com, and provide us with the following information:

- Number of Units (number of training Kits you need)
- Delivery Address (a full international address)

and we will get back to you as soon as possible. After processing your order, we will inform you of the total cost and delivery time.

The total cost and delivery would depend on the size of the order and your location. It would affect the time it would take us to procure items, and complete setup and installation, packaging, and shipping to you. You will be provided with this information before you confirm the order.

Part I

Theory and Concepts

1 The Internet of Things (IoT)

1.1 A NEW DESIGN PARADIGM: THE INTERNET OF THINGS

In 2016, there were 6.4 million Internet of Things (IoT) devices globally; this number is expected to become 20–50 billion by 2030. With the human population projected to be about 8–9 billion by then, which means in few years, there will be 5–6 IoT devices for each one of us (Jovanović, 2021; Kraijak & Tuwanut, 2015; Worldometer, 2021).

With technological breakthroughs such as 5G fuelling this growth, the real driving force behind this growth is integration; IoT is being integrated into all modern and emerging fields of technology, development, engineering, and manufacturing (Wang et al., 2021).

The IoT is all around us; it is becoming everywhere, in our homes, devices, vehicles, infrastructure, commerce, education, healthcare, services, buildings, machines, and of course, our industry. Furthermore, IoT is changing not only our products but also how we develop them (Beth Stackpole, 2016; Goto et al., 2016; Rehman et al., 2019).

The arrival of IoT introduces a new design paradigm into Mechanical and Industrial engineering fields that incorporate IoT into the design and development processes. This new paradigm can be further divided into two parts: design for IoT and design from IoT.

1.1.1 A New Design Paradigm: Design *for* IoT

With every "thing" being connected to the Internet, designers and developers need to integrate connectivity and programmability into the design of every machine, equipment, building component, infrastructure setting, machining centre, home appliance, etc.

IoT-ready systems would become more valuable in the future; systems with built-in stateless (cross-platform) network modules, embedded systems, and input/output ports would be easier to program, configure, and set up for IoT operations, making them more attractive for solution provider and system developers (Johnston et al., 2016).

Durability is another factor. Unlike standard networking devices, such as modems or routers, IoT devices are expected to operate in extreme conditions; in open agriculture fields, in hazardous industrial settings, or on moving vehicles. Therefore, these devices need protection; there is an actual demand for durable

DOI: 10.1201/9781003218395-2

casings and enclosures for IoT devices that can protect internal elements without impairing operations (Dofe et al., 2016; Tudosa et al., 2019).

1.1.2 A New Design Paradigm: Design *from* IoT

Traditionally, designers and manufacturers gather performance data while the product is still in-house, mainly during the prototype stages. Product field performance is often collected in the form of customer feedback through focus groups and surveys. IoT can change all that.

With devices/systems designed for IoT, i.e. connected and able to stream data, all developed products and equipment can stream their performance data back to the manufacturers in real time. This flow of in-field data is a game-changer; machines can directly report performance analysis of key parts, and record physical breakdowns and the conditions in which they occurred, thus helping engineers develop more creative designs (Goto et al., 2016; Kurtulus et al., 2020; Revetria et al., 2019).

1.1.3 IoT for Mechanical Engineers

Today, many major IoT applications directly involve Mechanical, Mechatronics, Industrial, and Civil engineering, namely, IoT Robotics, connected autonomous systems, Industry 4.0, Precision Agriculture, Infrastructure, energy and resources management, and more.

Yet, and understandably so, it is experts from the IT-related fields, i.e. Software, Electrical & Electronics, Networking, Web Development, Cloud Computing, etc., that often write about IoT. This makes it challenging for engineers from Mechanical or other non-IT fields to fully grasp IoT and adapt it successfully for their organizations and applications. This book aims to close this gap and provide a learning venue for non-IT-related professionals.

1.2 INTRODUCTION TO THE IoT FRAMEWORK

The first Internet-connected machine was developed in 1982, a modified vending machine at Carnegie Mellon University. The machine reported its current stock over the Internet, allowing the suppliers/vendor to know exactly when to restock the machine (Browning, 2018).

Without that information, scheduling the restocking trips would be very difficult. If the workers travel too often, the company will lose money on travel costs and wasted work hours. If they travel less often, the machine would be empty, and the company would lose revenue from lost sales. Finding the right balance is essential.

Remember, this is just one machine. The situation would be more complex if the company had ten, 100, or even 1,000 machines. The restocking operation would become exceedingly expensive and inefficient, as shown in Figure 1.1.

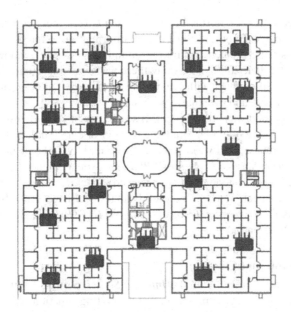

FIGURE 1.1   Restocking the vending machines problem.

The figure shows that the company has many vending machines; figuring out which machines need restocking and when to stock them would be a considerable challenge. Without this data, the operator would have to visit *every* machine at constant intervals. The resulting restocking operation would be very, very expensive.

By broadcasting their statuses to the vendor through the Internet, each vending machine would tell the operator *exactly* when it needs to be refilled, allowing them to plan efficient restocking trips. Furthermore, by logging this information over a prolonged period of time, the company can also capture its customer patterns, tastes, and location effects. That would allow them to identify popular products, capture seasonal changes, and further maximize profits.

But how does that happen? How can the machine connect to the Internet and send information? To fully understand the working principles of the IoT, we first need to understand how the Internet itself works.

1.2.1   A BRIEF REFRESHER ON THE INTERNET

When you check your feeds on social media, read your emails, or get news updates, what happens behind the scenes? How does all that data travel from its sources to your screen?

You might have a basic understanding of how the Internet works. Perhaps you have heard of words such as *Client, Server, Internet Protocol (IP) address, Browser,* and *IPs.* Maybe you are an expert on the subject. Nevertheless, it is essential to review these terms to understand the working principles of IoT better.

A computer network is formed by connecting two or more computers, where they can recognize each other and exchange information. In the beginning, computer networks were created by linking computers in labs to allow people to exchange data (Shuler, 2002). But, soon, there was a need to expand the scope of these networks and connect with the people in the next building, in the nearby town, in another city, and eventually worldwide.

Hence the *Internet* was born. Several IPs were established to govern our interactions over the Internet and facilitate the transfer of data (Shuler, 2002).

When you purchase a network connection service to your home or your mobile device, the *Internet Service Provider (ISP)* assigns you a unique *IP address*. Your IP address is like your phone number; it is used to identify you (specifically your modem) when connecting to the Internet. Data transfer is governed by other protocols, such as the *Hypertext Transfer Protocol (HTTP)*, and the *File Transfer Protocol (FTP)* (Lyon, 2020).

1.2.1.1 The Internet Client

You might be very familiar with the *Internet Server*, perhaps for the wrong reasons. After all, we all have experienced the frustrating situations when *the Server is down*, but what about the *Client*? In the Internet context, the term *Client* could mean different things (Shuler, 2002):

- **The Person**: When you access an online service on the web, to search for something, to watch a video, or read an email, then you are considered a *Client*.
- **The Machine**: The device you used to access the web could also be considered a client; this could be your computer, mobile device, laptop, or gaming console.
- **The Application**: You used to access the service or information from the web is also considered the *Client*. On the Internet, we use many clients for various purposes; we have email clients (Yahoo, Gmail, corporate emails), browser clients (Chrome, Explorer, Firefox), video streaming clients (Netflix, Amazon, etc.), social media clients, and more.

In this book, we will focus on the last definition and ignore the first two. Henceforth, the term *Internet Client* would refer to the web application or App we use on the web.

1.2.1.2 The Client–Server Connection Model

There are several connection models computers can employ to connect to one another and exchange information on the Internet. For our purposes, we will focus only on one model, the *Client–Server* connection model (*CIO Wiki*, 2021), as shown in Figure 1.2.

So, to access the net, we use a connected machine, such as a laptop or a mobile device, then on that machine, we use a browser to reach the webpage we want. In the browser, we type the name or the Universal Resource Locator (URL) of

FIGURE 1.2 The client–server connection model.

the page, click go, and after few moments, we receive the webpage we requested, including all text, images, and other media.

Behind the scenes, this is what happened; our client (the Internet browser) took the information we entered (website name or URL) and made a *request* to retrieve the information stored at a remote computer that is also connected to the network, i.e. the *Server*. We make similar requests all the time, such as the search keywords we enter in a search engine, the email address, the name of the video, and much more (Shuler, 2002).

That request is then sent through the web to the server. Upon confirming the validity of the information included in the request, the needed information is then retrieved from the server's *database*, which could be the contents of the website you requested, the results of your search query, the body of the email you selected, or the video you wanted to watch.

As discussed above, the whole process is governed by a set of Internet rules and guidelines or the *IPs*. They define how IP addresses work, how data is managed and transferred, the relationship between *Clients* and *Servers*, and much more (Lyon, 2020).

With this understanding, we are now ready to talk about the *IoT*.

1.2.2 The IoT Framework

The IoT builds upon the regular Internet and utilizes similar protocols. In the early days of IoT, standard IPs were used. Still, as the IoT became bigger and bigger, IoT-specific protocols were developed and established to optimize the performance of IoT systems and applications. Figure 1.3 shows the basic structure of the IoT framework.

In the IoT network, the sources of the data are the IoT devices or *things*. These can be considered the servers of the IoT framework. Anything can be a *thing*, as long as it can capture and broadcast data to the Cloud (Kraijak & Tuwanut, 2015).

Things could be as simple as a sensor connected to a modem, or any complex machine. Examples include, but not limited to, machining centres in smart factories, smart traffic lights, agriculture sensors, a driverless car, a connected water dam, and autonomous robots.

The data broadcast by things are often raw, large sets of numerical values that are too complex for us to comprehend. Therefore, this raw data is processed in

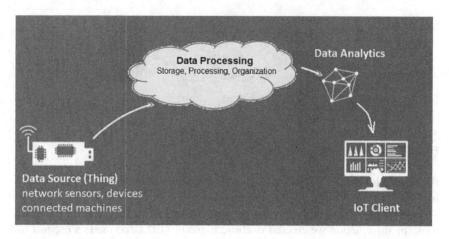

FIGURE 1.3 The IoT framework.

the Cloud. The *Cloud* is just a fancy way to describe a remote computer or server. Therefore, when we say *broadcast data to the Cloud*, we mean *send data to a remote computer or server* through the Internet.

In the Cloud, the raw data are put through several data processing and visualization algorithms that would convert the data into meaningful insights which we could understand and comprehend. These algorithms are referred to as the *Data Analytics (DA)* algorithms (Frankenfield, 2021). For example, a temperature sensor might capture and broadcast the following set of heat data [16.34, 18.24, 27.23, 31.23, 34.45].

As you can see, this is a collection of numbers that could mean anything. However, a DA algorithm might notice that the values increase with time, reporting an *upward trend*.

This is an example of *insight* we gained from the raw set of data. Of course, you could have noticed the trend yourself, but this was just a simple example of just one sensor and few readings. A standard IoT system might involve hundreds of sensors and thousands of readings, making it an arduous and time-consuming task to process all that data, filter out noise and anomalies, and make sense of it, if at all possible (Kraijak & Tuwanut, 2015).

These insights developed in Cloud are next delivered to the *IoT Client*, Internet clients dedicated to viewing the data and insights produced through the DA. An IoT client might resemble a regular Internet browser, but the difference is that it is populated with data procured from machines and things and not created by humans (Keil, 2020).

Returning to the vending machine example, through the IoT client (which could be a web application or an App), the operator would use the IoT client to view the status of every machine, delivery locations, and more, then make real-time delivery decisions.

As such, the principal elements of the IoT Framework are:

- The *Thing*; the device capturing and broadcasting raw data
- The *DA* Algorithm; converts the raw data into a meaningful insight
- The *IoT Client*; the application showing the processed data and insight.

This description of the IoT framework is somewhat classical or simplified. Indeed, *remote monitoring* was the initial purpose of all IoT systems. However, today IoT can do much than that. Furthermore, the methods of implementing IoT systems also vary, so depending on system and design considerations, the framework's structure might slightly vary, as we shall discuss in the following sections.

1.2.3 TYPES OF IoT SYSTEMS

IoT systems can be classified in several ways: by scope, by sector, by the implemented networking protocols, and by the direction or the flow of data. Classifying IoT systems into sub-types and genres is helpful to gather experts from these areas and focus their shared experiences and knowledge to develop great IoT systems.

1.2.3.1 By Flow of Data

IoT system can be classified by the direction of the flow of data. For example, Figure 1.4 shows an IoT system used to remotely interact with a group of robotic cameras for the TV and film industry. Using this example, we can understand this classification:

- **Remote Monitoring**: Data flows from the *thing* to the IoT client
- **Remote Controlling**: Remote commands flow from users to the device(s)

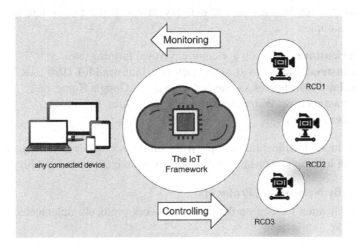

FIGURE 1.4   The types of IoT systems: By the flow of data.

- **Thing-to-Thing**: Data is shared among the IoT devices
- **Combinations**: Mixture of two or more of the above systems.

By understanding (or by setting) the direction of the data flow, several design decisions are affected. In *remote-monitoring* IoT systems, the focus would be implementing effective DA algorithms to create the best possible insight from the raw data.

In *remote-controlling* systems, the clients must capture user inputs (through buttons, sliders, etc.) and send them to the IoT devices, who themselves would be programmed to expect these commands and act on them when they arrive.

In *Thing-to-Thing* systems, the IoT devices would need to be programmed and configured to exchange, share, and combine raw data for the collective optimum performance. Examples include mesh systems (see below), multi-agent systems, and more.

1.2.3.2 By Scope (Type of Devices)

This classification focuses on the type of devices, or things, being connected to the cloud. Examples include the following:

- Internet of Nano Things (IoNT), covering nano-scale devices
- Internet of Mission-Control Things (IoMCT), for Military, Police, etc.
- Internet of Mobile Things (IoMT), for on-the-move IoT devices (OMIDs)
- Internet of Robotic Things (IoRT), for IoT Robotics.

Through these classifications, experts from those areas, i.e. Nanotechnology, Mission-Control, Robotics, etc., could focus their work together and develop more efficient IoT systems.

1.2.3.3 By Sector

This classification focuses on the industry in which the IoT system is implemented; examples:

- **Agriculture**: Precision agriculture, vertical farming, etc.
- **Industrial**: Industry 4.0, smart factories, Industrial IoT (IIoT), etc.
- **Social**: Smart homes, connected appliances, Google Home, etc.
- **Infrastructure**: Water management, smart cities, vehicle, etc.
- **Other Sectors**...

Through these classifications, people from similar sectors can work together on developing IoT applications that best suit their organizations and industry.

1.2.3.4 By Networking Protocols

This classification focuses on the type of network protocol implemented; examples include:

- **Cellular**: for mobile, moving, and portable systems,
- **LAN/PAN**: local/personal area networks, such as *Bluetooth* or *Wi-Fi*

- **LPWANs**: low-powered wide area networks, e.g. *LoRa* (Incháustegui et al., 2020)
- **Mesh Networks**: formed of a mesh of nodes collaborating to reach an Internet gateway, such as *ZigBee*.

The choice of network protocol often depends on the application requirements, whether the devices would be fixed or mobile, indoor or outdoor, etc. It also depends on data broadcasting requirements, such as the volume of data packets needed, frequency of broadcast, type of data required, and other considerations (Pazos et al., 2015).

1.2.3.5 The IoT Gateway

In the early days of IoT, the purpose of an IoT gateway was similar to a *network card* in a computer system; to establish a connection to the Internet and facilitate data transfer. However, with the development of network-ready controllers, such as the Raspberry Pi, Beaglebone, and NodeMCU, which are readily connected and can be easily programmed for IoT, the need for a dedicated *Network Card* diminished significantly (Guoqiang et al., 2013).

Today, the role of IoT gateways is to act as traffic police and govern the flow of data for optimum system performance and responsiveness. By monitoring the flow of information coming from each connected endpoint and prioritizing critical data, IoT gateways can prevent system overloading and traffic bottlenecks (Adesina & Osasona, 2019).

Nevertheless, for IoT systems with smaller volumes, the possibility of overloading and bottlenecks remains low, especially with the arrival of 5G capabilities. Therefore, for the purposes of this book, we will not focus on the design of the IoT gateways.

1.3 UNDERSTANDING THE FULL POTENTIAL OF IoT

As discussed earlier, Figure 1.3 represents the classical form of the IoT; IoT devices capture and broadcast raw data to the cloud, where *DA* algorithms convert the raw data into valuable insight, which is delivered to the IoT clients for us to view and use. In reality, IoT systems can be much more than that, as shown in Figure 1.5.

As shown in the figure, IoT systems can benefit organizations in three ways: *Streamline Operations*, *Repurposing Data*, and *Data Monetization*. We already briefly discussed the first benefit, through the vending machine example, but not the other two. This section discusses all of these potentials, with examples and case studies.

1.3.1 IoT POTENTIAL: STREAMLINING OPERATIONS

Streamlining operations refers to the practice of reducing operational costs, minimizing waste, and maximizing utilization. Streamlining would result in leaner operations, which would result in increasing profits (by lowering operations costs) (Aionys, 2019).

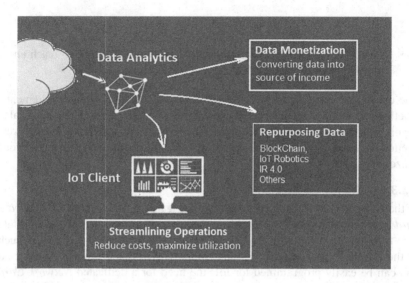

FIGURE 1.5   The full potential of IoT.

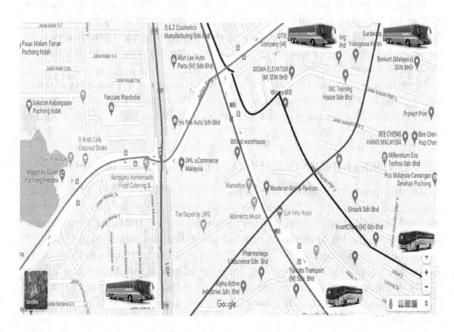

FIGURE 1.6   The bus operator problem.

Streamlining operations was the first purpose of all IoT systems, as we saw in the vending machine example discussed above. Let us consider another example from another industry; The Logistics and Transportation Sector, as shown in Figure 1.6.

Figure 1.6 shows the bus operator problem. As shown in the figure, the company operates five busses in five different routes, but due to rising costs, the company wants to drop one route and focus only on the remaining routes. The question now is, which route should the company drop? And to which route (of the remaining routes) should they assign the extra bus?

Once again, without reliable information, the bus operator will have to guess and hope, and mistakes will be very costly. If the company drops an in-demand route or assign a bus to the wrong route, they could lose more money than before. However, with a cleverly designed IoT system that utilizes mobile IoT devices, an elaborate set of DA algorithms, and a reliable IoT client, the bus operators would get all the information they need.

The system could identify passenger volume (for each route) on an hourly, daily, weekly, or monthly basis. Therefore, the system could locate in-demand routes, peak hours, traffic patterns, driver performance, and more. Then, based on that data, the operators could make informed decisions, drop the least in-demand routes, reward excellent drivers, capture user feedback, minimize their losses, and maximize the use of their busses and drivers.

In fact, the operators could also make *dynamic* changes to their operations to capitalize on passenger volumes and patterns. Since they already know their passenger volumes, trends, and patterns, they can re-route busses and drivers any time in the day, week, or month, to match passenger patterns. Not only will they be able to reduce costs but also maximize profits.

1.3.2 IoT Potential: Repurposing Data

Aside from just viewing the data and using that information to streamline operations, IoT data can benefit other frameworks and technologies (McFadin, 2015). We have seen an example of that already in Figure 1.4, which demonstrated another emerging technology; *IoT Robotics*.

Intelligent robots already have a set of data gathering devices for their odometry operations. Mobile robots capture map data for navigation, social robots capture human queues for effective human–robot interaction, and industrial robots use part data to select appropriate processing routines. By linking these robots to the Internet, we can turn them into *things*.

Once connected, robots can broadcast their data, information that can be used for various purposes, coordinate a group of search and rescue robots, log interactions with humans at home (or other social settings), and for industrial planning and operations.

Figure 1.4 is part of an IoT Robotics project that focused on robotic cameras. In that project, developers created two sets of robotic cameras remotely operated by a director through the Internet. The director could view life footage shot and broadcast by the cameras while at the same time able to manipulate the cameras through the Internet.

In **Agriculture**, IoT systems can be used to capture field data (such as water level, fertilization, and moisture levels) and use that information to streamline agriculture operations, i.e. re-direct resources, such as workers, machines, and consumables to where needed. These systems are examples of *Precision Agriculture* systems. However, that same data can be used for another purpose entirely; for the development and implementation of **Smart Contracts**.

Powered by ***BlockChain***, Smart Contracts are dynamic financial contract systems (much like a computer program) whose terms (prices, delivery dates, etc.) change based on current agriculture information. By integrating IoT data from their precision agriculture systems to a Smart Contract system, the organization can benefit twice from their data, streamlining their operations and obtaining the best deal for their produce.

1.3.3   IoT Potential: Data Monetization (Data as a Commodity)

Data monetization made Big Tech companies big; companies like Facebook or Google use and sell user data, and all insights developed from it for targeted advertising. We can do something similar in our IoT systems (Gudino, 2019).

For example, company A has developed a working IoT system that captures a constant flow of data in periodical reports filled with data-based findings and insights. On the other hand, company B does not have the technology to develop such a system, but they could use the information. In this case, company A can sell the data, in the form of insight reports, to company B. This concept is shown in Figure 1.7.

Since the data is continuously changing every day, week, or month, company B would need a constant supply of data reports from company A every day, week, or month, depending on the situation and the project at hand. Perhaps a third company, company C, is also interested in the same data, so company A can sell the same data reports to them as well.

As such, the IoT system developed by company A, aside from helping them streamline operations and integrate with other technologies, could have a third benefit. It could generate a product (IoT data reports) that it can sell for profit.

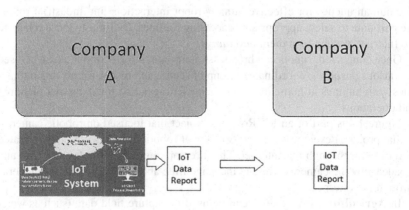

FIGURE 1.7   IoT data monetization.

Furthermore, since the data reports are updated constantly and can be sold to multiple buyers, the IoT system can generate a constant and scalable source of income.

As for concerns over data sensitivity or competition, company A can choose to hide its private or sensitive data, sell only the insights, or sell only to non-competitors.

An example of this idea, let us return to the bus operator example. Starting from Figure 1.6, if we zoom in on one of the in-demand routes, we will see the view shown in Figure 1.8.

Figure 1.8 shows a local area map, with the in-demand bus route highlighted (in black). The circles along the route represent the locations of two known bus stops along the route. The rectangular shapes near the bus stops with dollar signs represent buildings and businesses that happen to be near the bus stops.

Based on data obtained from the IoT bus system (as discussed above), the bus operator company has exact data passenger volume, foot traffic, and travel patterns in this area. This information would be vital for the business and properties near the bus stops.

Knowing in advance how much and when the maximum foot traffic would occur at the bus stops, the businesses nearby would be better prepared to capitalize on it. Property owners and agents would also want to know that information to better market and sell their units.

The bus company can capitalize on this; they can sell daily/weekly reports on passenger foot traffic to these business and properties, thus generating new income. In fact, they could do this along the whole bus route; create and sell data reports to every business and property near every bus stop. The best part is that these businesses are not competitors to the bus company, so the company does not risk sharing such information.

While this could be an attractive business model for company A, they still need to do some work to make it viable. How would they identify their target audience (who would need their data)? How to ensure (to potential buyers) that the data reports are authentic and reliable? And how to package raw IoT data (or its insights) into sellable data reports? We discuss that next.

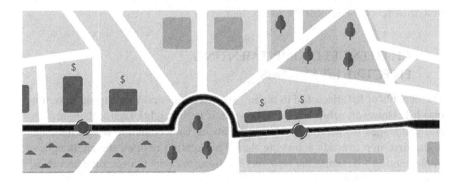

FIGURE 1.8 Data monetization: The IoT bus example.

1.3.3.1 IoT Data Monetization: How to

Monetizing IoT data can be achieved in two ways: after the fact or through a dedicated system. These two approaches are similar in result; they only differ in implementation.

After the fact means the company decides to monetize its IoT data after they had already developed a working IoT system and used it for another purpose (streamlining operations or repurposing data) to create an auxiliary source of income for the company.

A dedicated system means the company purposely built the IoT system for the sole purpose of selling its data as a commodity. Perhaps the company identified a potential market for some information (e.g. passenger volume or foot traffic), so they built a dedicated IoT system to develop that information and sell it to the potential market.

Either way, be it *after the fact* or *dedicated*, companies planning to monetize their IoT data and insights must follow this process:

1. Develop a working IoT system that can capture, process, and store data and insight.
2. Ensure proper encryption, security, and validation of the IoT data and insight.
3. Package the IoT data into periodic (daily/weekly/monthly) reports ready for purchase.
4. Research who else would be interested in this data, how much could it mean to them.
5. Armed with this information, approach possible customers and create the deals.

The only difference between after the fact or dedicated types of methods is where to start. In after the fact, companies would start the process at step 1; build the IoT system, use it to streamline operations, or repurposing data, then consider monetization as an option to further benefit from the IoT system and create a new revenue stream. In dedicated, the company would start at step 4; do the research first, then reverse-engineer the IoT system.

1.4 CHALLENGES OF IMPLEMENTING EFFECTIVE IoT SYSTEMS

The benefits of IoT discussed in the last section could motivate anyone to venture into IoT. However, achieving these benefits is not straightforward; there are several challenges we need to navigate and avoid. Understanding these challenges is the first step towards achieving that. This section reviews the challenges of implementing IoT, while the next section discusses how to overcome and eliminate these challenges.

1.4.1 The Multidisciplinary Nature of IoT

The field of IoT is multidisciplinary by definition (Kumar et al., 2019). To fully understand and implement IoT, one needs to have working knowledge in the following areas:

- Electrical and Electronics engineering
- Mechatronics or Electro-mechanical engineering
- Software engineering, specifically on programming and web applications development
- Sensors, actuators, and controllers selection, setup, and programming
- Networking setup and configuration
- Knowledge of economics and business development

This multidisciplinary nature of IoT makes it difficult for beginners to enter the field of IoT. This is further compounded by the very nature of engineering education, which usually focuses on specific disciplines, such as Mechanical, E&E, or Software engineering, at a time.

As a result, even after understanding the full potential of IoT, those interested in IoT might not know where or how to start, who to hire for the job, and how can you trust them (if you do not understand how the whole thing works). This is a common challenge among *Mechanical, Industrial, Civil,* and other engineers not from the *Software* or the E&E departments. So, for all of you out there, you are not alone; this book is meant for you.

1.4.2 Sector-Specific Challenges

Today, IoT is implemented in various sectors and fields; agriculture, industry, homes, cities, infrastructure, and more recently, embedded in all goods and products.

Each sector has its own unique set of challenges that might not apply in other sectors. Therefore, understanding the needs of your industry and the relevant challenges you may or may not face when implementing IoT is vital for a successful implementation. We will now discuss these challenges sector by sector.

1.4.2.1 Outdoor IoT Applications (Open-Field Agriculture, Outdoor Robotics)

As discussed before, in precision agriculture applications, IoT devices are placed in the agriculture field to collect data that would be used to streamline the agriculture operations, as shown in Figure 1.9.

For this sector, the primary challenge is to establish a reliable Internet connection for IoT devices in the field (collecting field data). Often, these devices are expected to be placed in isolated rural areas with a poor network connection and no access to electrical power (Romeo et al., 2020). The same applies to water management systems, which manage water flow in small canals through

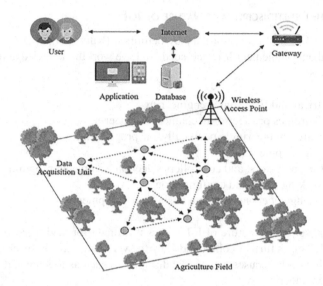

FIGURE 1.9   IoT for precision agriculture.

a network of autonomous and remotely monitored/operated *Watergates*, often found in rural environments (Hajjaj, Hafizuddin et al., 2020).

Another challenge is to protect the IoT devices from the elements, against heat from the sun, water from the rain, and attacks from animals and wildlife. Finally, the (mechanical) challenge is to develop the casings that can protect these devices, but without interfering with their operations, they still need to capture and broadcast data to the cloud.

Figure 1.10 shows an example of this situation. This picture is taken from one of our projects on IoT agriculture; you can find the complete report here (Gsangaya et al., 2020).

As shown in the image, we 3D printed the casing and used high-grade adhesives to protect the internal components yet not interrupt their operation; the transparent cover allows solar radiation inward, powering the system (Gsangaya et al., 2020).

FIGURE 1.10   Casing design of agriculture IoT devices.

Nevertheless, plants do not grow instantly, and water levels do not rise rapidly (unless we are in the monsoon season). Therefore, since changes occur relatively slowly, any IoT updates would also be minor and less often. In other words, IoT data packet size and broadcast frequencies would be small and manageable.

1.4.2.2 Industrial IoT Applications (Industry 4.0, Smart Factories, IIoT, etc.)

The situation here is the polar opposite of the outdoor sector. There would be no problem powering the IoT devices or connecting them to the Internet since all devices would be placed indoors, where power and connection are readily available.

Nevertheless, the industrial sector has its own challenges. Manufacturing and industrial machines are expected to operate for extended operational hours (perhaps even 24-hour shifts), processing hundreds or thousands of parts per machine per day, performing various tasks; processing, inspection, finishing, QC, packaging, and more (Figure 1.11).

Therefore, the sheer amount and complexity of data would be enormous, and it would need to be broadcast as fast as possible. That means large data packets and high-speed broadcasting frequencies would require a very powerful (therefore expensive) connection.

Another challenge is security and privacy of data. For most industries, manufacturing data are proprietary and cannot be exposed to competitors. So, added layers of security measures against cyber-attacks are a must for industrial IoT applications (Vakaloudis & O'Leary, 2019).

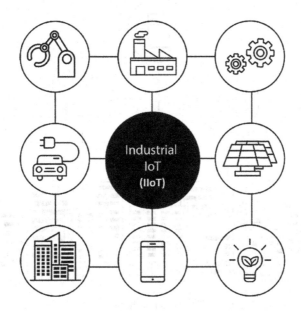

FIGURE 1.11 Industrial Internet of Things (IIoT).

1.4.2.3 Social IoT (Smart Homes, Smart Schools, Rehab Systems, Care for Adults and Disabled)

When it comes to IoT in any social setting, be it at home, school, hospitals, etc., the main challenge is to manage the *Impact of Technology on our Society*. In recent years, technology has become an integral part of our lives. In our fields, factories, schools, cities, and even our homes, not everyone is happy about it (Dhelim et al., 2021) (Figure 1.12).

Several social challenges related to technology exist in our societies. These range from *acceptance*, *fear*, and outright *rejection* of technology. As a result, the level of technology adoption may not be as high as developers had hoped. Therefore, social IoT systems, by extension, are also affected by these challenges.

An example of this phenomena comes from the TV and film industry. Figure 1.4 showed an IoT-enabled robotic camera system for a production crew to operate remotely. The intended effect was to help the camera crew to film events and activities remotely without being there. While the developed system worked adequately, and the camera crew were excited about it, 60% of the crew who tested the system expressed negative feelings towards the robotic camera system and worried about their future in the industry (Routh & Pal, 2018).

Therefore, developers of *social* IoT systems must consider their system's impact on the people. People with negative perceptions of IoT might not want to

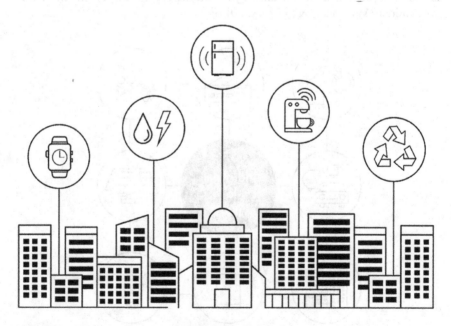

FIGURE 1.12   Social Internet of Things, smart homes.

use the technology that often or none at all. As a result, the full potential of these systems might not be realized. Designers must incorporate *positive re-enforcement* into the interfaces of their systems. Users must feel at ease and not intruded upon when using these applications.

1.4.2.4 Smart Cities and Infrastructure

Examples include smart public buildings, traffic control through IoT traffic lights, IoT parking lots, utility management, connected smart cities, and intelligent retail (Figure 1.13).

The biggest challenge in this sector is that everything is already built, so incorporating IoT would require a lot of *retrofitting* or *rebuilding* from scratch. Both options are expensive, complicated, and may require years to complete.

Another challenge is the sheer size of these projects. So far, we have talked about an agriculture field, a factory, a home, a building, but not an entire city. Managing this upgrade to a smart city requires collaboration and trust among all players: developers, businesses, and government bodies (Kumar et al., 2019; Yadav & Vishwakarma, 2018).

The political will of the nation/city may have to take the lead, but technology providers must be ready to play their roles as well. Leaders of technology (owners, managers, decision makers, etc.) need to be tuned to government plans and align their business strategies to match the government's long-term plan. That would be helpful to gain government support in the forms of grants, tax breaks, and other incentives.

1.4.2.5 Mobile IoT Applications (IoT for Vehicles, Logistics and Transportation, Drones, etc.)

Mobile IoT is yet another branch of IoT that has taken a life on its own in recent years. Unlike standard IoT applications, such as those shown in Figures 1.3 and 1.9, mobile IoT applications utilize OMIDs.

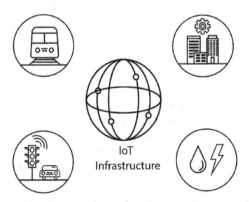

FIGURE 1.13 The Internet of Things for infrastructure.

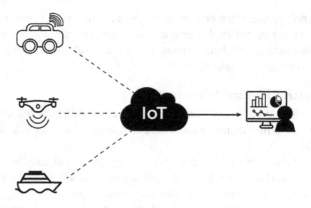

FIGURE 1.14   On-the-move IoT devices (OMIDs) for logistics.

In a standard IoT application, IoT devices are usually pre-installed in fixed locations, such as an agriculture field, a factory, a home, and a school. Therefore, their networking setup is usually pre-established before the launch of the IoT application, freeing the developers to focus on data management and insight development and delivery. On the other hand, for mobile IoT applications, the situation is different (Romeo et al., 2020) (Figure 1.14).

As the name implies, on-the-move IoT devices (OMIDs) could be directly installed on moving vehicles or embedded in products or packages transported in the moving vehicles. As they travel from one location to another, OMIDs would gather and broadcast raw data to the cloud, just like any other IoT system. OMIDs are often used mainly in the Logistics and Transportation industry; other applications include fleet management systems, agriculture drones, driverless cars, and search and research robots.

While on the move, OMIDs go through varying and changing network environments, i.e. changes in signal strength, latency, available bandwidth, current data traffic, etc. The location of an OMID relative to the nearest tower would directly impact its connection quality. The time of the day would impact available bandwidth. As OMIDs travel, they go through varying locations and at different times of the day. Therefore, the network environments they encounter become continuously changing and unpredictable (Hajjaj & Gsangaya, 2019).

By design, IoT devices (fixed or on the move) are designed to be simple nodes that live-stream data, i.e. continuously capture and broadcast data without storing (or caching) such data. Therefore, any network interruption would result in data losses. Incomplete data would result in unreliable insight, adversely affecting the IoT application's reliability, resulting in incorrect findings and recommendations, thus defeating their very purpose.

This problem is not unique to OMIDs. In general, all mobile devices encounter this situation while on the move. *Network Selection Algorithms (NSAs)* is a technology that allows mobile devices to scan for the best available network and automatically connect to it, thus maintaining a reliable connection to the cloud and preventing any data loss.

Unfortunately, though, current NSAs cater for mobile devices and not for OMIDs. This is an active research area; to develop effective network selection algorithms specifically for OMID and mobile IoT applications (Hajjaj & Gsangaya, 2019).

1.4.3 TECHNOLOGICAL CHALLENGES

Let us assume that we overcame the previous challenges; we have assembled a team of experts from multiple disciplines, and we fully understood our industry/sector challenges. Next, we need to contend with technological challenges, such as *software/hardware compatibility*, *networking capability and limits*, and *cybersecurity* measures.

1.4.3.1 Software/Hardware Compatibility

The beauty of IoT is that you can implement it with your choice of technology options. You can choose the type of sensors you want and the controllers you want. You can structure your data the way you want. You select the DA algorithm you prefer in the language you like. You can choose the IoT client you want, or you can custom-make your own. You can also scale your application however you like to match your needs.

Often, the technological choice comes down to availability and experience. Developers would choose options they are experienced with and are available to them. The clashes come when people select different or incompatible choices. For example, say developer A selected Arduino as the choice of the controller due to their experience with it. However, developer B defined the system parameters as too complex for the simple Arduino controller to match.

A common ground must be established among the design team. Technological choices must be discussed, vetted, and agreed upon from the start to avoid later headaches. This is something we will discuss in detail in a later section.

1.4.3.2 Network Capability and Limits

Network capability goes hand in hand with the required data size and broadcast frequency. As discussed above, in some applications (agriculture), we could work with small data packets broadcast every few minutes or even hours. Other applications (Industry 4.0) might require large data packets broadcast every few seconds.

The network must support data size requirements and frequency. Setup costs and limitation might force developers to make compromises and concessions. They could perhaps break the data packet size in half but make it more frequent or cache the data before broadcasting.

With the impending arrival of 5G networking capabilities, IoT applications are expected to experience a significant boom in the possible IoT data size and broadcast frequencies. With unprecedented bandwidth, data rates, and latencies, coupled with IoT-dedicated protocols and infrastructure, the impact is expected to be very major.

As a comparison, in the best 4G network, it would take us 16 minutes to download a 12 GB document. In 5G, it would take only 11 seconds. With these exceptional capabilities, 5G is expected to impact every facet of our lives: homes, industry, cities, infrastructure, and more, and IoT is expected to be part of all of that.

1.4.3.3 Cybersecurity and IoT Attacks

IoT devices are designed to be simple nodes that perform only one task: capture and broadcast data. This simplicity, however, makes these devices vulnerable to attacks and hacking. Also, the data itself being broadcast to the cloud, it too could be hacked.

This brings the role of IoT cybersecurity and data encryption. The level of security would directly depend on how critical the data is. If monetization is employed, then customers would want to know that their data is safe and hack-proof.

This area is perhaps best left to cybersecurity experts. We (the rest of the team) could contribute by adequately defining the data structure to facilitate better security and protection. We will discuss this issue in later chapters.

1.4.4 SOCIOECONOMIC CHALLENGES

We already discussed some social challenges related to IoT. Awareness and acceptance of IoT and related technology are essential for us to fully realize the benefits of IoT. We could have the best technology in the world, but if we choose not to use it, it would be a waste.

Another challenge is related to education, specifically **the lack of interdisciplinarity** in technology and engineering education. From early on, we are trained to focus only on one specific discipline and field to ensure specialization and excellence. This may work with specific fields, such as mechanical design or software development, but not for IoT.

IoT requires students and learners to be exposed to all related disciplines, as highlighted in Section 1.3.1. That does not mean one needs to be an expert in all fields, because that would require a lifetime of learning. Some working experience would suffice.

This book serves that purpose; to help those not from the Software or E&E departments to understand IoT and develop some working experience. This way, they would know how to relate it to their fields and participate effectively in IoT development teams.

The **availability of IoT-related laws and policies**, or lack of them, is also another challenge. IoT is still an emerging technology in many countries worldwide, and many governments are still learning to adapt to it. That is reflected in the available laws and policies guiding the implementation of IoT.

As a result, what is legal or accepted today might not be so tomorrow. Developers and organizations need to fully be aware and alert to new guidelines to avoid getting into trouble. The last thing any organization needs is to spend time, effort, and money on an IoT application, only to realize that it is no longer allowed or permitted. In the next section, we discuss the effective implementation of IoT, which would help us realize all the potentials of IoT while avoiding all of its challenges and problems (Routh & Pal, 2018).

1.5 THE EFFECTIVE IMPLEMENTATION OF IoT: THE DETAILED PROCEDURE

Effective implementation refers to implementing an IoT system at your organization or for your project to realize its potential benefits while avoiding its challenges entirely. The step-by-step procedure to achieve that is outlined below:

1. Set the *Common Ground* (differences and similarities, resources)
2. Define the system architecture (scope, sector, direction of data flow)
3. Define the data structure (needed insights, raw data, types, sizes, data sources)
4. Develop the IoT devices that would capture and broadcast the raw data (the *things*)
5. Obtain/setup networking to match system needs (data packet size, broadcast frequency)
6. Develop/select the DA algorithms to get the insights (*Analytics*)
7. Develop IoT clients (web applications) as per system architecture and DA algorithms
8. IoT outputs: protocols for streamlining operations
9. IoT outputs: protocols for repurposing data (reuse it for technologies)
10. IoT outputs: protocols for data monetization

The first three steps involve pre-analysis, setup, and making important decisions that would impact the rest of the process. Step 4 involves mechatronics/mechanical design, while step 5 involves networking systems. Step 6 involves software engineering, while step 7 involves web development. Steps 8 through 10 define how the outputs of the IoT system are delivered. In the following sub-sections, we will discuss each step of the process in detail.

1.5.1 SET A COMMON GROUND

Before an organization can embark on IoT, it must conduct a survey or take an inventory check of all in-house technologies, system, hardware, skills, and personnel education and experience. Only with a precise accounting of the organization's resources, both in people and technology, the organization can assemble an effective team for IoT development.

First and foremost, the available *technologies*, the organization needs to know what technologies are available in-house. This will be valuable later during development, as the company would utilize its in-house technologies rather than spend resources on importing new technologies. Specifically, the organization needs to review the following:

- Manufacturing systems (production layout, machines used, etc.) (if applicable)
- Open-source or *Proprietary* technologies (can you modify it, or is it a *Blackbox*)
- Operating systems (OS) available (Windows, Linux, Mac, others)
- Programming languages, software solutions (C++, Python, others, libraries)
- Custom/unique systems or designs available only in-house (developed internally)

Next, the *people*, the survey must query the organization's people and identify educational background and experience, especially with the in-house technologies (Knuckey, 2019). These experts would form the basis of the *IoT Team* for the organization.

The first task of the IoT team would be to *set the Common Ground* for everyone. The team must agree on technology choices; what hardware to use, which OS to use, which programming language to implement, which web development solutions to use, and so on.

Secondly, the team must identify any weakness in the organization related to IoT; any skills or technologies the organization lacks. Then based on the team's recommendations, the organization would act and *close the gaps*, setting up training, hiring experts, and procuring all the needed technologies, systems, and infrastructure.

1.5.2 Define Your System Architecture

Once the IoT team is in place and a technological common ground has been established, the team would be ready to develop its first IoT system for the organization.

IoT system architecture is related to the IoT classifications we discussed at the beginning of this chapter. Specifically, which sector would this system belong to? What would be the scope of the system? What would be the direction of data flow? (McFadin, 2015).

By defining or setting the *Sector* of the proposed IoT system, the team would identify which area it would be related to, such as industry, agriculture, infrastructure, sustainability, or others. This would allow the team to invite experts from these sectors for advice and guidance. Be it from within the organization or not, these experts would provide excellent input to the IoT team, especially in the next step (defining/setting the data structure).

For example, agriculture experts would know what a precision agriculture system needs to achieve. Energy experts would advise on the needed parameters for IoT sustainability projects. Educators would advise on smart classrooms and delivery/assessment methods.

A similar argument can be made for the *Scope* of the proposed project: *Roboticists* would define robot data needed for an IoT Robotics project, nanotechnology experts would advise on IoNT (IoT for nanotechnology) systems and so on.

Next, the *direction of data flow*, the team would decide if the proposed IoT system would implement *remote monitoring, remote controlling, thing-to-thing*, or combinations.

These three decisions, *Sector, Scope, and Data Flow*, would directly impact the design, setup, and programming of all parts of the IoT framework, specifically, the IoT devices, the DA algorithms, and the IoT clients. Therefore, the IoT team must clearly set these choices very early on and make sure not to make any changes along the way.

1.5.3 SET/DEFINE DATA REQUIREMENTS

One more important decision to make before developing the IoT system is to define or select the *Data Structure* of the proposed IoT system.

Data is the DNA of an IoT system; IoT devices capture and broadcast raw data to the cloud. There, DA algorithms convert the raw data into valuable *insights* and deliver them to the IoT clients, where users can utilize these insights for their purposes (McFadin, 2015).

Therefore, the development process begins from the end; we start from the *insights* and reverse-engineer the whole IoT system to obtain them. Specifically, the IoT team must answer the following questions:

1. What *insights* do we need from our IoT system?
2. What raw data would we need to develop these insights? Where to get it from?
3. What types of data would we need to capture?
4. How much data would we need? How often would we need it?

Using an IoT system for precision agriculture as an example, let us go through these questions and provide some sample answers.

1. What *insights* do we need our IoT system to deliver?
   Where (within the field) and when will the plants need more water or fertilizers
2. What raw data would we need to develop these insights? Where to get it from?
   Soil moisture level, fertilizer level, ambient temperature

3. What types of data would we need to capture?

Examples: Text, numbers (floats, integers), Booleans (True/False values), image, videos

4. How much data would we need? How often would we need it?

Do we have specific needs, or can we use rates provided by the available network?

Similarly, the IoT team needs to discuss these questions and come up with the best answers. Input from sector/scope experts would be vital here, as discussed in the last section.

1.5.4 DESIGN THE IoT DEVICES, THE *THINGS*

Figure 1.16 shows the design architecture and components of an IoT device, which would allow it to capture and broadcast data (Kjellby et al., 2019) (Figure 1.15).

The *Sensors*: These are the actual devices that capture the raw data and send it to the controller for analysis and processing. There is a wide variety of sensors that can capture any type of data. Sensors also vary in range, capability, and

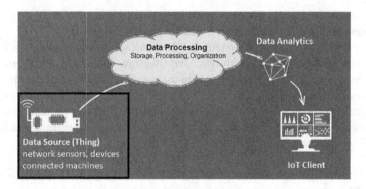

FIGURE 1.15   The IoT framework: The *Things*.

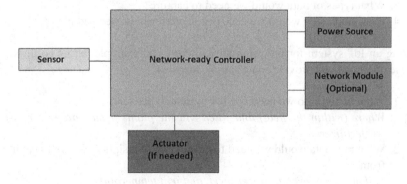

FIGURE 1.16   Design architecture of an IoT device.

cost. Sensors could be digital or analogue, each with its pros and cons. The field of *Sensor Selection* is beyond the scope of this book. Relevant experts include Mechatronics, Automation, and E&E engineers.

The Network-Ready *Controller*: The brains of the IoT device. Programmed to perform all primary tasks; receive data from sensors, package data to web-friendly formats, and broadcast data to the cloud. Optionally, to give motion commands to actuators, if included.

There are different types of IoT controllers, each with varying capabilities and features: *Controller Chip* controllers, such as the AT91SAM chip, an ARM architecture processor, the *Controller Board* controllers, such as the Arduino or the NodeMCU controllers, or the full-fledged *Computer-on-chip* controllers, such as the Raspberry Pi, or Beaglebone systems. For the sake of simplicity, we will refer to all of these types as *Controllers*. In later chapters, we will discuss these differences and their impact on IoT operations.

The Network Module (Optional): Regardless of the differences, all IoT controllers must be ready, both in hardware and software, to connect to the Internet. For some IoT controllers, connectivity is a built-in feature (Raspberry Pi, Beaglebone, NodeMCU). For others (Arduino, AT91SAM, etc.), a *network module* is needed. A network module is an external module device added to establish a network connection for the controller, as shown in Figure 1.17. We will discuss modules in detail in later chapters.

Nevertheless, sometimes this is something we cannot escape; perhaps the only controllers we have in-house are *Arduino Uno*. Perhaps our system requires a specific *ARM-based* controller that is not readily connected, and other reasons may apply. Therefore, in the later hands-on chapters, we will discuss both connectivity options (*built-in* and through a *module*).

The Power Source: Obviously, power is essential for the components of the IoT device. This is not an issue for indoor IoT applications, such as industry or

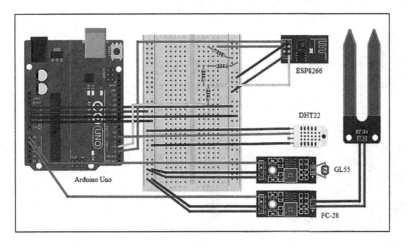

FIGURE 1.17 The ESP8266 network module for the Arduino Uno.

smart homes. However, the situation is different for *outdoor*, *mobile*, and *embedded* IoT applications.

For *Outdoor* applications, we could always extend power lines to wire up the devices, but that would be expensive, disruptive, and restrictive to the IoT devices. The better option is to use solar-powered rechargeable batteries or power banks. Free from the wires, the developers could freely experiment with the locations and arrangements of the devices with ease.

Mobile IoT devices, used in the logistics industry, could be recharged through the vehicles on which they are installed. *Embedded* IoT devices, installed within consumer products, could be recharged when the consumers power the products and use them.

Regardless of the recharging method, the power unit typically contains a rechargeable battery or a power bank and miscellaneous components for recharging.

The Actuators (If Needed): Adding the actuators to the IoT devices would comprehensively change their primary functions. As discussed before, IoT devices primarily capture and broadcast data. Adding actuators to the devices would add another function: *Automation*. Specifically, adding actuators, with miscellaneous components, would turn the IoT devices into remotely monitored/operated autonomous systems.

In many situations, we may need to create systems that can operate independently of human input. However, we may still need to monitor them and override their operations when needed. Examples of such systems include *Industry 4.0* (machining centres), *IoT Robotics*, and water management systems. An example of such an IoT device is shown in Figure 1.18.

As shown in the figure, a DC motor is connected to the controller, the Raspberry Pi 3, via a motor driver chip. Figure 1.18 also shows the rest of the circuit, showing sensors and override buttons, as well as the algorithm of the controller program. This design is part of an IoT system for *Centralized Water Management*, which we will discuss in detail in a later section.

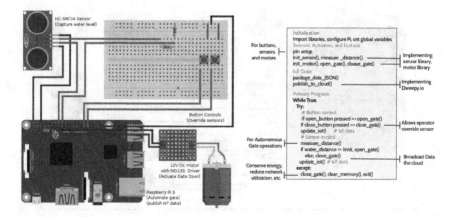

FIGURE 1.18   Adding actuators to IoT devices.

Obviously, adding actuators to the IoT devices is needed only if that was the primary purpose of the IoT application; to develop remotely monitored autonomous systems. This is another decision the IoT team must make at the start of the development process.

Also, adding actuators necessitates the addition of mechanical and electro-mechanical engineering. Specifically, motor selection, mechanism and gear train design for torque/speed control, power transmission and control, mechanical components design, and more.

Fortunately, these areas are the primary experience of mechanical engineers, making this type of IoT systems, remotely monitored autonomous systems, their speciality.

1.5.5 NETWORKING CONFIGURATION AND SETUP

Being *network-ready* and part of the IoT framework, as shown in Figure 1.19, does not mean that the IoT device can create its own connection. It only means that the device is ready to connect to a network if it is already established (Benazzouz et al., 2014). For example, your mobile phone device is network-ready; it can connect to a Wi-Fi or a cellular network, but it cannot create that connection on its own. You still need to have an established network already in place (Wi-Fi or cellular) to connect your phone with it.

This is not an issue for indoor IoT applications; devices can be connected to the local network through Wi-Fi, Bluetooth, or even by cable. The main challenge is for *outdoor*, *mobile*, and *embedded* IoT applications.

For *Outdoor* IoT applications, we could use Wireless Access Points (WAPs). It is similar to the hotspot connection we can create with our mobile devices. Except these are often devices sold directly by the cellular ISPs with a subscription contract. Each WAP would serve a group of nearby IoT devices, as shown in Figure 1.9. The number of WAPs required would depend on the size of the field and the number of IoT devices implemented in that application.

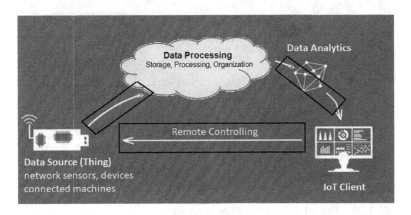

FIGURE 1.19   The IoT framework: *Networking setup.*

Alternatively, we could use a Long Range Wi-Fi connection (LoRa). The main advantage of LoRa is that it provides a range of connection 1,000 times bigger than a regular WAP, but that connection would be limited in terms of bandwidth and data size (Huh & Kim, 2019; Incháustegui et al., 2020). Recalling that we only need infrequent and small data packets in agriculture, LoRa could be a viable alternative.

For *Mobile* applications, IoT devices need a reliable connection. So, a built-in WAP is often added as part of the device itself. Coupled with a *Network-Selection* algorithm, the device could remain connected to whichever network is available nearby (Chen et al., 2018).

Just as in power requirements, *Embedded* IoT devices, installed within consumer products, could utilize the local Wi-Fi when the consumers power their products and use them.

1.5.6 Select/Develop the Required Data Analytics (DA) Algorithms

Data Analytics (DA) refers to all data analysis methods that we apply to raw data to obtain meaningful insights and lessons from the data, as shown in Figure 1.20.

As discussed earlier, the IoT team needs to identify the insights the IoT system needs to deliver. This includes defining or setting the *Purpose*, *Steps*, and *Methods* of DA used.

Purpose: Which could be any of the following (Frankenfield, 2021):

- **Descriptive**: *What is going on with our system?*
- **Diagnostic**: *Why is (something) happening?*
- **Predictive**: *What is likely to happen (to something)?*
- **Perspective**: *What can we do about it?*

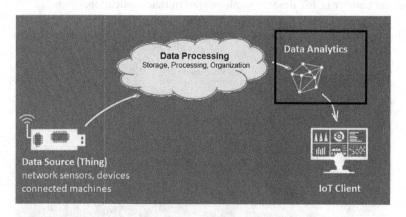

FIGURE 1.20   The IoT framework: *Data analytics.*

Steps: In general, DA involve the following steps: pre-processing (cleansing, transforming), integration (combining multiple sources), and modelling/visualization, as shown in Figure 1.21.

Methods: The methods and techniques used in implementing these steps involve various fields: Statistics & Probability, Fuzzy logic, Artificial Intelligence (AI), Machine Learning (ML), Deep Learning (DL), and other advanced Data Science topics.

Sometimes we cannot identify the insights in advance; the system is new, and we do not know what to expect, so we **let the data guide us**. At first, we focus on processing and visualizing the raw data, deduce any lessons and experimenting with methods and techniques. Hopefully, after few iterations, we would learn more about the system that would help us develop a more solid IoT application that would give us more valuable insights.

1.5.7 DEVELOP/SELECT YOUR IoT CLIENT

Next, the IoT team needs to decide how to implement the IoT Client (Keil, 2020). Like any other web application, that decision comes down to data privacy, security, costs, and skills. One of the oldest web applications out there is the *email*. There are three ways you could set up an email service. Let us review them (Figure 1.22).

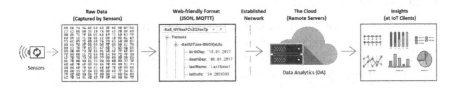

FIGURE 1.21   The conversion from raw data to meaningful insights.

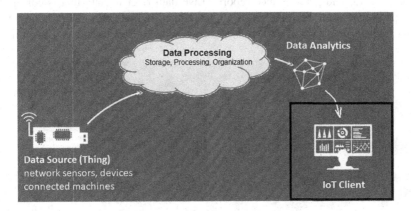

FIGURE 1.22   The IoT framework: *The IoT client.*

You could always use any free email services out there, such as Yahoo, Gmail, or your corporate or school email. It will cost you nothing, and setup will take minutes, but the contents of your email would be exposed to the administrators of your provider.

A second option; you create the email application yourself; perhaps you want a particular feature or a unique email ID. But you host the application using a hosting web service for a fee. You need to have some knowledge of web development for this option, and you need to spend money on hosting. Still, your email is exposed to the hosting service.

A third option; you do everything yourself; create the email application, launch it, and host it on your own physical server. While this option would give you complete control and privacy, you will need to be an expert in web development and spend more money on hosting.

For **IoT Clients**, the above choices and the implications are precisely the same. There are many free and *open-source* IoT client services, such as *ThingSpeak* and *Freeboard.io*. These services could be a great starting point for learners, beginners, and developers.

Beginners could implement these services during training; developers could use these open-source codes of these platforms as starting points and learning tools towards developing their customized versions for future applications.

1.5.8   IoT Outputs: Streamlining Operations

Now that the complete IoT application is running, IoT devices capture and broadcast data, data is being processed in the cloud, and insights are developed and delivered to the IoT clients. We can now use the results to our benefits, starting with *Streamlining Operations* (Figure 1.23).

We can obtain three types of outputs from the IoT Clients that we can use for streamlining operations: live (or interactive or *online*) data, historical (stored or *offline*) data, and performance reports. Live data refer to data that is currently happening as you look into the IoT Client. If the IoT system monitors water level and receives a new set of data, this data is considered live, interactive, or online.

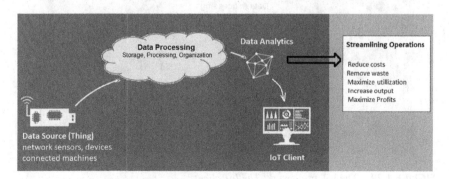

FIGURE 1.23   IoT outputs: *Streamlining operations.*

In some applications, such as agriculture, changes happen very slowly, so there is no point to wait for live updates. Instead, data is captured and stored in the cloud for later retrieval; therefore, it is considered offline. Though it would lack the interactivity of live data, it usually contains far more data and so would be readily available for season effects and user patterns.

In most cases, the actual users of IoT systems, who would learn from the developed insights and act upon them, are the decision makers and managers. These people may not have the time to view and process the data from the IoT clients. Instead, recommendation reports could be developed by the IoT team for their benefits.

It might take time for operations to be effectively streamlined; change always take time. So, a combination of live data, historical data, and performance reports could be helpful to bring about a change in the organization for the better.

1.5.9 IoT Outputs: Protocols for Repurposing Data

As discussed earlier, repurposing data involves reusing the IoT data for another technology (or technologies) and framework for the benefit of the organization. A few things need to be in place before we can achieve that (Figure 1.24).

Firstly, we need **to identify other areas/fields** where the IoT data could be useful. The IoT team should consider the following; what else we can do with this data? Which other project or activity can benefit from this insight? Who else would find this data beneficial?

Alternatively, we could develop IoT systems *specifically for other technologies*. Prime examples include BlockChain or Robotics; both fields need data extensively, so developers could create dedicated IoT systems to develop the data and insights they need.

Once we identify the target technology/framework, we need to develop the *Data Pipeline* to export the data from the IoT framework into that target technology/framework. The *Data Pipeline* is a set of data processing designed to facilitate this transfer, namely:

- **Data Conversion**: IoT data is converted into compatible units/settings based on the requirements of the target technology/framework.

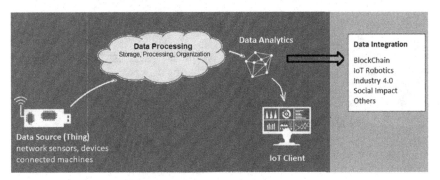

FIGURE 1.24 IoT outputs: *Repurposing data.*

- **Data Repackaging**: At this stage, data could be in the form of *insights*, so it is possible that data would need to be returned to the raw or basic form. Also, the data structure is reorganized as per the requirements of the target technology/framework.
- **Data Transfer**: Once ready, the converted and repackaged data is then transferred to the target technology/framework. The rate of transfer is, again, as per the requirements of the target technology/framework.

1.5.10 IoT Outputs: Protocols for Data Monetization

As discussed before, another organization might be interested in data and insights generated by our IoT system. So, they would be willing to pay a subscription fee to receive scheduled data updates, thus generating a continuous source of income (Figure 1.25).

It is also possible that the other company focuses on other technologies/ frameworks that could benefit from our IoT data, so we can combine *data monetization* with *repurposing data*. Still, to successfully monetize data (or repurposed data), we must first do the following:

- **Identify the Scope of Data to Be Monetized**: Define precisely what you are selling; your whole data set, a sub-set, a repurposed data set, others.
- **Ensure Validation of Data**: You need to show your prospective customers how you obtained your data, with evidence but without exposing propriety information.
- **Ensure Data Security and Encryption**: This could also be considered part of data validation, ensuring your data is also safe and protected.
- **Package Data in Periodic Reports**: Configure your system to create reports daily, weekly, monthly, or in other intervals.
- **Offer Data Subscription Services**: To your prospective customers for a profit.

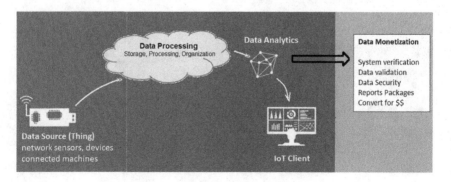

FIGURE 1.25 IoT outputs: *Data monetization.*

With this, the process is complete, and you have developed a working IoT system that brings benefits to your organization. In the later chapters, we will develop the technical skills you will need to complete this process for your organization. But first, we finish this chapter with a few case studies; few IoT projects completed by Mechanical engineers.

1.6 CASE STUDIES OF SUCCESSFUL IoT APPLICATIONS

The following projects were completed by use between 2017 and 2021. They cover several sectors, scopes, and applications. They also show a variety of IoT systems that include simple IoT devices and complex remotely operated autonomous systems.

1.6.1 THE CENTRALIZED WATER MANAGEMENT SYSTEM (2017–2020)

In this project, we utilized the IoT to create a system for centralized water management. In Malaysia, especially in the rural regions, water flow in small canals and waterways is controlled through many weir-type watergates, usually scattered over a large geographical area.

These gates utilize a manually operated worm gear mechanism to open/close the gateway. Therefore, to manage the water flow in each canal, someone needed to go to each gate to open or close the waterway, which is very inefficient, especially during the monsoon season.

The first step was to automate the watergate, so we re-designed the weir-type watergates to become autonomous. We installed sensors that measure the water level at the gate and actuated the gate mechanism through DC motors and a gearing system to control power/torque. Based on the data obtained from the sensor, the gate actuator mechanism would open/close the gate, thus automating the watergate, as shown in Figure 1.26.

Since the watergates are scattered over a large geographical area, *remote monitoring* became essential. We could not send people to each gate (to monitor performance) because that would defeat the point of automation (if the workers are there, they might as well operate it manually). As such, we employed the IoT.

The controller managing the gate was switch to the network-ready Raspberry Pi, and after the infrastructure setup was complete (power and connection), the gates went live.

Each IoT-enabled watergate was configured to broadcast its relevant data to the command centre for remote monitoring. Specifically, the water level, the gate status (opened or closed), and other information (other sensors were added to collect weather data, but we will focus only on the watergate operations), as shown in Figure 1.27.

As shown in the figure, as each gate broadcasts its data and sent them to the command centre, the collated data created a *Centralized* understanding of the water situation all over the region. Officials could monitor each gate, coordinate and share information with local authorities, and recommend action in the event of emergencies.

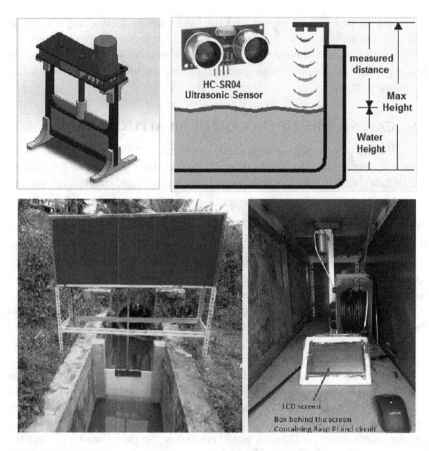

FIGURE 1.26   The centralized water management: *Autonomous watergates.*

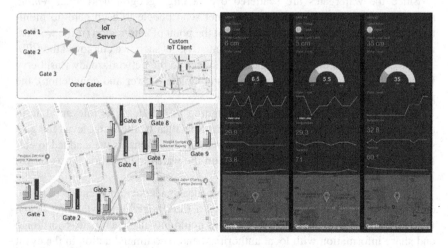

FIGURE 1.27   The centralized water management: *The IoT framework.*

Furthermore, the officials could also *control* these gates remotely. Again, based on gathered information, they could remotely override the sensors at each gate and open/close it as they see fit. This project was successfully demonstrated with three actual watergates scattered over an area of $3,000\,km^2$ in size. The data shown in Figure 1.27 is the actual data captured from these three gates.

Although originally developed for flood mitigation, the project was also helpful for other water-related projects, such as irrigation, industrial, and infrastructure. Also, the project is easily scalable and expandable.

This project won several Gold Awards and certificates for innovation. A full report on this project is presented in this paper (Hajjaj, Hafizuddin et al., 2020).

1.6.2   The IoT-Enabled Robotic Camera Dolly (2018–2019)

In this project, we utilized the IoT to remotely operate a robotic Camera Dolly for the TV and film industry. Although it was not originally designed for it, this work found new relevance due to the social distancing measure taken in the wake of the Covid-19 pandemic in 2020.

In the TV and film industry, the Camera Dolly is a trolley-like platform that carries the camera. A camera person usually operates the Dolly, taking commands from a director on how to take the shot, so each camera person would work to achieve the director's vision.

So, in this system, we utilized *IoT Robotics* to develop a remotely operated robotic camera. From the comfort of his laptop or mobile device, the director would control the camera, or multiple cameras, remotely. We divided the work into two parts: developing the robotic Camera Dolly and establishing the IoT framework to control it remotely.

Figure 1.28 showcases the design and development of the robotic Camera Dolly. It is essentially a mobile robot moving along a fixed track. We added actuators to automate the various movements to move the camera or to manipulate the shot angle.

The architecture of the IoT framework of this system was already shown in Figure 1.4. Figure 1.29 shows the actual system that implements this framework, showing how remote user commands can control camera movements and shot angles (Hajjaj & Karim, 2021).

1.6.3   Portable, Wireless, Interactive IoT Sensors for Agriculture (2018–2020)

This project was introduced to solve several problems we discovered when we reviewed the practices of precision agriculture systems at the time. We discovered most companies used wired agriculture sensors, which significantly disrupted operations, were very limited yet very expensive. So, we sat out to develop portable and interactive IoT devices for agriculture. The resulting system was shown in Figure 1.9; the developed sensors were shown in Figure 1.10.

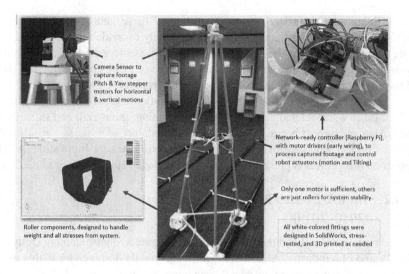

FIGURE 1.28   The IoT-enabled robotic Camera Dolly: *Robot system design.*

FIGURE 1.29   IoT-enabled robotic Camera Dolly: *Remote monitoring & controlling.*

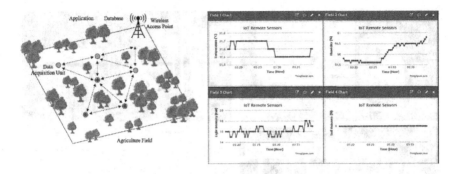

FIGURE 1.30 The IoT framework for interactive precision agriculture.

Aside from collecting data for field managers, we also wanted our sensors to be interactive, i.e. give information locally for the workers in the field. So, we installed multi-coloured LED lights on each IoT device and programmed them to light up a specific colour based on a pre-defined condition; red = low water, yellow = low fertilizer, and so on. This way, as workers come to the field, they would be welcomed with a colourful set of sensors, telling them exactly what each resource is needed and where.

We also solar-powered each sensor, freeing them from the wires and significantly reducing costs, thus creating a solution for precision agriculture far more powerful than the original system at a fraction of the price. Figure 1.30 shows an interactive field (notice the dots) and IoT client we implemented (ThingSpeak).

A full report on this project is presented in this paper (Gsangaya et al., 2020), which includes design analysis, IoT framework, mechanical system design (for Thing design to operate in the outdoors), networking setup, and results and findings.

1.6.4 IoT Vehicle Management System with Network Selection (2019–Current)

In this project, we developed an IoT framework for fleet vehicle management and monitoring. The target industry is the Transportation and Logistics (T&L) sector.

In this IoT framework, vehicles are equipped with our *mobile* IoT devices to gather raw data about the passengers or cargo they are transporting. This work supports passenger busses or delivery/transportation trucks.

This information is broadcast to the cloud, where it would be processed and evaluated at our servers through our patented (filed) IoT Vehicle Management System (IVMS) set of DA algorithms. This includes passenger count, available seats (for busses), cargo status, and item tracing (for delivery trucks). Other information also includes drivers' performance, such as punctuality, adhering to traffic laws, passenger feedback, and travel records.

There are two types of users for the bus service version of this application: passengers and bus operators. Each is provided with a dedicated client showing

FIGURE 1.31   The IoT framework for vehicle fleet management.

relevant information. For the passengers, they receive updates on bus location, estimated time of arrival (ETA), available seating, and driver ratings. For the operator, the system provides updates on utilization patterns, active routes, vehicle tracking, traffic incidents (if any), and more (Figure 1.31).

The project won two GOLD awards for innovation in 2020. First, the original project (IVMS) won at the *Malaysia Technology Expo (MTE 2020)*. The updated project (AS-IVMS), enhanced with the *Auto-Select* network selection algorithm, also won at the *Seoul International Invention Fair 2020 (SIIF2020)* (Hajjaj, Gsangaya et al., 2020).

1.7   IoT OF TOMORROW: EMERGING TRENDS OF THE INTERNET OF THINGS

Understanding IoT trends and their expected changes is vital for anyone involved in IoT, be it the IoT team, the decision makers, or investors. Armed with that understanding, organizations can develop/upgrade their IoT systems to become future-ready; decision makers and investors can make long-term decisions to help them capitalize on these developments and trends. This section reviews the emerging IoT trends at the time of writing this book, May 2021.

1.7.1   IoT Applications of Tomorrow

Today, IoT is applied in many applications, in industry, agriculture, smart homes, infrastructure, and more. With the arrival of 5G and the expected boost of connectivity, you can expect *IoT to be Anywhere and Everywhere*: IoT for retail, services, productivity, healthcare, predictive maintenance, logistics, etc. Any sector can be IoT-enabled in the future, as long as it is data-driven (Kumar, 2021; Smith, 2021).

One of the biggest emerging fields to embrace IoT is **Healthcare**. In 2020, remote medicine, or *Telemedicine*, became mainstream. With developments in connected wearables, monitors, sensors, and medical dispensers, providers would be able to care for patients remotely from a convenient distance. This brings about a massive opportunity in healthcare facilities and equipment, with connectivity a must-have requirement (Kumar, 2021; Weinert, 2021).

The **Retail Industry** is also expected to fully embrace IoT due to the social distancing rules enforced on shoppers after the pandemic. As a result, IoT is expected to make shopping safer, efficient, and very highly customized for its market (Weinert, 2021).

In the past, and indeed today, IoT applications focus on specific tasks or functionalities. In the near future, expect **Large-scale IoT** implementation: city-wide IoT systems, smart buildings, and complete IoT-enabled organizations to become the norm (Weinert, 2021).

1.7.2 INNOVATIVE SOLUTIONS FOR IoT

There is no doubt 5G will boost IoT applications and technologies, but that will also boost the demand for **5G-IoT-ready products**. Creating IoT-ready products is acceptable for today's standards; being 5G-ready (as well) is being ready for tomorrow.

Aside from delivering a great connectivity boost to IoT and creating new opportunities, 5G is also expected to cause challenges. The sheer number of expected devices (20–50 billion devices by 2030) would bring **Cybersecurity & Data Protection** issues on an unprecedented scale. As a result, entities providing solutions in these areas would be in great demand.

Hyper-Automation is the process of combining *Automation* with advanced technologies, such as *AI, ML, DL*, and *Robotic Process Automation (RPA)*, to transform the whole organization rather than just automate a process or a function, with IoT being the glue linking the various processes within the organization (Smith, 2021) (Figure 1.32).

The Cloud is moving; although a fundamental element of IoT, researchers are investigating new technologies that could change the role the *Cloud* plays in IoT or even eliminate it. The motivation behind this is that most IoT challenges are Cloud-related: data security, compliance, broadcast delays, and networking issues (Smith, 2021).

Distributed Cloud, Hybrid Cloud, MultiCloud, Private Cloud, and even *Cloud-less IoT* are all active research fields in this area. Collectively, they refer to how remote servers are managed to minimize Cloud-related challenges. **Edge Computing** is a new development paradigm that combines several of these terms and ideas. In the post-pandemic and the need to accelerate remote

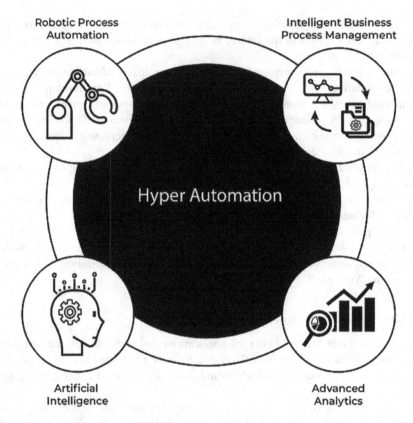

FIGURE 1.32 Hyperautomation and IoT.

services, Edge Computing is becoming an element of tomorrow's IoT (Marr, 2020) (Figure 1.33).

Another exciting trend is the development of ***battery-less IoT devices***. Due to the relatively small power requirements, utilization of solar or hybrid luminaires could bring an end to power-related issues and problems in the near future (Weinert, 2021).

1.7.3 IoT AND OTHER EMERGING TECHNOLOGIES

With IoT being *Anywhere & Everywhere* and enhanced with innovative solutions, integrating IoT with other emerging technologies of the future is expected to skyrocket.

We have already discussed ***BlockChain*** and remotely monitored **automated systems**. However, if we also include *5G* and *Hyper-Automation*, the possibilities become endless: tele-operated medical robots, remote Human-Robot Interaction systems (***remote HRI***), connected social robots (interacting remotely with each other), and more (Newman, 2020).

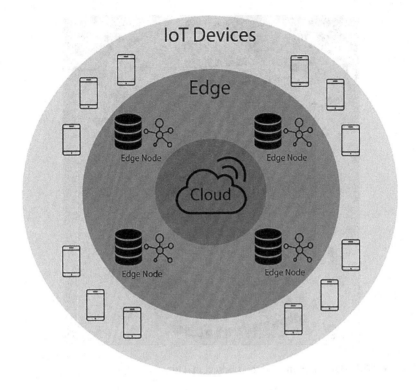

FIGURE 1.33 *Edge computing* for tomorrow's IoT applications.

As more and more sectors embrace IoT, such as the *Productivity*, *Retail*, and *Healthcare* sectors, the ***Anything-as-a-service*** (**XaaS**) model is also expected to skyrocket. Furthermore, with Edge-Computing and other innovative Cloud implementations, *Anything* can be delivered safely, securely, and promptly to the consumer. Therefore, service providers need to adopt the XaaS model to expand their reach (Smith, 2021; Weinert, 2021).

IoT can provide us with clear insights into the full *Product Lifecycle*, starting from consumer requirements, design ideas, manufacturing operations, testing and evaluation, and delivery logistics (to the consumer), and in few years, *in-service* product performance. As such, the enhanced IoT of tomorrow is expected to become the ideal technology to help create and realize the full potential of ***Digital Twins*** (Kumar, 2021; Newman, 2020) (Figure 1.34).

A Digital Twin of a physical system is the real-time virtual representation of that system, which could be a machine, a consumer product, a robot, a building, etc. Digital Twins are the highest level of system modelling, considered the next step after *paper drafting*, *computer drafting/design*, and *model-based engineering systems (MBSE)* (Yang et al., 2018).

FIGURE 1.34   Digital twins and the Internet of Things.

REFERENCES

Adesina, T., & Osasona, O. (2019). A Novel Cognitive IoT Gateway Framework: Towards a Holistic Approach to IoT Interoperability. *2019 IEEE 5th World Forum on Internet of Things (WF-IoT)*, 53–58. https://doi.org/10.1109/WF-IoT.2019.8767248

Aionys. (2019). *How IoT Sensors Can Streamline Business Processes – Aionys.* https://aionys.com/how-iot-sensors-can-streamline-business-processes/

Benazzouz, Y., Munilla, C., Günalp, O., Gallissot, M., & Gürgen, L. (2014). Sharing user IoT devices in the cloud. *2014 IEEE World Forum on Internet of Things (WF-IoT)*, 373–374. https://doi.org/10.1109/WF-IoT.2014.6803193

Browning, D. (2018). *IoT Started with a Vending Machine|Machine Design.* MachineDesign. https://www.machinedesign.com/automation-iiot/article/21836968/iot-started-with-a-vending-machine

Chen, J., Zhang, D., Liu, D., & Pan, Z. (2018). A Network Selection Algorithm Based on Improved Genetic Algorithm. *2018 IEEE 18th International Conference on Communication Technology (ICCT)*, 209–214, Chongqing, China.

CIO Wiki – Client Server. (2021). CIO Index. https://cio-wiki.org/wiki/Client_Server_Architecture

Dhelim, S., Ning, H., Farha, F., Chen, L., Atzori, L., & Daneshmand, M. (2021). IoT-Enabled Social Relationships Meet Artificial Social Intelligence. *IEEE Internet of Things Journal*, 1. https://doi.org/10.1109/JIOT.2021.3081556

Frankenfield, J. (2021). *Data Analytics Definition.* Investopedia. https://www.investopedia.com/terms/d/data-analytics.asp

Gsangaya, K., Hajjaj, S. et al. (2020). Portable, wireless, and effective Internet of things-based sensors for precision agriculture. *International Journal of Environmental Science and Technology, 17*(9), 3901–3916. https://doi.org/10.1007/s13762-020-02737-6

Gudino, M. (2019). *IoT Data Monetization: Turn Your IoT Data into Additional Revenue – IoT Times.* IoT Times. https://iot.eetimes.com/iot-data-monetization-turn-your-iot-data-into-additional-revenue/

Guoqiang, S., Yanming, C., Chao, Z., & Yanxu, Z. (2013). Design and Implementation of a Smart IoT Gateway. *2013 IEEE International Conference on Green Computing and Communications and IEEE Internet of Things and IEEE Cyber, Physical and Social Computing,* 720–723. https://doi.org/10.1109/GreenCom-iThings-CPSCom.2013.130

Hajjaj, S., & Gsangaya, K. (2019). *Vehicle Location and Performance Monitoring System for Resources Management and Effective Utilization.* https://tinyurl.com/yddw4uq2

Hajjaj, S., Gsangaya, K., & Hashim, W. (2020). *AS-IVMS|SIIF2020.* Seol International Invention Fair 2020. http://kipa.org/siif_en/fair/index.jsp

Hajjaj, S., Hafizuddin, M. et al. (2020). Utilizing the Internet of Things (IoT) to develop a remotely monitored autonomous floodgate for water management and control. *Water (Switzerland), 12*(2). https://doi.org/10.3390/w12020502

Hajjaj, S., & Karim, N. (2021). Adoption of Robotics in the TV & Film Industry: The IoT-enabled Robotic Camera Dolly. *30th IEEE International Conference on Robot & Human Interactive Communication (RO-MAN),* Vancouver, BC, Canada.

Huh, H., & Kim, J. Y. (2019). LoRa-based Mesh Network for IoT Applications. *2019 IEEE 5th World Forum on Internet of Things (WF-IoT),* 524–527. https://doi.org/10.1109/WF-IoT.2019.8767242

Incháustegui, C. I. R., Rodríguez, F., & Gutiérrez, S. (2020). Development and Testing of Gateway LoRa for Cloudino IoT Open Source Platform. *2020 IEEE ANDESCON,* 1–5. https://doi.org/10.1109/ANDESCON50619.2020.9272130

Jovanović, B. (2021). *Internet of Things statistics for 2021 – Taking Things Apart.* Data Prot. https://dataprot.net/statistics/iot-statistics/

Keil, A. (2020). *IoT clients.* Arm Keil. https://www2.keil.com/iot

Kjellby, R. A., Cenkeramaddi, L. R., Frøytlog, A., Lozano, B. B., Soumya, J., & Bhange, M. (2019). Long-Range & Self-powered IoT Devices for Agriculture & Aquaponics Based on Multi-Hop Topology. *2019 IEEE 5th World Forum on Internet of Things (WF-IoT),* 545–549. https://doi.org/10.1109/WF-IoT.2019.8767196

Knuckey, E. (2019). *Practical Steps Towards a More Diverse Tech Team|by Makers|Medium.* Makers Academy. https://tinyurl.com/25y6d5br

Kraijak, S., & Tuwanut, P. (2015). A Survey on IoT Architectures, Protocols, Applications, Security, Privacy, Real-World Implementation and Future Trends. *11th International Conference on Wireless Communications, Networking and Mobile Computing (WiCOM 2015),* 1–6. https://doi.org/10.1049/cp.2015.0714

Kumar, S., Tiwari, P., & Zymbler, M. (2019). Internet of Things Is a Revolutionary Approach for Future Technology Enhancement: A Review. *Journal of Big Data, 6*(1). https://doi.org/10.1186/s40537-019-0268-2

Kumar, V. (2021). *Top Emerging IoT Trends Business Should Look for in 2021.* Fintech News. https://www.fintechnews.org/top-emerging-iot-trends-business-should-look-for-in-2021/

Marr, B. (2020). *The 5 Biggest Internet Of Things (IoT) Trends In 2021 Everyone Must Get Ready For Now.* 123 Internet Group. https://www.bernardmarr.com/default.asp?contentID=2125

McFadin, P. (2015). *Internet of Things: Where Does the Data Go?.* Wired. https://www.wired.com/insights/2015/03/internet-things-data-go/

Newman, D. (2020). *5 IoT Trends To Watch in 2021*. Forbes. https://www.forbes.com/sites/danielnewman/2020/11/25/5-iot-trends-to-watch-in-2021/?sh=7028612f201b

Lyon, P. (2020). *How Does the Internet Work? A Simple Explanation of the Internet*. IoT for All. https://www.iotforall.com/how-does-the-internet-work

Pazos, N., Müller, M., Aeberli, M., & Ouerhani, N. (2015). ConnectOpen – Automatic Integration of IoT Devices. *2015 IEEE 2nd World Forum on Internet of Things (WF-IoT)*, 640–644. https://doi.org/10.1109/WF-IoT.2015.7389129

Romeo, L., Petitti, A., Colella, R., Valecce, G., Boccadoro, P., Milella, A., & Grieco, L. A. (2020). Automated Deployment of IoT Networks in Outdoor Scenarios using an Unmanned Ground Vehicle. *2020 IEEE International Conference on Industrial Technology (ICIT)*, 369–374. https://doi.org/10.1109/ICIT45562.2020.9067099

Routh, K., & Pal, T. (2018). A Survey on Technological, Business and Societal Aspects of Internet of Things by Q3, 2017. *2018 3rd International Conference On Internet of Things: Smart Innovation and Usages (IoT-SIU)*, 1–4. https://doi.org/10.1109/IoT-SIU.2018.8519898

Shuler, R. (2002). *How Does the Internet Work?* Stanford University (Class Material). https://web.stanford.edu/class/msande91si/www-spr04/readings/week1/InternetWhitepaper.htm

Smith, J. (2021). *10 IoT Trends to Disrupt the Tech World in 2021*. IoT for All. https://www.iotforall.com/10-iot-trends-to-disrupt-in-2021

Vakaloudis, A., & O'Leary, C. (2019). A Framework for Rapid Integration of IoT Systems with Industrial Environments. *2019 IEEE 5th World Forum on Internet of Things (WF-IoT)*, 601–605. https://doi.org/10.1109/WF-IoT.2019.8767224

Wang, J., Lim, M. K., Wang, C., & Tseng, M. L. (2021). The evolution of the Internet of Things (IoT) over the past 20 years. *Computers and Industrial Engineering*, *155*(May), 107174. https://doi.org/10.1016/j.cie.2021.107174

Weinert, J. (2021). *11 IoT Trends That Will Define 2021*. Interact. https://www.interact-lighting.com/global/iot-insights/11-iot-trends-2021

Worldometer. (2021). *World Population Clock: (2021)*. Worldometer – Real Time World Statistics. https://www.worldometers.info/world-population/

Yadav, P., & Vishwakarma, S. (2018). Application of Internet of Things and Big Data Towards a Smart City. *2018 3rd International Conference On Internet of Things: Smart Innovation and Usages (IoT-SIU)*, 1–5. https://doi.org/10.1109/IoT-SIU.2018.8519920

Yang, C., Shen, W., & Wang, X. (2018). The Internet of Things in Manufacturing: Key Issues and Potential Applications. *IEEE Systems, Man, and Cybernetics Magazine*, *4*(1), 6–15. https://doi.org/10.1109/msmc.2017.2702391

2 Foundation Topics
Concepts

2.1 TERMINOLOGIES AND FUNDAMENTALS

Before you begin your journey in developing Internet of Things (IoT) systems, you must develop a set of skills and working knowledge in few areas related to Electrical & Electronics (E&E) and Software.

Different readers might have different experiences in these fields. You may indeed be familiar with some of the topics discussed in this chapter, perhaps an expert. Nevertheless, we would still recommend that you read the contents of this chapter and consider it a review.

We selected the topics of this chapter due to their relevance to IoT, especially the hands-on work presented in Chapters 4 and 5. So, while you could be familiar with a topic now, you still need to develop a working experience to be ready to perform the tasks presented in the later chapters. If you skipped a section from this chapter, you could always return here for a quick refresher or review on the topic.

Finally, topics discussed in this chapter are presented from the perspective of *Mechanical* engineers. Therefore, the depth and breadth of each topic reflect that philosophy, being deep enough just for the purposes and needs of Mechanical, Industrial, Civil, or related fields.

2.1.1 ELECTRICAL & ELECTRONICS SYSTEMS

In *Electrical* systems, the primary focus is on the production and distribution of *Electricity*, from the energy sources to the end users. The analysis involved in electrical systems includes generation, transmission, distribution, storage, and electrical power management.

In *Electronics* systems, the primary focus is on the management and transmission of *Data*. The analysis involves systems and machines for capturing data (sensors), processing data (controllers), and performing actions based on the data (actuators) (*E vs. E*, 2012).

2.1.2 HARDWARE ABSTRACTION

Hardware abstraction is the process of linking hardware to software; it is the process of defining a hardware element, such as a sensor or an actuator, as an *Object* in the controller program, thus allowing us to interact with it (Wolf, 2014). This concept is shown in Figure 2.1.

FIGURE 2.1   Hardware abstraction.

When you plug in a device to your computer, you must wait until it is *Properly Installed*, i.e. until its *Drivers* are installed. A driver of a hardware device is a program that contains hardware abstraction definitions of that device. Without the proper driver, that hardware would not be properly *abstracted*; therefore, the system would not be able to interact with it.

In electro-mechanical systems, including IoT systems, hardware abstraction and setup is an essential early step in creating effective controller programs (Wolf, 2014).

2.1.3   A PROGRAM VS. AN ALGORITHM

Although the terms *Program* and *Algorithm* are related and seem similar, they are, in fact, different. Understanding that difference and using that understanding when creating controller programs (or any computer program for that matter) is a powerful skill for any developer.

Essentially, both an algorithm and a program contain a set of steps, instructions, and *logic* to be performed by a system (a sensor, a machine, a robot, an application, etc.). The difference between them is *how* these instructions are written. Figure 2.2 shows a visualization of the difference between a program and an algorithm (Verma, 2018).

An algorithm is written in a human language (English, Spanish, your native language, etc.); it could also contain symbols and pseudo code that you would understand. You can also visualize your algorithm with flow charts and block diagrams. In other words, you create your algorithm in your own words or in any visualization you prefer.

On the other hand, a program is written in a properly formulated programming language, governed by a strict set of language rules, called the language *Syntax*. A common beginner's mistake is to skip the algorithm and focus entirely on writing the program, which is unfortunate.

If you begin with the program directly, you would have to contend with two tasks simultaneously, creating the steps and logic of your program *and* program errors. This could be disruptive, confusing, and a very time-consuming exercise, especially if you are a beginner and not yet familiar with program troubleshooting.

Instead, you should always *begin* with the algorithm; starting from your ideas and objectives (what you want your system to do), and based on the given input

A Computer Program	The Equivalent Algorithm

```
import traffic_library

# setup
tl = traffic_library.Traffic_Light()
carl = traffic_library.vehicle(personal)

# Operations: while car is on the road
while isCarOnRoad(carl) == True:

    # Traffic law 1 = Traffic Lights
    if tl.color == "green":
        carl.status = maintain_speed()
    elif tl.color == "yellow":
        carl.status = slowdown_speed()
    elif tl.color == "red":
        carl.status = set_speed(0)
```

Obtain a driving license
Procure a Vehicle (buy, lease)

While driving on the road,
when you encounter a traffic light:

If the light is green, keep going.
If it's yellow, then slow down.
If it's red, then stop the vehicle.

FIGURE 2.2 A computer program vs. an algorithm.

parameters, create the set of rules and instructions in your own words. This way, you would not need to worry about the Syntax or its errors; you would instead focus on creating the building blocks of your code.

Once your algorithm is ready or complete, then it would be a matter of conversion. Based on the Syntax rules of your chosen language, you can then convert your algorithm into a working program. If you decided to change language, you could simply repeat the process. Only now, you would need to apply the Syntax rules of the new language, and so on.

Having an algorithm at hand is an excellent tool to check your program if it is not performing as expected. You can use the algorithm as a reference point or as a troubleshooting tool. The algorithm can act like a general guideline to help you conceptualize your ideas and convert them into reality while creating the intricate components of your program.

2.1.4 THE PROGRAM SYNTAX

The Syntax of a computer language defines how words, symbols, and their combinations form the elements of that language. It is analogous to the *Grammar* of a human language, only more critical. If you break some grammar rules in a human language, your audience could still understand the intended message. However, in a computer system, any Syntax violation would result in program errors and system failures (Woz U, 2020).

Therefore, understanding the Syntax rules of your programming language is essential. Luckily, you need not memorize anything or keep notes anywhere. All you need to do is to search online for the task you need+language, and you will find plenty of references online. For example, if you search *if statement C++*, you will see plenty of references online. We will revisit *Online Sources* later in this chapter.

2.1.5   Microprocessors vs. CPUs

As discussed earlier, a computer program receives a set of input information (from sensors, user input, another program, etc.), processes that information (based on the algorithm), and then gives out a set of instructions to other components (actuators, memory, other programs, etc.)

In a computer system, a *Processor* unit performs the above activities, i.e. give output commands based on input data as per program instructions. After decades of miniaturization, it is commonly known today as the *Microprocessor*. A typical microprocessor consists of thousands of micro-electronic components (transistors) that allow it to be programmable to perform the arithmetic and logical tasks discussed above. Microprocessors vary in capabilities, sizes, and features. As a result, different microprocessors are built for different applications.

A *Central Processing Unit* (*CPU*) is a powerful microprocessor that can perform all primary operations needed for a stand-alone computer system. Aside from the components of a typical microprocessor, it also consists of registrars, an arithmetic unit, a logic unit, a control unit, a small memory unit (known as the cache), and others. Figure 2.3 shows a comparison.

The CPU can perform all math, logic, memory operations, memory slots tracking, and interact with all linked systems. Therefore, CPUs are often used to operate complex systems such as computers, operating systems (OSs), and complex machines.

On the other hand, microprocessors (or microcontrollers) are often limited to specific tasks or sub-tasks of a complex system. Though they also perform arithmetic and logic operations, these are often not on the same scale as those performed by the CPUs (Munoz, 2020).

2.2   EMBEDDED SYSTEMS: AN INTRODUCTION

As shown in Figure 2.4, an embedded system is a microcontroller-based system (a controller with sensors, actuators, and misc. components) inserted, or embedded, into another system to perform a dedicated function and add that functionality to the host system.

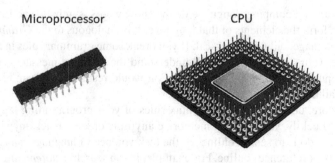

Microprocessor   CPU

FIGURE 2.3   A single-chip microprocessor vs. a CPU.

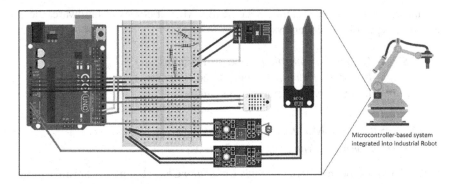

FIGURE 2.4 An industrial robot with an embedded system for Industry 4.0.

As seen in the figure, the embedded system adds few features to the industrial robot, such as *Data Collection* and *Connectivity (to the Cloud)*, thus making it ready for Industry 4.0 and Industrial IoT (IIoT).

The design of embedded systems involves *Hardware, Software*, and *System Architecture* considerations. Hardware issues include components, types, and peripherals. Software issues include controller programming, inputs, outputs, and network operations.

System architecture involves advanced concepts such as embedded system *Type* (mobile, network-enabled, stand-alone, real-time), *Control Software Architecture* (simple loop, interrupt-controlled, cooperative multitasking, multi-threading), and *Scale* (small-scale, medium-scale, sophisticated-scale embedded systems) (Serpanos & Wolf, 2011).

For this book, however, we will focus only on the *Hardware* and *Software* factors, as these issues serve as a prerequisite before considering the advanced system architecture issues.

For example, before you can decide on the scale of your embedded systems and their sophistication, you would need to understand the hardware and software needs for each implementation, and so on.

2.3   EMBEDDED SYSTEMS: HARDWARE CONSIDERATIONS

The key to the success of embedded systems is miniaturization. Embedding a desktop or laptop into a Robot is not practical, but embedding a miniaturized version of that computer is possible, hence, the concept of *System-on-Chip (SoC)* (Risset, 2011).

Thanks to the advances in microelectronics manufacturing, microcontrollers and CPUs continue to shrink in physical size while exploding in performance. Also, with advances in system integration, it is possible today to build *pocket-sized* computers or controller systems. Specifically, when it comes to hardware, there are three types of embedded systems:

1. *Single-Chip microcontroller* embedded systems
2. *Single-Board microcontroller* embedded systems
3. *Single-Board computer* embedded systems

2.3.1 SINGLE-CHIP MICROCONTROLLER SYSTEMS (CONTROLLER CHIP EMBEDDED SYSTEMS)

Single-Chip microcontrollers, or simply *Controller Chips*, Figure 2.3, are microcontrollers enclosed in a single chip that can be embedded into any electro-mechanical system. However, to perform their tasks, Controller Chips need some support components to be embedded; these may include input/output ports, memory, and miscellaneous (Vaglica & Gilmour, 1990).

2.3.2 SINGLE-BOARD MICROCONTROLLER SYSTEMS (CONTROLLER BOARD EMBEDDED SYSTEMS)

As the name implies, *Single-Board microcontrollers*, or simply *Board Controllers*, are microcontrollers integrated with their support components on single printed circuit boards (PCBs). Examples include Arduino, Figure 2.5, NodeMCU, and others (Khan, 2021).

While Controller Boards are easier to embed into electro-mechanical systems, Controller Chips allow customization and user-specific application development. However, both types still require a separate computer system for programming, configuration, and troubleshooting.

2.3.3 SINGLE-BOARD COMPUTER SYSTEMS (COMPUTER BOARD EMBEDDED SYSTEMS)

Single-Board Computer systems, or simply *Computer Boards*, go a step further; they are a complete computer system on a single board, as shown in Figure 2.6.

The figure shows the Raspberry Pi 3 board, and as shown in the figure, the board contains all major components of a computer system, all miniaturized to fit the size of a credit card. Being a stand-alone system allows for more complex applications and systems. In addition, Computer Boards are relatively easier to embed in electro-mechanical systems than other types.

However, the differences in performance between these types are a different discussion altogether; sometimes, all we need is a single controller chip, sometimes a controller board is more suitable, and sometimes we would need a full-fledged computer. Therefore, we need to understand the difference between these systems (*The Raspberry Pi*, 2021).

Nevertheless, the design and development Controller Chip is outside the scope of this book (since it is targeted for mechanical engineers). Therefore, for the

FIGURE 2.5   The *Arduino Uno* controller board.

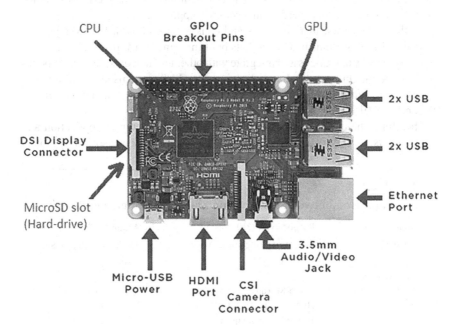

FIGURE 2.6   The *Raspberry Pi 3* computer board.

remainder of this book, we will focus entirely on *Controller Boards* and *Computer Boards* embedded systems.

2.3.4 EMBEDDED SYSTEMS: FEATURES, COMPARISONS, AND COMBINATIONS

The following few subsections provide comparisons between Controller Boards and Computer Boards, represented by the *Arduino, Raspberry Pi*, and *Beaglebone* boards. The comparisons focus on system features, performance, and readiness for IoT.

2.3.4.1 The Raspberry Pi vs. the Arduino

Table 2.1 summarizes the difference between the Arduino and Raspberry Pi boards. As the table shows, the Raspberry Pi is a full-fledged computer that can perform complex operations. In contrast, the Arduino is limited in scope to simple switch operations for smaller projects.

As seen in the table, the Raspberry Pi comes ready with multiple connectivity options, making it *Network-Ready*; ready to perform network-related operations without added hardware or software (aside from importing relevant libraries). Arduino, on the other hand, requires external *modules* to enable networking. The same applies to the number of available ports, and therefore available features (Orsini, 2014).

2.3.4.2 Arduino IoT Systems vs. Raspberry Pi IoT Systems

Table 2.2 shows another comparison between Arduino and Raspberry Pi systems, this time in terms of their performances in IoT applications.

As the table shows, there are pros and cons for each board. For example, the Raspberry Pi IoT systems benefit from its built-in connectivity, ports, and ability to perform complex operations and integrate with other technologies, such as Robotics or BlockChain. On the other hand, Arduino-based IoT systems are ideal for simple tasks, consume less power, relatively cheaper, and support analogue sensors (Pedamkar, 2015).

Therefore, the decision on board type depends on the target application and requirements; is the task simple or complicated (network sensor vs. remotely

TABLE 2.1
A Comparison between the Arduino and the Raspberry Pi Boards

Area	Raspberry Pi (3B)	Arduino (Uno)
Processor	1.4 GHz, Quad-core, ARMv8	16 MHz, ATMega328P
RAM	1 GB SDRAM	2 KB SRAM
Input voltage	5 V	7–12 V
Storage	Micro-SD (up to 16 GB), USB	32 kb flash memory
Ports	HDMI, Audio Jack, LCD USB×4 (input/output)	USB×1 (input only)

TABLE 2.2

A Comparison between the Arduino and the Raspberry Pi Boards

Comparison	Raspberry Pi (3) IoT Systems	Arduino (Uno) IoT Systems
Networking	Ethernet, Wi-Fi, Bluetooth	Only with external modules
Pins	GPIO: 40, analog: 0	GPIO: 14, analog: 6
Power consumption	260 mA (idle)	11.45 – 27.85 mA (idle)
IDE (language)	Any Linux-supported IDE (any programming language)	Arduino IDE (Arduino language, C/C++)
Applications (recommended)	Complex, multithreaded tasks, for integration with other technologies (Robotics, BlockChain, ROS)	Simple, real-time tasks, when speed is critical, if analog sensors used

monitored autonomous system)? Is system speed a concern, or can we afford a delay? Do we use the built-in features of the Raspberry Pi or build our own Arduino+modules system?

Another critical factor is the programming language. As shown in Table 2.2, Arduino boards generally support C++ only since the Arduino language is an extension of C/C++, while the Raspberry Pi can be programmed with virtually any language. Language choice is not just about personal preference or experience; it is also related to available libraries and resources.

Say you found a feature online and want to incorporate it into your system, but unfortunately, the library you found is written in Python and you are using *Arduino*. Therefore, you cannot use this library directly unless you create a conversion library or re-implement it (re-write it from scratch) in Arduino, assuming that is possible.

The same thing could apply to external modules, perhaps the manufacturer created the device's drivers only in C++, but you are now working on Python. But this is a lesser problem because you can always select appropriate modules with matching drivers. Also, most module manufacturers today create drivers for all major systems and languages.

2.3.4.3 The Raspberry Pi vs. the Beaglebone

We could have replaced the Raspberry Pi with the Beaglebone, and Tables 2.1 and 2.2 would not change much (except the GPIO configuration). That is because Raspberry Pi and Beaglebone are both considered *Computer Boards* (Pedamkar, 2018).

Historically speaking, the Beaglebone came first. It was launched in 2008, while the Raspberry Pi was launched in 2012. Both systems were initially meant as educational tools to help students learn about computer systems, mechatronics, and microcontrollers.

Soon, however, their popularity grew outside their intended markets. Today, they are widely used by students, hobbyists, engineers, and professionals for Robotics, embedded systems, automation, and of course, IoT systems. Nevertheless, there

TABLE 2.3

A Comparison between the Raspberry Pi and the Beaglebone Computer Boards

Comparison	The Raspberry Pi (3)	The Beaglebone (Black)
Processor	1.4 GHz, Quad-core, ARMv8	1 GHz, ARM Cortex A8
RAM	1 GB SDRAM	512 MB DDR3
Input voltage	5 V	5 V
Storage	Micro-SD	2 GB on board, micro-SD
Ports	HDMI, audio jack, USB×4 (in/out), LCD	Micro HDMI, USB×1 (in/out)
Networking	Gigabit Ethernet, Wi-Fi, Bluetooth	Fast Ethernet
Pins	GPIO: 40 pins, Analog: 0	GPIO: 2×46 pins (92 total pins)
Operating systems	Raspberry Pi OS, Risc OS, Ubuntu (Mate, snappy only) Windows IoT	Ubuntu, Debian, Android, Windows IoT

are differences between the Raspberry Pi and Beaglebone boards (Long, 2019), as shown in Table 2.3.

As seen in the table, there are once again pros and cons between the two boards. The Raspberry Pi supports more connectivity options (a more powerful Ethernet, Wi-Fi, and Bluetooth), while the Beaglebone supports more than double GPIO pins (92 total) (Nikhil, 2021).

Beaglebone supports more powerful OSs, such as Android, Ubuntu, and Debian. In contrast, the Raspberry Pi boards support special versions (distributions) of Linux, such as *Raspbian*, a unique Linux distribution specifically for the Raspberry Pi.

2.3.4.4   Combinations of Embedded Systems

By combining different types of embedded systems, such as the Arduino (a Controller Board) with a Raspberry Pi (a Computer Board), you can develop systems that benefit from both worlds; why choose when you can have both!

The Controller Boards can be dedicated to capture and respond to sensor data in real time, including analogue sensors. Then, based on the data, they can act quickly and accordingly.

On the other hand, the Computer Boards could handle more complex and multi-tasked operations; they can receive system updates from the Controller Boards, handle networking, package and broadcast data to the cloud, wait for remote instructions (if any), and more.

Over the years, there have been many successful applications of these combinations, mainly for remotely monitored/operated autonomous systems. One example that stands out is the *Farmbot* project, as shown in Figure 2.7.

The Farmbot project is a backyard autonomous agriculture robot that can perform generic agriculture tasks. It is a *Cartesian Robot* controlled via a combination of local Controller Boards and a Raspberry Pi board (*FarmBot|Open-Source CNC Farming*, 2021).

FIGURE 2.7   The *Farmbot* remotely operated agriculture robot. (*FarmBot*, 2019.)

The local controllers operate the three motors corresponding to the x, y, z motions that make up the Cartesian Robot's movements. At the same time, the Raspberry Pi updates system behaviour (watering, picking, seeding, etc.), broadcasts data to the cloud, and receives remote commands from its user, which are sent through their mobile devices.

This is also an excellent example of *IoT Robotics*, where IoT data (current status of field and growth of produce) can directly impact Robot operations (task/behaviour selection).

2.4   EMBEDDED SYSTEMS: PERIPHERALS

Embedded systems consist of a wide range of hardware components, modules, sensors, actuators, and miscellaneous components; collectively, these components are referred to as *Peripherals*. They can be utilized in conjunction with all types of embedded systems to achieve various effects. This section presents a list of peripherals for embedded systems.

2.4.1   MODULES (CONNECTIVITY, OTHERS)

Modules are electronic components that add specific functionalities, such as the wireless network modules (Wi-Fi, Bluetooth, cellular modules) and others. These modules are ideal for boards that do not originally have these features, such as the Arduino Uno, Nano, and Mega.

2.4.1.1   The ESP8266 Wi-Fi Module

The ESP8266 Wi-Fi Module is a low-cost, self-contained controller-on-chip with an integrated Transmission Control Protocol/Internet Protocol (TCP/IP) stack that can provide access to a Wi-Fi network, providing wireless connectivity (*Esp8266 Module*, 2015) (Figure 2.8).

Pin 7: RX	Pin 8: VCC (3.3V)
Pin 5: GPIO0	Pin 6: Reset
Pin 3: GPIO2	Pin 4: CH_EN
Pin 1: Ground	Pin 2: TX

FIGURE 2.8   An ESP8266 Wi-Fi module.

The ESP8266 is powered by a 32-bit Tensilica Xtensa microcontroller at 80 MHz, with 96 kb of flash memory and 64 kb of SRAM. Additionally, it comes with factory-installed firmware and can be controlled using standard AT commands. The module supports 2.4 GHz Wi-Fi connections based on the 802.11 b/g/n protocol.

Furthermore, the module can connect to a router and function as both a client and an access point (AP). Lastly, the module is IP addressable and can also function as a web server.

2.4.1.2   The HC05 Bluetooth Module

Bluetooth is an affordable communication protocol with a maximum data rate of 1 Mbps, with a nominal working range of 100 m using a 2.4 GHz frequency. The HC-05 is an inexpensive, low-power Bluetooth module that enables two-way (full-duplex) wireless functionality in any embedded system (*HC-05 Bluetooth Module*, 2018) (Figure 2.9).

The module can be used for communication between two embedded systems and is compatible with a wide range of Bluetooth compatible devices such as smartphones, laptops, and tablets. In addition, the built-in data mode enables the module to send and receive data from other Bluetooth devices. Thus, devices such as smartphones can be used as data loggers and remote controllers, i.e. remotely switch components on or off.

2.4.1.3   The SIM800L GSM/GPRS Module

The SIM800L is a standard wireless network module for IoT systems. The SIM800L module is a low-cost, miniature cellular modem. It can be integrated with embedded systems to achieve cellular phone functionalities, such as sending and receiving SMSs, placing or receiving phone calls, and connecting to the Internet via the General System for Mobile Communication (GSM) and General Packet Radio Service (GPRS) protocols. The module supports quad-band GSM/GPRS network; therefore, it can provide reliable connectivity to embedded systems almost anywhere in the world (*SIM800L GSM Module*, 2019) (Figure 2.10).

2.4.1.4   The Ublox Neo-6M GPS Module

The Global Positioning System (GPS) is a satellite-based navigation system. GPS satellites circle the Earth twice a day in a precise orbit. GPS technology uses

FIGURE 2.9   An HC-05 Bluetooth module.

FIGURE 2.10   A SIM800L GSM/GPRS module.

unique signals and orbital parameters sent by these satellites in space to receivers on Earth, in this case, the GPS module, to decode its location accurately and precisely (Figure 2.11).

GPS satellites transmit low-power radio signals that travel by line of sight, wherein they can pass through clouds, glass, and plastic but will not go through most solid objects, such as buildings and mountains. The signals received from the satellites by the module contain timestamps of when they were transmitted. Using information from these satellites, the exact position of the GPS receiver can be triangulated. For example, to calculate a 2D position, namely latitude and longitude, and track movement, a GPS receiver must be locked on to the signal of at least three satellites.

With four or more satellites in view, the receiver can determine 3D position with the addition of the altitude. Once the receiver position has been determined,

FIGURE 2.11   A Ublox Neo-6M GPS module.

the GPS module can then calculate relevant information, including the speed, bearing, trip, and destination distances.

The Ublox Neo-6M GPS module consists of a built-in antenna and a low-power receiver core for highly accurate positioning information. The module can track up to 22 satellites on 50 channels and achieve the industry's highest sensitivity tracking level at 161 dB while consuming only 45 mA supply current. In addition, it has a horizontal position accuracy of 2.5 m and a navigation update rate of 1 Hz.

One great feature of the module is Power Save Mode (PSM), which dramatically reduces the module's power consumption to just 11 mA, making it suitable for power-sensitive applications like a GPS wristwatch. The module also contains a rechargeable button battery which helps retain the battery-backed RAM (BBR). As the battery retains the clock and last positional data, the time-to-first-fix (TTFF) is significantly reduced to 1 second with much faster position locks.

Without the battery, the GPS module would always cold-start, so the initial GPS lock takes more time, up to 27 seconds. The battery is automatically charged when power is applied and maintains data for up to 2 weeks without power. In addition, the module supports the National Marine Electronics Association (NMEA) output data format, a standard supported by all GPS manufacturers (*Ublox NEO-6M GPS Module*, 2017).

2.4.2   INPUT DEVICES (SENSORS, BUTTONS)

As discussed earlier, input devices capture and deliver information to the microcontroller. This could be environment data captured by sensors or user commands captured by buttons, touch screens, or similar devices. Sensors are classified as *Analogue* or *Digital* sensors.

Analogue sensors produce a continuous analogue voltage output proportional to the measured parameter, ranging from 0 to 3.3 V or 5 V, depending on the microcontroller. Also, analogue sensors are made from analogue components, such as resistors, capacitors, amplifiers, diodes, and transistors, so they are often prone to environmental noise.

Digital sensors, on the other hand, consist of logic gates and built-in microcontroller chips that convert the measured parameter into a digital signal output; binary values of 0 or 1, that correspond to *low* or *high*, or *true* or *false* outputs, respectively. As a result, digital sensors are considered more accurate and precise compared to analogue sensors.

2.4.2.1 The ADXL335 Accelerometer Sensor

The ADXL335 sensor measures acceleration or the change in motion with a full sensing range of ±3 g. It can measure the static acceleration due to gravity in tilt-sensing applications and dynamic acceleration resulting from motion, shock, or vibration. The force caused by vibration or acceleration causes a mass to squeeze the piezoelectric material in the sensor, which produces an electrical charge that is proportional to the force exerted upon it (Figure 2.12).

Since the charge is proportional to the force, and the mass in the sensor is a constant, then the charge is also proportional to the acceleration. Therefore, by measuring this charge or voltage, the acceleration can be determined. The sensor has three analogue outputs, X-out, Y-out, and Z-out, which outputs an analogue voltage proportional to acceleration exerted on the X-axis, Y-axis, and Z-axis.

Accelerometers are commonly used in electronic devices such as video game controllers to detect movement and actions from the user (*ADXL335 Accelerometer*, 2018).

2.4.2.2 The Water Level Sensor

A water level sensor is used to measure water level, detect rainfall, or detect leakage. The sensor has a series of ten exposed copper traces, five power traces, and five sense traces. These traces are interlaced so that there is one sense trace

FIGURE 2.12 An ADXL335 accelerometer sensor.

FIGURE 2.13 A general-purpose water level sensor.

between every two power traces. The traces are not connected but are bridged by water when submerged (Figure 2.13).

The exposed parallel conductors act as a variable resistor whose resistance varies according to the water level. The change in resistance corresponds to the distance from the top of the sensor to the water's surface and is inversely proportional to the height of the water.

The more immersed in water the sensor is, the better its conductivity and resistance, and vice versa. Water level can be determined by measuring the resistance and corresponding analogue output voltage (*Water Sensor*, 2017).

2.4.2.3   The FC-28 Soil Moisture Sensor

A soil moisture sensor is a type of variable resistor with a resistance that decreases as the volumetric content of water in the soil increases. The sensor consists of two exposed probes that allow current to pass through the soil. The soil conducts more electricity when there is more water in the soil, resulting in less resistance. Since dry soil is a poor conductor of electricity, the soil is less conductive, and there will be more resistance when the moisture level is low (Figure 2.14).

As the soil moisture sensor's resistance depends on the water content in the soil, the soil moisture level can be determined by measuring its resistance and corresponding analogue output voltage. In addition, the sensor includes a digital output that outputs a high signal when the moisture is above a certain threshold. This sensor is often used in automated greenhouse and sprinkler systems (*Soil Moisture Sensor*, 2015).

FIGURE 2.14   An FC-28 soil moisture sensor.

2.4.2.4   The GL55 Light Intensity Sensor

A light intensity sensor consists of a photoresistor or light-dependent resistor (LDR), a variable resistor with a resistance that decreases as the ambient light intensity increases. Simply put, the flow of electric current through the photoresistor increases with increasing light intensity. Inversely, decreasing ambient light intensity increases the photoresistor resistance (Figure 2.15).

The photoresistor's resistance depends on the amount of light falling on it. The ambient light intensity value, measured in Lux, can be determined by measuring the photoresistor's resistance and corresponding analogue output voltage. The sensor also provides a digital output based on the amount of light contacting the surface of the photoresistor, ideal for sensing whether it is daylight or nighttime conditions. A built-in potentiometer can be used to adjust the threshold of the digital output (*Light Sensor*, 2016).

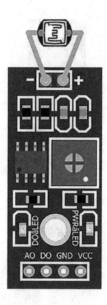

FIGURE 2.15 A GL55 light intensity sensor.

2.4.2.5 The Infrared Flame Detection Sensor

The infrared (IR) flame detection sensor is sensitive to the IR radiation emitted by open flames. It is used for short-range fire detection up to 1 m and is usually used as a fire alarm. The sensor can detect a flame or a light source with IR radiation wavelength in the range of 760–1,100 nm. It can produce both analogue output; a real-time voltage signal based on the thermal resistance, and digital output. On the other hand, a high output signal is produced when the IR value reaches a certain threshold (*Flame Sensor*, 2018) (Figure 2.16).

2.4.2.6 The MQ Gas Quality Sensor

The MQ series of gas quality sensors are metal oxide semiconductor (MOS) type of sensors. The sensor can detect combustible gases such as liquefied petroleum gas (LPG), methane, propane, butane, alcohol (ethanol), hydrogen, carbon monoxide, and smoke (Figure 2.17).

A nickel–chromium coil and aluminium oxide ceramic coating forms a heating element. When the tin dioxide (SnO_2) semiconductor layer is heated at a high temperature, oxygen is adsorbed on the surface. In clean air, electrons from the conduction band in tin dioxide are attracted to oxygen molecules. This forms an electron depletion layer just below the surface of SnO_2 particles and forms a potential barrier. As a result, the SnO_2 film becomes highly resistive and prevents electric current flow.

In the presence of combustible gases, however, the surface density of adsorbed oxygen decreases as it reacts with the gases, which lowers the potential barrier. Electrons are then released into the tin dioxide, allowing current to flow freely through the sensor.

FIGURE 2.16   An infrared flame detection sensor.

FIGURE 2.17   An MQ gas quality sensor.

Metal oxide sensors are also known as *Chemiresistors* since the working principle is based on the change of resistance of the sensing material when exposed to combustible gases. Thus, by measuring the change in resistance and corresponding output voltage, combustible gas concentrations can be detected.

It can detect gas concentrations anywhere from 200 to 10,000 ppm. The MQ gas sensor provides a digital output based on combustible gases and a variable analogue output based on the proportion of gas concentration in the air. The higher

FIGURE 2.18   An HC-SR04 ultrasonic distance sensor.

the gas concentration in the air, the higher the output voltage, and vice versa. The sensor has a built-in potentiometer for adjusting the threshold of the digital output. This sensor is mainly used in smoke alarms and gas leakage detection (*MQ2 Gas Sensor*, 2019).

2.4.2.7   The HC-SR04 Ultrasonic Distance Sensor

The HC-SR04 ultrasonic sensor uses sonar to determine the distance to an object. The ultrasonic transmitter emits a high-frequency 40 kHz ultrasonic pulse reflecting off an object and back to the ultrasonic receiver. The time delay between when the sound wave was transmitted and when it was received is also measured (Figure 2.18).

Since distance is related to speed and time, by knowing the speed of the sound wave and the time taken for the sound wave to travel back and forth from an object, the distance from the sensor to the object can be calculated. The sensor offers a large non-contact range detection between 2 and 400 cm with excellent accuracy of 3 mm (*HC-SR04 Sensor*, 2017).

2.4.2.8   The FC-51 Obstacle Detection Sensor

An obstacle detection sensor emits IR light that is bounced back by objects in proximity. When an object is detected, a high digital output is produced. We can adjust the sensitivity using the onboard potentiometer. This sensor is typically used in Obstacle Avoidance Robots to detect when the Capitalize Robot is about to impact walls or other objects. The sensor detects objects at a distance of 2–30 cm and a detection angle of 35° (*IR Sensor*, 2017) (Figure 2.19).

2.4.2.9   The Sound Detection Sensor

A sound detection sensor is a highly sensitive module for picking up audio and triggers a digital output based on the sound intensity. The threshold value can be adjusted with the onboard potentiometer. The sensor consists of a microphone with a diaphragm and a backplate. When sound waves are channelled into the microphone, the diaphragm vibrates, and the capacitance changes as the diaphragm and backplate get closer together or farther apart (Figure 2.20).

This change in capacitance causes a change in voltage which can be measured to determine the amplitude of the sound. This signal is fed to an LM393 comparator and converted to a digital output (*Sound Sensor*, 2019).

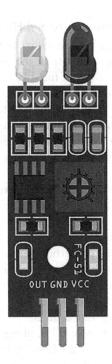

FIGURE 2.19 An object detection sensor.

FIGURE 2.20 A sound detection sensor.

2.4.2.10   The DHT11/22 Temperature and Humidity Sensor

The DHT11/22 are low-cost digital temperature and humidity sensors, Two electrodes with a moisture-holding substrate in the middle make up the humidity sensing component. The conductivity of the substrate and resistance between the electrodes changes according to the ambient humidity (Figure 2.21).

Furthermore, the DHT11/22 includes a negative temperature coefficient (NTC) sensor, wherein a change in temperature causes a change in resistance of the resistor. These sensors provide more significant changes in the resistance with small temperature changes and are made by sintering semiconductive materials such as ceramics or polymers.

The term NTC means that the resistance decreases proportionally with an increase in the temperature. An IC measures and processes this change in resistance and converts the signals into a digital output about the ambient humidity and temperature (*DHT11, DHT12*, 2016).

The DHT22 has slightly better properties compared to the DHT11; the DHT22 has a humidity range of 0%–100%, a humidity accuracy of ±2%, a humidity resolution of 0.1%, a temperature range of −40°C to 125°C, a temperature accuracy of ±0.5°C, and temperature resolution of 0.1°C.

The DHT11 has a humidity range of 20%–80%, with humidity accuracy of ±5%, and a humidity resolution of 0.1%, along with a temperature range of 0°C–50°C, temperature accuracy of ±2%, and temperature resolution of 0.1°C. However, the DHT22 sensor is also much more expensive than the DHT11 (*DHT11, DHT12*, 2016).

In addition, the DHT22 is also slower at updating readings with a sampling rate of 0.5 Hz and a refresh rate of 2 seconds than a sampling rate of 1 Hz and a refresh rate of 1 second on the DHT11.

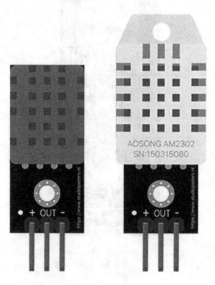

FIGURE 2.21   A DHT11/22 temperature and humidity sensor.

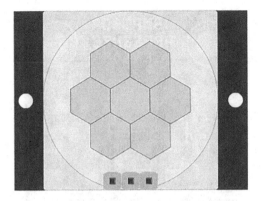

FIGURE 2.22   An HC-SR501 pyroelectric infrared sensor.

2.4.2.11   The HC-SR501 Pyroelectric Infrared Sensor

The HC-SR501 pyroelectric infrared (PIR) sensor detects movement from humans or objects. All objects emit heat energy in the form of IR radiation. The hotter an object is, the more radiation it emits. PIR sensors are specially designed to detect such levels of IR radiation. When an object passes in front of the sensor, the change in IR levels is detected, and high digital output is produced (*HC-SR501 PIR Sensor*, 2018) (Figure 2.22).

2.4.2.12   The Pushbutton

A pushbutton is a component that connects two points in a circuit when pressed. It is a simple, two-state switch mechanism used to control a process such as turning on or off actuators, including motors, buzzers, and LEDs (Figure 2.23).

Inside a pushbutton is a small spring that makes contact with two wires, allowing electricity to flow when pressed. When released, the spring retracts, and the contact is interrupted, and the current flow immediately stops.

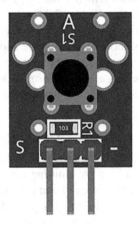

FIGURE 2.23   A general-purpose three-pin pushbutton module.

FIGURE 2.24 A BMP180 barometric pressure sensor.

In a pushbutton module, when the button is open or unpressed, there is no connection in the pushbutton circuit, so a low reading is produced on the digital output. However, when the button is closed or pressed, a connection is made in the pushbutton circuit, producing a high digital output (*Button Module*, 2018).

2.4.2.13   The BMP180 Barometric Pressure Sensor

The BMP180 sensor is used to measure the atmospheric pressure of the environment. The sensor contains a diaphragm with one capacitive plate in contact with the atmosphere. Atmospheric pressure is detected through how much the diaphragm is deformed due to resulting pressure. The higher the pressure exerted, the more the diaphragm moves, which results in a change in resistance and higher barometer reading. Such measurements mainly allow for the forecasting of short-term changes in the weather (Figure 2.24).

A decrease in air pressure often indicates a higher chance of rain incoming, while air pressure increases indicate clear skies and incoming warm and dry air. By measuring atmospheric pressure, the altitude of an object can be determined as well. The pressure range of the sensor is 300–1,100 hPa. This sensor produces a digital output that the microcontroller can read via the I2C protocol (Pattabiraman, 2018).

2.4.2.14   The MAX30100 Pulse Oximeter and Heart Rate Sensor

The MAX30100 is an optical pulse oximetry and heart rate sensor. It derives SpO_2 level and heart rate readings by emitting two wavelengths of light from two light-emitting diodes (LEDs), one red and one IR LED, then measuring the optical density of the pulsing blood through a photodetector. This specific LED colour arrangement is enhanced for detecting pulsing blood through the tip of the finger under indoor conditions (Figure 2.25).

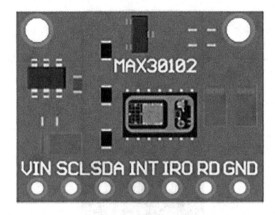

FIGURE 2.25 A MAX30100 pulse oximeter and heart rate sensor.

When the heart pumps blood, there is an increase in oxygenated blood in the blood vessels. As the heart relaxes, the volume of oxygenated blood also decreases. As it turns out, oxygenated blood absorbs more IR light and passes more red light, while deoxygenated blood absorbs red light and passes more IR light.

By reading the absorption levels for both light sources, the SpO_2 level can be determined by the sensor. In addition, by knowing the time between the increase and decrease of oxygenated blood, the heart rate can be determined. This sensor produces a digital output that the microcontroller can read via the I2C protocol (Newton, 2020).

2.4.2.15   The AS608 Optical Fingerprint Sensor

Optical fingerprint sensors work by shining a bright light and taking low-resolution snapshots of the tip of a finger to create arrays of identifiers that are then used to identify a given fingerprint uniquely. The AS608 can store up to 128 individual fingerprints. This sensor helps detect, record, or verify fingerprints via Universal Asynchronous Receiver/Transmitter (UART) protocol (Hrisko, 2019) (Figure 2.26).

2.4.3   OUTPUT DEVICES (ACTUATORS, LEDS, BUZZERS)

As discussed earlier, an actuator is a device that performs an action sanctioned by the microcontroller. Specifically, actuators convert electrical signals into a corresponding physical quantity such as movement, force, sound, light, and heat. Thus, actuators are sometimes classified as *transducers* because they change one type of physical quantity into another.

Actuators can be classified as *Binary* or *Continuous* based on the number of output states. For example, a direct current (DC) motor is a continuous actuator as it runs non-stop until it receives a stop command, whereas a servo motor rotates at a pre-defined angle and then stops by itself.

Some actuators, such as LEDs and buzzers, do not involve motion but rather serve as *indicators* that get activated (light on, buzzer on) when certain conditions

FIGURE 2.26   An AS608 optical fingerprint sensor.

occur. These actuators are excellent training and learning tools for beginners as they can simulate the performance of the real actuators without the need for complex electro-mechanical systems.

2.4.3.1   The Relay

A relay is a binary actuator as it has two stable states, either energized and closed or de-energized and open. A relay is an electromagnetic switch operated by a relatively small control signal that can turn on or off a much larger electric current. Relays control one electrical circuit by opening and closing contacts in another circuit using electromagnetism (Figure 2.27).

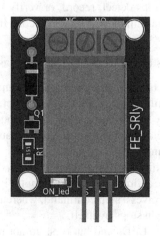

FIGURE 2.27   A single-channel relay.

Relays may be normally open (NO) or normally closed (NC). Most relays are NO, wherein the output circuit is in the off position by default. In a NO relay, power flows through the input circuit, activating an electromagnet. This generates a magnetic field that attracts a contact to join with the output circuit, allowing current flow. When the source of power is removed, a spring draws the contact away from the output circuit, stopping the flow of electricity and turning off the end device (Diffley, 2015).

The fundamentals of NC relays are the same as NO relays; only the default states are reversed. When the input circuit is activated, the electromagnet draws the contact away from the output circuit. As such, NC relays keep the output circuit in the on position by default. In either case, applying electrical current to the contacts will change their state.

Relays can also be classified based on the type of trigger; a low-level trigger will allow the current to go through the power line when the control signal is below a specific voltage, while a high-level trigger will allow the current to go through the power line when the control signal is above a specific voltage (Diffley, 2015).

Relays are generally used to switch smaller currents in a control circuit that do not usually control power-consuming devices. For example, since Arduino boards can only drive a voltage of 5 V at their output pins, a relay is required to drive further higher-powered devices, including 12 V actuators such as DC motors and pumps. In addition, protective relays prevent equipment damage by detecting electrical abnormalities and overloads (Diffley, 2015).

2.4.3.2 The Direct Current (DC) Motor

A motor is a continuous actuator because it can rotate through a full 360° motion. Electric motors turn electricity into motion by exploiting electromagnetic induction. At the most basic level, there are *brushed* and *brushless* motors and DC and alternating current (AC) motors (Figure 2.28).

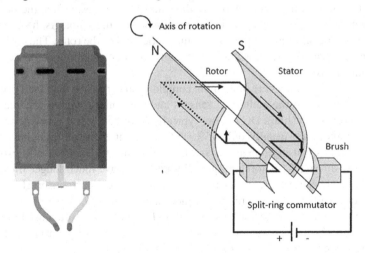

FIGURE 2.28 A brushed direct current motor.

A brushed DC motor has permanent magnets outside its structure, with a spinning armature on the inside. The permanent magnets, which are stationary on the outside, are called the stator. The armature, which rotates and contains an electromagnet, is called the rotor. The key to producing motion is positioning the electromagnet within the magnetic field of the permanent magnet. As a current-carrying wire generates a magnetic field, the rotor spins 180° due to magnetic force when an electric current is run through the armature.

To go any further, the electromagnet poles must flip, which is enabled by the split-ring commutator that connects the armature to the circuit (*Brushless vs. Brushed DC Motors*, 2005).

Electricity flows from the battery's positive terminal through the circuit, passes through a copper brush to the commutator, and then to the armature. But this flow is reversed midway through every full rotation, thanks to the two gaps in the commutator.

For the first half of every rotation, current flows into the armature via the first portion of the commutator, causing the current to flow in a specific direction. For the second half of the rotation, electricity enters through the second half of the commutator, causing current to flow into and through the armature in the opposite direction. This constant reversal essentially turns the DC power supply into AC, allowing the armature to experience torque in the right direction at the right time to keep it spinning a full 360° (*Brushless vs. Brushed DC Motors*, 2005).

A brushless DC motor is essentially flipped inside out, eliminating the need for brushes to flip the electromagnetic field. Instead, the permanent magnets are on the rotor in brushless DC motors, and the electromagnets are on the stator. A controller then charges the electromagnets in the stator to rotate the rotor a full 360°.

To properly rotate the field, the controller needs to know the physical position of the magnets on the rotor relative to the stator at all times. Often, the position information is obtained using hall sensors mounted on the stator. As the magnetic rotor turns, the hall sensors pick up the magnetic field of the rotor. The controller uses this information to pass current through the stator windings in a sequence that spins the rotor.

Brushless DC motors are often more complex and expensive than their brushed counterparts due to the additional sensors and controller required for functionality. However, brushless DC motors typically have 85%–90% efficiency, while brushed motors are usually only 75%–80% efficient. Brushes eventually wear out, sometimes causing dangerous sparking, limiting the lifespan of a brushed motor. Brushless DC motors are quiet, lighter, and have much longer lifespans. In addition, because a controller regulates the electrical current, brushless DC motors can achieve much more precise motion control.

Because of all these advantages, brushless DC motors are often used in modern devices where low noise and low heat are required, especially in continuously running devices (*Brushless vs. Brushed DC Motors*, 2005).

2.4.3.3 Servo Motors

A servo motor is an electro-mechanical device that produces torque and velocity based on the supplied current and voltage. Essentially, a servo motor is a closed-loop mechanism that uses position feedback to control its motion and final position. It contains a small DC motor connected to the output shaft through the gears (*Servo Motors*, 2013) (Figure 2.29).

The output shaft drives a servo arm and is also connected to a potentiometer. The potentiometer provides position feedback to the servo control unit, where the current position of the motor is compared to the target position. According to the error, the control unit corrects the motor's actual position to match the target position.

If the shaft is at the correct angle, then the motor shuts off, but if the angle is not correct, it will turn the motor until it is at the desired angle. Unlike DC motors, the positioning of servo motors can be controlled precisely (*Servo Motors*, 2013).

Servo motors are available in a wide variety of types, shapes, and sizes. Most servo motors are capable of 0°–180° rotations. However, it is mechanically not capable of turning any farther due to a mechanical stop built onto the main output gear. Servo motors can be controlled by sending a series of pulses to the pulse–width modulation (PWM) signal line.

A conventional servo motor expects to receive a pulse roughly every 20 ms, or 50 Hz. The length of the pulse determines the position of the servo motor. Pulses ranging between 0.5 and 2.5 ms will move the servo shaft through the full 180° of its travel, though this may sometimes vary with different brands. If the pulse is high for 0.5 ms, then the servo angle will be zero. If the pulse is high for 1.5 ms, then the servo will be at its centre position, or 90°. If the pulse is high for 2.5 ms, then the servo will be at 180°.

Servo motors are useful in many robotics projects, such as turning the front wheels on a remote control (RC) car for steering, moving a Robotic arm across multiple planes, and pivoting a camera or sensor on a Robot to look around (*Servo Motors*, 2013).

2.4.3.4 Light-Emitting Diodes (LEDs)

In its simplest terms, an LED is a semiconductor device that converts electrical energy into light energy. LEDs emit light when an electric current is passed through

Command
Power
Ground

FIGURE 2.29 A general-purpose servo motor.

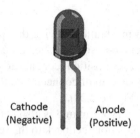

Cathode   Anode
(Negative)   (Positive)

FIGURE 2.30   A light-emitting diode (LED).

the semiconductor material. Since light is generated within the solid semiconductor material, LEDs are described as solid-state devices (Figure 2.30).

The term solid-state lighting distinguishes this lighting technology from other sources that use heated filaments, such as incandescent and tungsten halogen lamps, or gas discharge, such as fluorescent lamps (*LEDs*, 2004). Since an LED does not rely on heat to produce light, it runs cooler and is much more energy-efficient and long-lasting than incandescent light bulbs.

LEDs come in different shapes and types, though the most common are through-hole LEDs with two legs of different lengths. The long leg is the anode (positive), and the short leg is the cathode (negative). LEDs only work in one direction, wherein electric current flows from the anode to the cathode.

LEDs come in a variety of colours, depending on their material. For example, a red LED is made with gallium arsenide. LEDs come in all sorts of sizes as well, such as 3, 5, and 10 mm, denoting the diameter of the LED. Five millimetre LEDs are the most common and are often used as illumination, such as in flashlights as they can be extremely bright. On the other hand, 3 mm LEDs are not as bright but are smaller and suitable for on/off indication; to indicate if a system is switched on or off (*LEDs*, 2004).

2.4.3.5   Active Piezoelectric Buzzer

Piezoelectric buzzers are simple devices that can generate basic beeps and tones. These buzzers convert an electric signal into sound energy. They work using a piezo crystal, a unique material that changes shape when voltage is applied to it. When the crystal pushes against a diaphragm, similar to a speaker cone, it generates a pressure wave which the human ear picks up as sound (Figure 2.31).

Active buzzers have an internal driving circuit with an oscillating source and will sound as soon as it is energized with a DC voltage. However, it can only produce a continuous or pulsed audio signal since the frequency is fixed (Kim, 2019).

Passive buzzers do not have an internal oscillating source and must be driven via PWM. Since PWM signal is just a fast on/off signal, or a square wave, by changing the frequency, or how often the square wave changes from high to low, the frequency of the buzzer tone can be altered as well.

The simple way to distinguish between active and passive buzzers is to drive them with a battery.

FIGURE 2.31   An active piezoelectric buzzer module.

If the buzzer sounds, it is an active buzzer. If it is soundless, then it is a passive buzzer. Active buzzers can be easily controlled using HIGH/LOW digital signal, while the **Tone**() function controls passive buzzers (Kim, 2019).

2.4.4   MISCELLANEOUS COMPONENTS

Miscellaneous components are components that do not fit under any of the categories already discussed but are still very important for the setup and development of embedded systems.

2.4.4.1   The Solderless Breadboard

Using a solderless breadboard to connect electronic components can simplify the prototyping process and reduce the time taken to build a circuit. As breadboards do not require soldering, they are reusable, making it ideal for quick prototypes and experimenting with circuit design. The breadboard has many holes into which components such as ICs, LEDs, and resistors can be inserted. Each hole is connected by a metal strip beneath it, forming a node (Short, 2009) (Figure 2.32).

A node is a point in a circuit where two or more components are connected. Connections between different components are made by inserting their leads in a common node. The tops of the metal rows have clips to hold the components in place. Once inserted, that component will be electrically connected to anything else placed in that row. The metal rows are conductive and allow current to flow from any point in that strip.

The long top and bottom row of holes, indicated by the red and blue stripes, are used for power supply connections. The rest of the circuit is built by inserting components and connecting them with jumper cables. It should be noted that the top and bottom rows of holes are connected horizontally and split in the middle

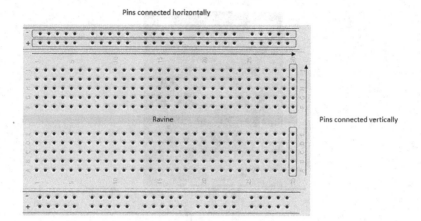

FIGURE 2.32   A solderless breadboard with pin connections.

while the remaining holes are connected vertically. The separation in the middle of the breadboard, called a ravine, isolates both sides of a given row from one another and is not electrically connected (Short, 2009).

This ravine serves an essential purpose. Many ICs are manufactured specifically to fit onto breadboards. To minimize the amount of space they take up on the breadboard, they come in what is known as a dual-in-line package (DIP). These DIP chips have legs that come out of both sides and fit perfectly over the ravine.

Since each leg on the IC is unique, they should not be connected. That is where the separation in the middle of the board comes in handy. Thus, components can be connected to each side of the IC without interfering with the opposite side. In addition, breadboards come in various types and sizes to suit different prototyping requirements (Short, 2009).

2.4.4.2   Resistors
A resistor is a passive electrical component that provides electrical resistance in a circuit. In electronic circuits, resistors reduce current flow, adjust signal levels, and divide voltages, among other uses. The ability of a resistor to reduce the current is called resistance and is measured in units of Ohms (Ω). Following Ohm's law, if the voltage in a circuit remains the same, the current will decrease if the resistance is increased.

The total resistance of resistors connected in series is the sum of their resistance values, while the total resistance of resistors connected in parallel is the reciprocal of the sum of the reciprocals of the individual resistors. The power dissipation of a resistor is calculated by multiplying voltage and current.

Fixed resistors have resistances that only change slightly with temperature, time, or operating voltage. Variable resistors have resistances that can be adjusted and used to manage circuit elements, such as volume control or a lamp dimmer, or as sensing devices for heat, light, humidity, force, or chemical activity photoresistors and thermistors (Jimblom, 2017).

The resistance of fixed resistors can be determined based on the colour of the bands on the exterior. In the standard four-band resistors, the first two bands indicate the two most significant resistor values. The third band is a weight value, which multiplies the first two digits by a power of ten. The final band indicates the tolerance of the resistor.

The tolerance explains how much more or less the actual resistance of the resistor can be compared to its nominal value. Table 2.4 shows the colour codes and corresponding values.

Wire-wound resistors consist of an insulating ceramic rod running through the middle with copper wire wrapped around the outside and covered by an insulating material.

The number of copper turns controls the resistance very precisely, wherein the more copper turns, and the thinner the copper wire, the higher the resistance. In smaller-value resistors, designed for lower-power circuits, the copper winding is replaced by a spiral pattern of a thin film of conductive material.

Resistors like this are much cheaper to make and can be constructed out of various materials, such as carbon, metal, or metal-oxide film (Jimblom, 2017). Once again, the greater the number of turns, the higher the resistance. Generally, wire-wound resistors are more precise and more stable at higher operating temperatures.

2.4.4.3   Jumper Cables

Jumper cables are simply wiring with connector pins at each end, allowing them to connect two points without soldering. Jumper cables are typically used with breadboards and other prototyping tools to make it easy to change a circuit as needed. Though jumper cables come in various colours, the colours do not serve

TABLE 2.4

Fixed Resistors and List of Resistance Values

Colour	Band 1–2 Primary Values	Band 3 Multiplier	Band 4 Tolerance (%)
Silver	–	0.01	±10
Gold	–	0.1	±5
Black	0	1	–
Brown	1	10	±1
Red	2	100	±2
Orange	3	1 K	–
Yellow	4	10 K	–
Green	5	100 K	±0.5
Blue	6	1 M	±0.25
Violet	7	10 M	±0.1
Grey	8	–	–
White	9	–	–

Male header

Female header

FIGURE 2.33   An example of male to female jumper cables.

any purpose other than differentiating between types of connections, such as ground or power (Hemmings, 2018) (Figure 2.33).

Jumper cables typically come in three versions, namely male-to-male, male-to-female, and female-to-female. The difference between each is in the end-point of the wire. Male ends have a pin protruding and can plug into sockets, while female ends have openings to plug components. Jumper cables are ideally made of 22 American Wire Gauge (AWG) solid-core wire (Hemmings, 2018).

2.5   EMBEDDED SYSTEMS: SOFTWARE CONSIDERATIONS

After selecting the type of controller for your system, the next consideration you need to make is how you will *talk* to it; this is referred to as Controller Programming. In many ways, a controller is just as good as its program, you could have the best hardware in the world, but it would only run based on the instructions you define in its *Controller Program.*

2.5.1   THE MAIN ELEMENTS OF A CONTROLLER PROGRAM

Although controller programs vary greatly depending on the hardware being implemented or controlled, the main elements of a controller program remain relatively the same. Figure 2.34 shows the main elements of a typical controller program (*Controller Programming*, 2021).

The program showed in Figure 2.34 is simplified for clarity. Hopefully, you can see items we already discussed, such as *Libraries*, *GPIO*, and *Hardware Abstraction*. Next, we discuss these items in more detail:

- **Libraries**: usually at the very beginning of the program. This is where you import libraries that you will use in your program. In the program shown in Figure 2.34, we import GPIO, Dweepy (an IoT library), and some items from the time library.

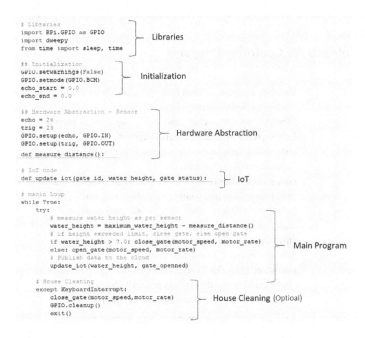

```
# Libraries
import RPi.GPIO as GPIO              ⎤
import dweepy                        ⎬ ─ Libraries
from time import sleep, time         ⎦

## Initialization
GPIO.setwarnings(False)             ⎤
GPIO.setmode(GPIO.BCM)              ⎬ ─ Initialization
echo_start = 0.0                     ⎦
echo_end = 0.0

## Hardware Abstraction - Sensor
echo = 24                            ⎤
trig = 23                            ⎬ ─ Hardware Abstraction
GPIO.setup(echo, GPIO.IN)           ⎪
GPIO.setup(trig, GPIO.OUT)          ⎪
def measure_distance():              ⎦

# IoT code
def update_iot(gate_id, water_height, gate_status):   ⎬ ─ IoT

# main Loop
while True:
    try:
        # measure water height as per sensor
        water_height = maximum_water_height - measure_distance()    ⎤
        # if height exceeded limit, close gate, else open gate      ⎪
        if water_height > 7.0: close_gate(motor_speed, motor_rate)  ⎬ ─ Main Program
        else: open_gate(motor_speed, motor_rate)                    ⎪
        # Publish data to the cloud                                 ⎪
        update_iot(water_height, gate_openned)                      ⎦

    # House Cleaning
    except KeyboardInterrupt:                           ⎤
        close_gate(motor_speed,motor_rate)              ⎬ ─ House Cleaning (Optional)
        GPIO.cleanup()                                  ⎪
        exit()                                          ⎦
```

FIGURE 2.34   Elements of an IoT-enabled controller program.

- **Initialization**: also near the top of the program, where variables and utility functions are defined and initialized (defined with initial values).
- **Hardware Abstraction**: this program interacts with an ultrasonic distance sensor, so here, we define the *measure distance* function/method, which is used later.
- **IoT Code**: this is the code we use to package data in JSON objects and broadcast it to the cloud. We will discuss the details of this code in Chapter 5.
- **Main Program**: the primary part of the program (control gate based on sensor data).
- **House Cleaning**: an optional part of the program, defines what happens when the program is closed/ended, such as shutting down motors and returning to defaults.

This program is part of the *IoT Water Management System* discussed in earlier chapters. The entire program is discussed in this paper (Hajjaj et al., 2020).

2.5.2 Sources of Data for Controller Programs

In controller programs, data could come from various sources. For example, it could be defined by the programmer or the end user, read from a data file or a database, imported as part of a library (including sensor libraries), or received from remote IoT sources. Table 2.5 reviews these different sources of data.

TABLE 2.5

Sources of Data for Controller Programs

Source	Details
Programmed	Variables and items defined in the program, directly defined by the program creators and developers
	Variables could be declared and used at any point in the program
User input	Data captured from human users directly through a dedicated system–human interface. Examples include computer–human interface or robot–human interaction (HRI) frameworks
Data files	Data procured from files, documents, and databases stored on the local machine or in remote sources (through the cloud)
	Data files come in a variety of types and configurations
Libraries	Data included in libraries imported onto the current program, such as mathematical constants included in the *math* library
	This also includes user-created programs and classes
Remote sources	Internet of Things (IoT)-related sources; through the *receive data* protocols, these could be live data or remote user commands
	Programs could be configured to *wait* for specific values

For this book, since we focus on developing controller programs for autonomous systems and IoT applications, we will focus primarily on *Programmed*, *Libraries*, and *Remote Sources*. We might also touch on *Data Files*, but very briefly.

Regardless of the source, once the data is captured and assigned to a *variable* or a *collection of variables* within the program, we can then apply our logic (algorithm) to it to achieve the purpose of the program, as we shall see later in the hands-on sessions.

2.5.3 Programming Languages for Controllers

The next consideration you need to make is what language you will use when talking to your controller, i.e. the programming language. There are many languages out there that can be used for controller programming. However, for this book, we will focus on the two most widely used languages; *C++ & Python*.

Both languages are considered *general-purpose* programming languages; they can be used for many uses and domains. Also, they both support *multi-paradigm* programming; they both support *structural*, *functional*, *procedural*, and *object-oriented* programming paradigms, which describe different ways of how program elements are constructed and deployed.

C++ is considered a *low-level, compiled* language; it requires separate procedures for *garbage collection* (memory management). It also needs a *Compiler* to translate instructions to *machine language*, the language understood by the processor. This, however, makes C++ more efficient and flexible, especially for resource-constrained systems and environments, which was ideal for computer and control systems back in the 1980s (Anderson, 2018).

On the other hand, Python is a *high-level, interpreted* language; it comes built-in with memory management, and it does not require a compiler; its code can execute directly. It also incorporates natural (human) language elements. This made Python very popular as developers could easily read and understand its code. Python is also known as *batteries included* as it comes with a very comprehensive standard (core) library.

C++ was released in 1985, while Python was first released in 1991. Today, both languages are among the most popular programming languages in the world in terms of applications, core and third-party libraries, and development communities. We will use C++ for Arduino boards since the Arduino language is an extension of C/C++ and Python for Raspberry Pi. Although we could use any language for Raspberry Pi, Python is the most widely used language in terms of hardware support, libraries, and online learning material (Sharma, 2021).

Table 2.6 shows a more detailed comparison between Python and C++ (Sayantini, 2020), which will be very useful for us before we start coding in later sections.

While C++ needs a compiler and does not support garbage collection, that actually makes it faster and efficient. On the other hand, Python is much easier to write and read code and usually requires fewer code lines. The last three comparison points might not be readily apparent for some readers because they relate to programming issues. You can return here after completing the programming exercises of later chapters; only then these three points would make sense.

TABLE 2.6
A Comparison between C++ and Python Programming Languages

Area	Python	C++
Size	Fewer lines of code needed	More lines of code needed
Garbage collection	Supports garbage collection (built-in feature)	Does not support (needs to be done separately)
Syntax	Very easy to learn, (similar to human language)	Very steep learning curve, (complex syntax structures)
Program speed	Slower, due to interpreter (as if compile and run simultaneously)	Faster, since it is pre-compiled, (compile program *before* run)
Code maintenance	Easier to maintain, (high readability, fewer lines)	Difficult to maintain, (complex syntax, more lines)
Lists	Lists/vectors can only contain variables of the same type	Lists can contain variables of different types
Scope of variables	Variables accessible outside loops	Variables limited within loops
Types of functions	Need not be pre-defined and followed	Must be pre-defined and followed

2.5.4   THE INTEGRATED DEVELOPMENT ENVIRONMENT (IDE)

The first decision to make is to decide *where* to create that program. Theoretically, you can use any text editor application to write a computer program, including Window's *Notepad*. You can also write some commands and instructions on your system's *Command Prompt*.

While these methods are helpful for quick debugging purposes, they are not practical. Aside from writing your program, you also need to debug it, test it, compile it, and run it. Only then you would know if you have successfully developed the program you intended. Simple text editors do not have these capabilities. The practical way to create programs is to utilize an *Integrated Development Environment (IDE)* (Škorić et al., 2016).

An IDE is a software application that provides comprehensive facilities for software development. These facilities include automated editing, language support, debugging tools, library support, and visualization and emulation tools (App/Web development IDEs).

The choice of an IDE depends on the target language, OS, and even personal preference. Some languages require specific IDEs. For example, Arduino boards require the use of the Arduino IDE. Some IDEs are limited to specific OSs. Sometimes, it comes down to the personal preference and convenience of the developer.

In this book, we will work with two IDEs; in Chapter 4, when we work with Arduino IoT systems, we will use the Arduino IDE. In Chapter 5, when we work with Raspberry Pi IoT systems, we will use *Geany*, an open-source IDE pre-installed with Raspberry Pi OS.

2.5.5   BEST PRACTICES FOR PROGRAM DEVELOPMENT AND TROUBLESHOOTING

For best results, especially for beginners in programming, we strongly recommend adopting the following suggestions for program development and troubleshooting.

- **Algorithm First**: As we discussed at the beginning of this chapter, create your algorithm and visualize all your ideas, *then* after that, convert your ideas into code.
- **Bit by Bit**: Do not attempt to write the whole program in one go or big chunks. Instead, write in small blocks, test and verify, then move on to the next block.
- **Error Codes**: If you get errors, that is actually great, just read the error codes and follow their instructions. Sometimes error codes are self-explanatory. You can also search the error codes online for solutions from others (see below).
- **Start at the Top**: In many cases, one error could cause other errors. So if you get multiple errors, deal with the first error in the list. Chances other errors will also be corrected or at least reduced. Never start from the middle or bottom of the list.

- **Trace the Bug**: If you get a *bug* (no errors, but the program is not behaving as planned), this is more challenging, as you might not know where the problem is. In this case, you may have to start from the beginning and trace the logic (flow) of your program, and hopefully, you will identify the source of the bug and remove it (*debugging*).
- **Use the Comments**: Comments are a powerful tool to organize your code and leave notes for your future self. You can also *comment-out* (temporarily disable) part of your program while debugging and troubleshooting your code.
- **Indentation (Python)**: Indentation plays an essential role in Python, and if you are careless, you could cause the *Indentation Errors*. We will address this issue later.
- **Online Resources**: On the Internet, you can find sample code, tutorials, training, and best of all, solutions and advice from programming experts, as we shall see later.

2.6 ONLINE RESOURCES

With this book, we hope you will gain the knowledge and experience to *start* working on IoT, but once you begin that journey, we recommend utilizing online resources.

We have already worked with some online resources in previous sections and chapters, so we discuss online resources in more detail in this section. In general, online resources can be divided into the following categories: *Learning Resources, IoT Clients, IoT Resources, and IoT Data Analytics Algorithms.*

2.6.1 LEARNING RESOURCES

Learning Resources provide you with the means to learn new concepts or find solutions to system and programming problems; few prominent examples are listed in Table 2.7.

Googling the error code is something you will do a lot in your programming journey. In many cases, as you shall see, it is the fastest way to solve a coding problem or situation. The rest of the sources are excellent to gain theoretical knowledge and practice experience.

2.6.2 IoT CLIENTS

IoT Clients are online platforms that allow you to create working IoT systems even if you do not have any experience or knowledge in web development, as shown in Table 2.8.

Some IoT clients listed in the table are open source (Freeboard), allowing users to fork their customized versions. All are free to use, but the free versions are usually limited, where the paid versions are more powerful, allowing for more visualization tools, historical data, and more advanced features.

TABLE 2.7

List of Learning Resources and Their Features

Name	URL	Features
Google	www.google.com	You can google error message, find solutions online
Wikipedia	www.wikipedia.org/	Great for learning about new topics and concepts
StackOverFlow	https://stackoverflow.com/	To find solutions for programming errors and bugs
YouTube	www.youtube.com/	You can watch hands-on demos and step by step
Arduino	https://forum.arduino.cc/	For Arduino and Arduino-compatible boards
Raspberry Pi	www.raspberrypi.org/	For Raspberry Pi boards
Beaglebone	https://beagleboard.org/	For Beaglebone boards

TABLE 2.8

List of IoT Clients and Their Features

Name	URL	Special Features
ThingsSpeak	https://thingspeak.com/	Data collection, processing, and visualization tool (we will use for Arduino systems)
Freeboard	http://freeboard.io/	Data collection, processing, and visualization tool (we will use for Raspberry Pi)
Blynk	https://blynk.io/	Especially for mobile IoT clients (we will use for Arduino and Raspberry Pi)
Node-RED	https://nodered.org/	Data collection, processing, and visualization tool For visual programming (blocks)
M2Mlabs	http://www.m2mlabs.com/	Data collection, processing, and visualization tool For machine-to-machine systems
ThingsBoard	https://thingsboard.io/	Data collection, processing, and visualization tool
Openremote	https://openremote.io/	For energy management, crowd management, and asset management applications
Kaa	https://www.kaaiot.com/	For establishing end-to-end IoT solutions, connected applications, and smart devices
DSA	http://iot-dsa.org/	Distributed service architecture (DSA) for inter-device communication and logic
Thinger	https://thinger.io/	Provides scalable cloud base for connecting devices
SiteWhere	https://sitewhere.io/en/	For ingestion, repository, processing, and assimilation of device inputs (data broadcast from devices)

2.6.3 IoT Resources and Vendor Solutions

IoT Resources are online platforms that provide support technologies and features useful for any IoT developer, as shown in Table 2.9.

Finally, most of the established technology organizations offer their own IoT platforms. These are useful when the company already uses a technology or a system from these provides. For example, if the company uses an Apache-based system, it is probably helpful to use the Apache IoT platform. Table 2.10 lists few examples.

TABLE 2.9

List of Resources Useful for IoT Applications

Name	URL	Features
Adafruit	www.adafruit.com/	Hardware/software support for components
TinkerCad	www.tinkercad.com/	Simulation tool for Arduino boards
TensorFlow	www.tensorflow.org/	Machine learning (ML) algorithm (open source)
Algorithemia	https://algorithmia.com/	Machine learning (ML) algorithm (proprietary)
OpenCV	https://opencv.org/	Real-time computer vision and image processing

TABLE 2.10

List of Vendor-Linked IoT Platforms

Name	URL
Google IoT Core	https://cloud.google.com/iot-core
AWS IoT Services	https://aws.amazon.com/iot/
Oracle IoT	https://www.oracle.com/internet-of-things/
Apache IoT	https://apachecon.com/acna19/iot.html
Bosch	https://developer.bosch-iot-suite.com/

With this, we have successfully reviewed all foundation topics and concepts you would need to learn before embarking on IoT systems development, which we will do starting from the next chapter, Chapter 3, where we cover refreshers on programming and coding.

REFERENCES

ADXL335 Accelerometer. (2018). *Last Minute Engineers.* https://lastminuteengineers. com/adxl335-accelerometer-arduino-tutorial/

Anderson, J. (2018). *Python vs C++: Selecting the Right Tool for the Job – Real Python.* Real Python. https://realpython.com/python-vs-cpp/

Brushless vs. Brushed DC Motors. (2005). Monolithic Power Systems (MPS). https:// www.monolithicpower.com/en/brushless-vs-brushed-dc-motors

Button Module. (2018). *Starting Electronics.* https://startingelectronics.org/tutorials/ arduino/modules/push-button/

Controller Programming. (2021). *Cyberbotics.* https://cyberbotics.com/doc/guide/controller-programming

DHT11, DHT12. (2016). *How to Mechatronics.* https://howtomechatronics.com/tutorials/ arduino/dht11-dht22-sensors-temperature-and-humidity-tutorial-using-arduino/

Diffley, J. A. (2015). *How to Use Relays to Control High-Voltage Circuits with an Arduino – Projects.* All About Circuits. https://www.allaboutcircuits.com/projects/ use-relays-to-control-high-voltage-circuitswwith-an-arduino/

E vs. E. (2012). *Bright Knowledge.* https://brightknowledge.org/engineering/electrical-and-electronic-engineering-what-s-the-difference

Esp8266 Module. (2015). *Electronic Wings.* https://www.electronicwings.com/sensors-modules/esp8266-wifi-module

FarmBot. (2019). *Farmbot Media Kit.* https://farm.bot/

FarmBot|Open-Source CNC Farming. (2021). https://farm.bot/

Flame Sensor. (2018). *Arduino Project Hub.* https://create.arduino.cc/projecthub/ SURYATEJA/arduino-modules-flame-sensor-6322fb

Hajjaj, S., Hafizuddin, M. et al. (2020). Utilizing the Internet of Things (IoT) to develop a remotely monitored autonomous floodgate for water management and control. *Water (Switzerland), 12*(2). https://doi.org/10.3390/w12020502

HC-05 Bluetooth Module. (2018). *Arduino Project Hub.* https://create.arduino.cc/projecthub/ electropeak/getting-started-with-hc-05-bluetooth-module-arduino-e0ca81

HC-SR04 Sensor. (2017). *Random Nerd Tutorials.* https://randomnerdtutorials.com/ complete-guide-for-ultrasonic-sensor-hc-sr04/

HC-SR501 PIR Sensor. (2018). *Last Minute Engineers.* https://lastminuteengineers. com/pir-sensor-arduino-tutorial/

Hemmings, M. (2018). *What Is a Jumper Wire?* Sparkfun, Start Something. http://blog. sparkfuneducation.com/what-is-jumper-wire

Hrisko, J. (2019). *Arduino Optical Fingerprint Sensor (AS608) – Maker Portal.* Maker Portal. https://makersportal.com/blog/2019/6/9/arduino-optical-fingerprint-sensor-as608

IR Sensor. (2017). *OSOYOO.* https://osoyoo.com/2017/07/24/arduino-lesson-obstacle-avoidance-sensor/

Jimblom. (2017). *Resistors – learn.sparkfun.com.* Sparkfun, Start Something. https:// learn.sparkfun.com/tutorials/resistors/all

Khan, A. (2021). *10 Best Microcontroller Boards for Engineers and Geeks – Engineering Passion.* Engineering Passion. https://www.engineeringpassion.com/10-best-microcontroller-boards-for-engineers-and-geeks/

Kim. (2019). *What's the Difference between Active Buzzers and Passive Buzzers? Active Buzzers and Passive Buzzers.* Manorshi. https://www.manorshi.com/What-s-the-difference-between-active-buzzers-and-passive-buzzers-id3333285.html

LEDs. (2004). *LEDs Magazine.* https://www.ledsmagazine.com/leds-ssl-design/materials/ article/16701292/what-is-an-led

Light Sensor. (2016). *Circuits4you.Com.* https://circuits4you.com/2016/05/13/arduino-light-sensor/

Long, M. (2019). *Beaglebone Black vs Raspberry Pi.* ElectroMaker. https://www. electromaker.io/blog/article/beaglebone-black-vs-raspberry-pi

MQ2 Gas Sensor. (2019). *Last Minute Engineers.* https://lastminuteengineers.com/mq2-gas-senser-arduino-tutorial/

Munoz, S. (2020). *CPU vs. Microprocessor: What are the Differences?* TechTarget. https://searchservervirtualization.techtarget.com/tip/CPU-vs-microprocessor-What-are-the-differences

Newton, A. (2020). *Interfacing MAX30100 Pulse Oximeter Sensor with Arduino.* How to Electronics. https://how2electronics.com/interfacing-max30100-pulse-oximeter-sensor-arduino/

Nikhil, A. (2021). *Raspberry Pi 2 & 3 vs Beaglebone Black.* Engineers Garage. https:// www.engineersgarage.com/raspberry-pi-2-3-vs-beaglebone-black/

Orsini, L. (2014). *Arduino Vs. Raspberry Pi: Which Is The Right DIY Platform For You?.* ReadWrite. https://readwrite.com/2014/05/07/arduino-vs-raspberry-pi-projects-diy-platform/

Pattabiraman, K. (2018). *How to Set Up the BMP180 Barometric Pressure Sensor on an Arduino.* Circuit Basics. https://www.circuitbasics.com/set-bmp180-barometric-pressure-sensor-arduino/

Pedamkar, P. (2015). *Raspberry Pi 3 vs Arduino|Learn The 6 Amazing Differences.* EDUCBA. https://www.educba.com/raspberry-pi-3-vs-arduino/

Pedamkar, P. (2018). *Raspberry Pi 3 vs BeagleBone Black|Which One Is More Useful.* EDUCBA. https://www.educba.com/raspberry-pi-3-vs-beaglebone-black/

Risset, T. (2011). SoC (System on Chip). In D. Padua (Ed.), *Encyclopedia of Parallel Computing* (pp. 1837–1842). Springer US. https://doi.org/10.1007/978-0-387-09766-4_5

Sayantini, D. (2020). *Python vs C++|What are the Differences between the Two?.* Edureka. https://www.edureka.co/blog/python-vs-cpp/

Serpanos, D., & Wolf, T. (2011). Architecture of Network Systems Overview. In D. Serpanos & T. Wolf (Eds.), *Architecture of Network Systems* (pp. 1–9). Morgan Kaufmann. https://doi.org/10.1016/B978-0-12-374494-4.00001_3

Servo Motors. (2013). *Last Minute Engineers.* https://lastminuteengineers.com/servo-motor-arduino-tutorial/

Sharma, R. (2021). *Python vs C++: Difference between Python and C++.* UpGrad Blog. https://www.upgrad.com/blog/python-vs-cplusplus/

Short, M., & Joel, E. B. (2009). How to Use a Breadboard – learn.sparkfun.com. Sparfun, Start Something. https://learn.sparkfun.com/tutorials/how-to-use-a-breadboard/all

SIM800L GSM Module. (2019). *Last Minute Engineers.* https://lastminuteengineers.com/sim800l-gsm-module-arduino-tutorial/

Škorić, I., Pein, B., & Orehovački, T. (2016). Selecting the Most Appropriate Web IDE for Learning Programming Using AHP. *2016 39th International Convention on Information and Communication Technology, Electronics and Microelectronics (MIPRO)*, 877–882. https://doi.org/10.1109/MIPRO.2016.7522263

Soil Moisture Sensor. (2015). *Last Minute Engineers.* https://lastminuteengineers.com/soil-moisture-sensor-arduino-tutorial/

Sound Sensor. (2019). *Last Minute Engineers.* https://lastminuteengineers.com/sound-sensor-arduino-tutorial/

The Raspberry Pi. (2021). *The Rasbperry Pi Organizaton.* https://www.raspberrypi.org/products/raspberry-pi-4-model-b/

Ublox NEO-6M GPS Module. (2017). *Last Minute Engineers.* https://lastminuteengineers.com/neo6m-gps-arduino-tutorial/

Vaglica, J. J., & Gilmour, P. S. (1990). How to Select a Microcontroller. *IEEE Spectrum*, 27(11), 106–109. https://doi.org/10.1109/6.62226

Verma, A. (2018). *Difference between Algorithm, Pseudocode and Program.* Geeks for Geeks. https://www.geeksforgeeks.org/difference-between-algorithm-pseudocode-and-program/

Water Sensor. (2017). *Last Minute Engineering.* https://lastminuteengineers.com/water-level-sensor-arduino-tutorial/

Wolf, M. (2014). Multiprocessor Software. In M. Wolf (Ed.), *High-Performance Embedded Computing)* (Second Edition, pp. 301–339). Morgan Kaufmann. https://doi.org/10.1016/B978-0-12-410511-9.00006-X

Woz U. (2020). *What is Syntax in Computer Programming?.* Woz U. https://woz-u.com/blog/what-is-syntax-in-computer-programming/

Part II

Hands-On System Development

3 Foundation Topics
Programming

3.1 PROGRAMMING LANGUAGES: C++

This section provides a comprehensive guide into the C++ programming language from the IoT perspective. We would revise concepts and tools in the C++ language that we would use later in IoT controller programming, data packaging, and broadcasting. Therefore, even if you are an expert in C++, we recommend you review this section.

3.1.1 GETTING STARTING WITH C++

The very first step of learning C++ is to ensure that it is correctly installed on your machine. That involves downloading and installing the *Geany* IDE, the C++ compiler, and setting them up properly to produce a sample C++ program. Luckily, the *Geany* IDE and the C++ compilers are available for all operating systems (OSs) and distributions.

If you prefer to work with another IDE, we recommend Geany because we will use it later for Python and Raspberry Pi programming. Similarly, you could use a different C++ compiler than the one we recommend below. However, we recommend using the same compiler we used to follow along in our hands-on exercise in this chapter.

3.1.1.1 Installation and Setup

Download and install Geany and the C++ compiler, the order of installation (which one to install first) is not essential. The sources shown in Table 3.1 are valid at the time of writing.

TABLE 3.1
Installation Sources for C++

Item	Name	Source
IDE	Geany	https://www.geany.org/download/releases/
		(select a release for your *Operating System*)
		Or search for: *Geany IDE download*
C++ compiler	MinGW-W64 (Windows)	https://sourceforge.net/projects/mingw-w64/
		(then click the *Download* button)
		Or search for: *C++ compiler sourceforge*

DOI: 10.1201/9781003218395-5

For the C++ compiler, the link shown in Table 3.5 is for *Windows* only. For other OSs, you can use the same search suggestion shown in the table; only add the name of your OS at the end. For example, if you use *Ubuntu*, you can search for C++ *compiler sourceforge Ubuntu* to find the correct compiler. You can do the same thing for any other OS or distribution.

After successfully installing the IDE and compiler, you can now write your first C++ program. Start the Geany IDE program and do the following:

- **Start a New Document**: Click on *New* or *File>New*, or hit the *Ctrl & N* keys on your keyboard. Any of these actions will start a new document. At this stage, this document could be any text file.
- **Set as C++ Program**: You need to tell Geany that your new document will be a C++ program. Click *File>Save As*, or hit the *Ctrl & S*, and a new pop-up window will ask you to set the filename and location, as shown in Figure 3.1.
- **Filename and Location**: *Convention* suggests using all small letters, no spaces, descriptive words for program file names, so things like *myfirst* or *firstprogram* or *program1* are all OK. You need, however, to end your file name with **.cpp** to tell Geany that this is a C++ (C Plus Plus) program file. The location is entirely arbitrary; a good practice is to create an individual folder for each project.

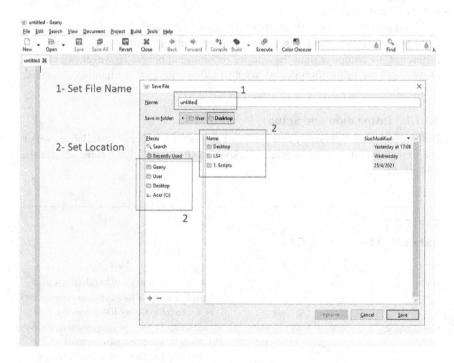

FIGURE 3.1. File naming and location setting in Geany IDE (C++).

- **Write Your Code**: Now that you have created the document and told Geany that it would be a C++ program, you can now write your C++ code.
- **Run Your Program**: *Compile*, then *Build*, then *Execute* your program.

For simplicity, or more like a convention, we will begin with the good old "Hello World" program. Write the simple code shown in Figure 3.2 in your new document, *Save* the file, then run your program. In C++, to run a program, you need to *Compile* it, wait for success, then *Build* it, wait for success, and then *Execute* it, as shown in Figure 3.2. If everything went smoothly, you should see the output also shown in Figure 3.2.

If you can see the output shown in Figure 3.2, you have successfully installed the Geany IDE and the correct C++ compiler for your system. This also means that you are now ready to proceed with to following sections and hands-on programming exercises.

If not, that means something went wrong; perhaps you downloaded a wrong file or did not follow the above steps accurately. So, we suggest you review your steps and ensure success before proceeding to the next section.

3.1.2 WORKING WITH DATA (VARIABLES AND COLLECTIONS)

As discussed before, the purpose of Electronics Systems, including all *Controller Programs*, is to manage *data*; controllers receive, process, and *produce* data (in the form of output data or commands based on output data). Therefore, in this section, we review the following concepts: *Variable Types*, and *Data Collections (lists)* in C++ (*C++ Documentation*, 2021).

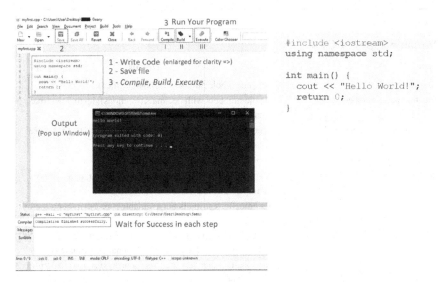

FIGURE 3.2   The Hello World program (C++) in Geany and its output.

3.1.2.1   Program Variables

In C++, a *variable* is a space holder where we can store a value temporarily. For example, let *roomTemp* be a variable that indicates the room temperature, and let us assign it a value of 24. Let us also assume the temperature room rose to 26.5°, so, in our program, we can update *roomTemp* with the new value, this time, it would be equal to 26.5.

We could then use *roomTemp* to *automate* a fan or an air conditioner unit to *control* the temperature in the room. For example, based on the current value of *roomTemp*, we could autonomously switch on or off the fan or air conditioner unit (or set fan speed or AC temperature). That was a simple example of a controller program used in *Automation*.

In the above example, the *value* assigned to *roomTemp* was a number with decimals. Other variables in other situations might use different *Types* of values, such as integers, logical operators, or even text characters; Table 3.2 lists different *Variable Types*.

3.1.2.2   Working with Variables

In C++, data is assigned to *variables* which the program can then manipulate to produce the needed results. For example, suppose you want to write a program to convert room temperature from Celsius to Fahrenheit. In that case, your program must include two variables: *C* and *F*, the conversion formula, and the interface to input values and display results.

So, in your program, you would need to *Declare*, *Manipulate*, and *Display* variables to perform the temperature conversion. We will first focus on declaring and displaying variables; then, we will discuss data manipulation.

TABLE 3.2
Variable Types in C++

Type	Details
Integer (int)	Integers, whole numbers without decimals
Floating point number (float)	Whole numbers with decimals (fractions), up to 7 decimal places
Floating point number, high precision (double)	Whole numbers with decimals (fractions), up to 15 decimal places
Logical output (boolean)	Logical values, either *True = 1, or False = 0*
A character (char)	A single ASCII character, i.e. a letter, a digit, or a symbol. Examples include 's', '5', or '('
A string	Technically, a string is not a variable type but rather a list of *Chars*. So, the *Hello* string is an array of Chars, ['H', 'e', 'l', 'l', 'o']. Still, Strings are often treated as a separate variable type, and the fact that they are lists (or arrays) is used in *String Operations*

3.1.2.3 Declaring Variables in C++

Before you can work with a variable, you need to declare it. In C++, you can do so through the *declare variable* structure, which includes three elements; the variable's *type*, *name*, and *value*, as shown in Figure 3.3.

The figure also shows examples of variable declarations for all variable types discussed above. As seen in the figure, you *must* declare the variable type in C++, as the compiler needs to know how to deal with this variable (allocate memory, call up appropriate functions, etc.).

Another thing to notice in the figure is that you can declare a variable without a value. Perhaps you do not know what initial value it could take, or perhaps that is unimportant now, as the value would be *assigned* later in the program.

Other things to notice in the figure is the general syntax of C++, such as the use of the *Semicolon* ";" to each line of code, and the use of two *Forward Slashes* "//" to create the C++ *Comments*, which could be a powerful tool for any developer.

3.1.2.4 Manipulating Variables in C++

After variables have been declared, we can use *Operators* to manipulate their values to achieve the effects we intend with our program. Returning to the example above, after declaring two variables, *C* and *F*, we can now use operators to perform the conversion. Operators are divided into several types: *arithmetic, assignment, comparisons, logical,* and *custom* operators. We will see these operators in action in the next section.

3.1.2.5 Displaying Variables in C++

In C++, displaying variables could be part of a *system–human* interface to show the program's output to the end user. Using the same example, a user inputs a temperature in *C*; the program performs the conversion (manipulation), then displays the output, converted in *F*.

Furthermore, displaying variables could be an excellent tool for troubleshooting and debugging your program and verifying the values it is producing against your algorithm, as we shall see later. Figure 3.4 shows the use of the *cout* module to display data.

```
// Declaring Variables
// Type   variableName = value;

int myAge = 27;                    // Integer
float roomTemp = 26.4;             // Float (fraction with 7 digits)
double clearance = 8.44395433;     // Double (fraction with 15 digits)
bool isCondition = true;           // Boolean (Logical values)
char firstLetter = 's';            // a Single Character
string welcomeMsg = "hello";       // An array of Characters

int numbStudents;      // variable declared, value assigned later
```

FIGURE 3.3 Declaring variables in C++.

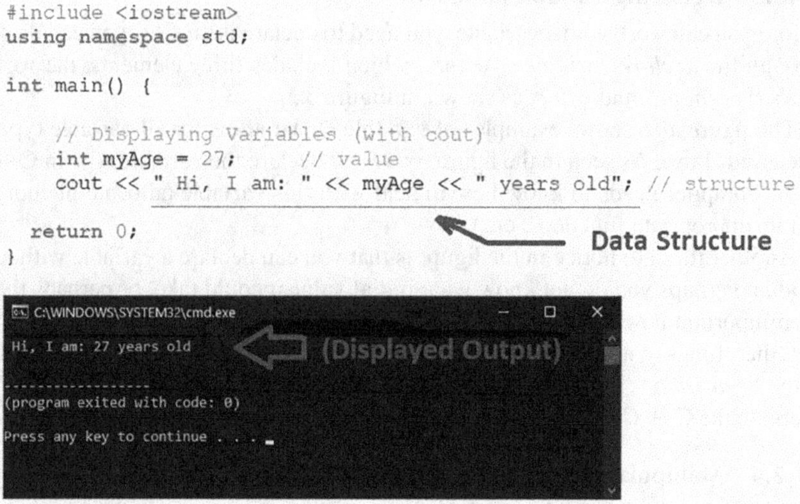

```
#include <iostream>
using namespace std;

int main() {

    // Displaying Variables (with cout)
    int myAge = 27;        // value
    cout << " Hi, I am: " << myAge << " years old"; // structure

    return 0;
}
```
Data Structure

```
Hi, I am: 27 years old

--------------------
(program exited with code: 0)
Press any key to continue . . . _
```
(Displayed Output)

FIGURE 3.4 Displaying variables in C++ using the *cout* module.

The *cout* module uses the "<<" *overload* operator to construct the output string, which could be constructed of text only, as shown in Figure 3.2, or a combination of text and data, as shown in Figure 3.4.

Printf could also be used to display output, but *cout* is preferable for many reasons; output formatting (structuring output before displaying it) is more complicated in *Printf* due to the inclusion of formatting specifiers, %d, %s, %e, %f, which is not needed in *cout*. Secondly, *cout* is a variable while *Printf* is a function; this makes it even easier to manipulate and construct the outputs. For this book, we will use *cout* exclusively in our C++ code.

3.1.2.6   Variable Collections

In many situations, it is easier or more effective to work with data as a collection or a set of data points. In C++, there are different types of collections or *Containers*; each describes a different structure of collections, including *arrays*, *vectors*, *lists*, and others. For this book, we will focus only on *arrays* when working on C++ (and later Arduino).

In C++, arrays are *fixed-sized sequence* containers. They hold a pre-defined number of items that cannot be changed, and each item holds a specific position in the list. Figure 3.5 shows an example of an array in C++.

The figure shows that an array is declared with a *type*, *name*, and *values*, just like any other variable. Only in an array, we must also declare the size or number of its items, the number enclosed in the square brackets, as shown in line 8 in the figure.

In C++, pre-setting the size of the array is optional, but there will be effects. For example, if we declared the *temps* array in line 8 as *temps[ ] = {23.4, 23.4,*

```
 1
 2      #include <iostream>
 3      using namespace std;
 4
 5  ⊟   int main() {
 6
 7          // Declaring an Array with values
 8          float temps[7] = {23.4, 23.4, 24.0, 25.1};
 9
10          // working with individual items within the Array
11          // Display value
12          cout << "First value in Array: " << temps[0] << "\n";
13
14          // Update value
15          temps[0] = 26.4;
16          cout << "UPDATED first value in Array: " << temps[0];
17
18          return 0;
19  └   }
20
21
22
23
24
25
26
27
28
29
30
31
32
```

```
C:\WINDOWS\SYSTEM32\cmd.exe                    —    □    ×
First value in Array: 23.4
UPDATED first value in Array: 26.4

---------------------
(program exited with code: 0)

Press any key to continue . . .
```

FIGURE 3.5   An example of arrays in C++.

24.0, 25.1}, the program would run just fine, but the array would have only four items. In Figure 3.5, we declared an array with seven items but provided only four, which leaves us with three more available slots to be assigned later if needed.

As also shown in Figure 3.5, we can access, manipulate, and update individual values from arrays, shown in lines 12, 14, and 16. Other advanced operations, such as adding new items (to the array), removing items, and combining lists, would need other container types, such as *vectors* or *Lists*, which we will not cover in C++.

Another thing to notice in Figure 3.5 is the "\n" character added at the end of line 12. This character indicates a *new line*, allowing the following statement to be printed in a new line.

3.1.3   MANIPULATING DATA (OPERATORS & CONDITIONALS)

In C++, we can manipulate data with *Operators* and *Conditionals*. Operators are pre-defined commands that perform specific operations, while Conditionals are sub-routines that execute only when certain conditions are met. With Operators and Conditionals, we can translate our algorithms from ideas or diagrams into code.

3.1.3.1 C++ Operators

As briefly discussed earlier, C++ operators can be divided into several categories, depending on functionality: *arithmetic, assignment, comparisons, logical,* and *custom* operators. In the following few subsections, we discuss these operators with examples.

3.1.3.2 C++ Operators: Arithmetic

Table 3.3 shows the arithmetic operators available in C++. These are the familiar operators we use in simple arithmetic operations, such as addition or subtraction.

The last two operators, the *Increment* and *Decrement* operators, are interesting because they are uniquely used in programming. They are often used when working with data sets or iterating through loops, which we will see later.

3.1.3.3 C++ Operators: Assignment

Table 3.4 shows some of the assignment operators available in the C++ language. As the name implies, these operators are used when assigning a value to a variable.

From an algebraic point of view, the operations shown in this table do not make sense; how can x be equal to x+1? But in C++, and indeed any other

TABLE 3.3

Arithmetic Operators in C++

Operator	Name	Description	Example
+	Addition	Adds together two values	x+y
−	Subtraction	Subtracts one value from another	x−y
*	Multiplication	Multiplies two values	x * y
/	Division	Divides one value from another	x / y
%	Modulus	Returns the division remainder	x % y
++	Increment	Increases the value of a variable by 1	++x
——	Decrement	Decreases the value of a variable by 1	——x

TABLE 3.4

Assignment Operators in C++

Operator	Example	Equivalent to	Description
=	x=5	x=5	Assign 5 to variable x
+=	x += 3	x=x+3	Update x; assign x its current value +3
−=	x −= 3	x=x−3	Update x; assign x its current value −3
*=	x *= 3	x=x * 3	Update x; assign x its current value multiplied by 3
/=	x /= 3	x=x / 3	Update x; assign x its current value divided by 3

```
1
2      #include <iostream>
3      using namespace std;
4
5   ┌  int main() {
6
7          float roomTemp = 23.4;   // Original value
8          cout << "Orignal value: " << roomTemp << "\n";
9
10         roomTemp += 3;            // Update value
11         cout << "UPDATED value: " << roomTemp << "\n";
12
13         roomTemp = roomTemp - 3;  // Restore value
14         cout << "RESTORED value: " << roomTemp;
15
16         return 0;
17  └  }
18
19
20
21
22
23
24
25
26
27
28
29
30
```

```
C:\WINDOWS\SYSTEM32\cmd.exe                    —    □    ×

Orignal value: 23.4
UPDATED value: 26.4
RESTORED value: 23.4

------------------
(program exited with code: 0)

Press any key to continue . . .
```

FIGURE 3.6 Assigning and updating variables in C++.

programming language, the equal sign is not as a comparison (x = 5), but rather as an *assignment* (*assign* 5 to *variable* x).

Furthermore, the equal sign is also used to *update* variables, as shown in the rest of the table, by first performing an arithmetic operation on the current value of the variable and then assigning the result to become the new value of the variable. An example of an update operation is also shown in Figure 3.6.

The figure shows two versions of the update commands, the extended operation (x = x + 3) and the *shorthand* (x += 3). There is no difference in performance between the two versions, so it is just personal preference and code readability.

3.1.3.4   C++ Operators: Comparison and Logical Operators

Tables 3.5 and 3.6 show the *Comparison* and the *Logical* operators available in C++. These operators are presented here together because they are often used together.

TABLE 3.5

Comparison Operators in C++

Operator	Example	Description
==	x == y	x equals to y
!=	x != y	x not equals to y
>	x > y	x greater than y
<	x < y	x less than y
>=	x >= y	x greater than or equal to y
<=	x <= y	x less than or equal to y

TABLE 3.6

Logical Operators in C++

Operator	Name	Example	Effect
&&	AND	Condition A && condition B	returns True if **both** conditions are True
||	OR	Condition A || condition B	returns True if **any** condition is True
!	NOT	! (Condition A)	returns **opposite** of condition (inverse)

As the names imply, the comparison operators compare two variables, while the logical operators combine multiple comparisons with the logical gates. They are often used together in *Conditionals*, *Loops*, and *Functions*, allowing developers to convert algorithms and process flows into program blocks and structures.

It is worth noting that the above comparisons and logical operations apply not only to numerals, such as Integers, Floats, and Doubles but also to *Booleans* and somewhat to *Strings*. The *String* class provides, among other things, the *compare* method.

3.1.3.5   C++ Operators: Math

Table 3.7 shows some of the math operators available in the C++ language. Math operators are advanced mathematical operations that can be used for data processing.

The operators listed in Table 3.7 are just samples; the math library is very extensive, and it also includes mathematical constants such as *Pi*, *g*, and much more. Therefore, the easiest way to find the command for an operation you need is to search for it online. For example, if you want to find the square root in C++, just search for *square root C++*, and you will find plenty of online resources that include the original application programming interfaces (APIs), sample code, and tutorials.

3.1.3.6   C++ Conditionals

As discussed before, Conditionals are programming constructs that allow you to execute parts of your codes based on specific conditions or situations. Conditionals

TABLE 3.7

Math Operators (Samples) in C++

Function	Description
max(x,y)	Find the highest value between x and y
min(x,y)	Find the lowest value between x and y
sqrt(x)	Finds the square root of x
round(x)	Round x (rounding factor can be set)
ceil(x)	Returns the value of x rounded up to its nearest integer (RoundUp)
floor(x)	Returns the value of x rounded down to its nearest integer
abs(x)	Returns the absolute value of x (removes negative sign, if any)
cos(x)	Returns the cosine of x, in radians
acos(x)	Returns the arccosine of x, in radians
cosh(x)	Returns the hyperbolic cosine of x, in radians
asin(x)	Returns the arcsine of x, in radians
atan(x)	Returns the arctangent, given (x=sin/cos), in radians
atan2(x,y)	Returns the arctangent, given (x=sin, y=cos), in radians

could be purely logical or functional. For example, they could capture different conditions or ensure successful program operations (without errors). We can use several types of conditionals in C++; the most common ones are the *If Statements*, *Switch Case*, and *Exceptions*.

3.1.3.7   C++ Conditionals: If Statements

The structure of an *If Statement* in C++ is shown in Figure 3.7. The *If Statement* is the most common Conditional in C++ and any programming language, for that matter.

The figure also shows the *else if* and *else* statements, which we can use to capture multiple *related* conditions. For example, a person must be a registered student first (condition1 = True) before checking their class attendance record (condition 2).

We could use multiple *if* or *else if* statements in different combinations to account for different scenarios or use the *Switch Case* construct, as shown in Figure 3.8.

3.1.3.8   C++ Conditionals: Switch Case

As shown in the figure, the process begins with evaluating the value of the *expression*, which could be a Boolean, a mathematical formula, a custom function, or anything else.

Next, the expression is compared against all possible *cases*; if the expression is found to equal a specific case, its code is executed. The *break* command is added to ensure only the block of the matching case is executed. If we remove the break commands in Figure 3.8, all blocks in the diagram (x, y, and *default*) will execute.

```
// The If Statement
if (condition1) {
    // execute if condition1 is true

} else if (condition2) {
    // execute condition1 is FALSE & if condition2 is TRUE

} else {
    // execute if both conditions1 & conditions2 are FALSE
}



// Multiple If Statements (independent conditions)
if (condition1) {
    // if condition1 is True
}

if (condition2) {
    // if condition2 is True
}
```

FIGURE 3.7 The structure and syntax of the *If Statement* in C++.

```
switch(expression) { // find value of expression

    case x:
        // execute this block if expression == x
        break;

    case y:
        // execute this block if expression == y
        break;

    default:
        // execute this block if expression does not equal any case

}
```

FIGURE 3.8 The *Switch Case* construct in C++.

Sometimes, the purpose of the conditional is operational. However, in some cases, we cannot fully predict what will happen when the program runs, so we tell the program first to *Try* certain things and *Catch* any possible errors if they occur, as shown in Figure 3.9.

3.1.3.9 C++ Conditionals: Exceptions

There are many situations where *Exceptions* are helpful; a typical example is handling user input. The program might instruct the user to input an integer, but the user could ignore that and input something else, which, if unchecked, could cause failure and crash the program.

The program would ask the user to input an integer; then, it would *Try* to capture that input. If the user inputted an integer, that input is *accepted* (a successful

```
try {
    // A block of code (with possible problems) to try
}
catch () {
    // a block of code to run in case errors happen
}
```

FIGURE 3.9   The exceptions construct in C++ (simplified).

Try), and the program proceeds. However, if the user inputted something else, the *Try* fails, triggering the code in the *Catch*, which could print out an error message. Furthermore, if we put the Try/Catch construct in a loop, then the program will never proceed till the user inputs the valid input, and this is the premise of *User Input Validation*.

The *Exception* construct shown in Figure 3.9 is the simplest form of this construct; we could have multiple catch blocks for different errors/situations. We could throw an error code to go along with the error (remember *error codes*). We could also insert more elaborate constructs, such as If statements, Switch Cases, loops, and functions.

3.1.4   REUSING CODE (LOOPS, FUNCTIONS, AND LIBRARIES)

In many cases, we need to reuse parts of our code; perhaps we need to perform a specific task on every item in a list, or while a particular condition is true, or whenever we need it.

There are several constructs in C++ for reusing code; these include *Loops*, *Functions*, and on a bigger scale, *Classes*, *Libraries*, and *Frameworks*. For this book, we will focus only on Loops, Functions, and Libraries.

3.1.4.1   Reusing C++ Code: Loops

In general, there are two types of loops in C++, the *For* and the *While* loops. As the names imply, the For loops reuse code *for* every item in a list or within a range, and the While loops reuse code *while* a particular condition is true. Both types are shown in Figure 3.10.

As shown in the figure, the For loop is designed to reuse a block of the program for every item in a list (or array) or every item within a range of values. This could be useful when working with structured data, such as data stored in lists, arrays, and ranges.

On the other hand, the While loop is best suited to operate on data based on situations and scenarios, often combined with *Conditionals*. The if statement could be configured to check if a specific situation is true/false, which could be a combination of several conditions. As a real-life example, if tuition fees are paid, a student registration remains valid/active. So while a student is active (true), they could receive service (education, use of facilities, etc.)

```
for (range/list){
    // execute block for every item in list/within range
}

while (condition){
    // execute block while condition is true
}
```

FIGURE 3.10   The *For* and *While* loops in C++.

There are other variations of loops, such as the *Do while* loop, *nested* loops (loops within loops or multi-dimensional loops), and *shorthand* (single line) loops. We will discuss these loops if and when we encounter them.

3.1.4.2   Reusing C++ Code: Functions

Sometimes, we need to reuse blocks of code only *when needed*; for that purpose, we use the *function* construct, as shown in Figure 3.11.

As seen in the figure, the function construct contains two main elements, the *declaration*, which defines the body of the function, or what it does, and the *call*, which is how we call the function to act from the main body of the program.

The figure shows that this function is a *void* function; it performs a task alright but does not return a value. Sometimes we need functions to perform miscellaneous tasks (print a message, close a file, etc.), and Void functions are best used for these kinds of situations.

Some other times, however, we need the function to return a value; a great example of this is the **main**() function in C++, shown in Figures 3.2, 3.4–3.6, which returns an integer, and *function2*, shown in Figure 3.12, which returns a Boolean.

If you have already noticed, the structure of the function declaration follows a similar structure to the variable declaration: *type*, *name*, and *body* (instead of value). In C++, the type of a variable or a function must be declared beforehand,

```
// function declaration
void myfunction(){
    // body of function
    //(block to execute when needed or called)
}


// to call the function
myfunction() ;
```

FIGURE 3.11   The *Function* construct in C++.

```
// void function; Performs task only
void myfunction(){
    // body of function
    //(block to execute when called
}

// Boolean function; Performs task & returns boolean
bool myfunction2(){
    // body of function
    //(block to execute when called

    return true;    // same Type as function
}
```

FIGURE 3.12   Functions with or without a *Return value* in C++.

as discussed in Table 3.2. Also, the type of the returned variable must correspond to the type of its function.

For example, the type of the *main()* function in C++ is **int**, so it returns an integer, while the type of *function2* in Figure 3.12 is **bool**, so it returns a Boolean, and so on.

3.1.4.3   Functions Parameters

Some functions need data to perform their tasks; the temperature conversion program discussed earlier is a good example. Figure 3.13 shows a complete version of this program.

The figure shows the function to convert from Celsius to Fahrenheit. As seen in the figure, the function takes input data (temperature in C), performs the conversion (data manipulation), then displays the output data (temperature in F). The input data is called the function *Parameters*.

As shown in Figure 3.13, parameters are declared as part of the function declaration, where we declare their types and implement them. For example, in the *convertCtoF* function, we declared that this function accepts a *float*, which will then be processed in a mathematical formula, as shown in the function definition (function body).

As also seen in the figure, the variables *temperature_C* and *temperature_F* are available only inside the function. So, if we attempt to *cout temperature_C* instead of *tempC* we would get a "variable not declared in this scope" error. You should try and see it for yourself.

We could have changed *temperature_C* and *temperature_F* to *tempC* and *tempF* inside the function, and this program would still work, but this is not a good idea as we might encounter bugs and operational issues. So instead, a good practice is to use different variable names within function bodies to avoid errors and bugs and improve program readability.

```
#include <iostream>
using namespace std;

// initialiazation
float tempC, tempF;

// Function to convert Celsius to Fahrenheit
float convertCtoF(float temperature_C){
    float temperature_F = temperature_C*(9/5) + 32;
    return temperature_F;
}

int main() {
    tempC = 24.5;    // set here as an example

    // call conversion function, and pass it the parameter
    tempF = convertCtoF(tempC) ;

    // Display output
    cout << "Temperature: " << tempC << " (C)\n";
    cout << "Temperature: " << tempF << " (F)\n";

    return 0;
}
```

FIGURE 3.13   A function with parameters in C++.

3.1.4.4   C++: We Are Done

At this point, we have covered all major areas of C++ concepts. Of course, there is plenty to learn, and we encourage you to use online resources for more practice. But for this book, we covered enough material to begin working with IoT systems where C++ is used, such as Arduino and Arduino-compatible systems.

3.2   PROGRAMMING LANGUAGES: PYTHON

This section provides a comprehensive guide into the Python programming language from the IoT perspective. We revise concepts and tools in Python that we would use later in IoT controller programming, data packaging, and broadcasting. Therefore, even if you are an expert in Python, we recommend you review this section.

For those who completed the C++ section, this section will feel like a repeat. Few concepts and issues covered in C++ are revisited here but in Python. This is done by design because some readers might have skipped the C++ sections altogether. On the other hand, this section will feel much easier if you have finished the C++ section. Also, you will get the chance to see the difference between the two languages, especially in syntax and program readability.

3.2.1   Getting Starting with Python

The first step of learning Python is to ensure that it is correctly installed on your machine. That involves downloading and installing the *Geany* IDE, the Python interpreter, and setting them up properly to produce a sample Python program. Luckily, the *Geany* IDE and Python are available for all OSs and distributions. So it is OK if you prefer to work with another IDE, but we recommend Geany because we will use it for Raspberry Pi programming.

3.2.1.1   Installation and Setup

Download and install Geany and Python. The order of installation (which one to install first) is not essential. The sources shown in Table 3.8 are valid at the time of writing.

You need to add Python to the PATH variable so your system would recognize Python files (.py extension). We recommend doing this during installation, as shown in Figure 3.14. You can also do this after installation; instructions are here (*Adding Python to PATH*, 2019).

After successfully installing the IDE and Python 3.x, you can now write your first Python program. Start the Geany IDE program and do the following:

- **Start a New Document**: Click on *New* or *File>New*, or hit the *Ctrl* and *N* keys on your keyboard. Any of these actions will start a new document. At this stage, this document could be any text file.

TABLE 3.8
Installation Sources for Python

Item	Name	Source
IDE	Geany	https://www.geany.org/download/releases/ (select a release for your *Operating System*)
Python	Python 3.9.5 (Windows)	https://www.python.org/downloads/ (Remember: Select *Add Python 3.x to PATH* option)

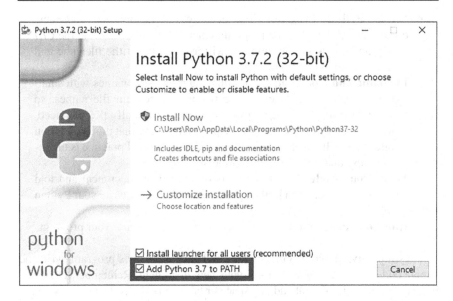

FIGURE 3.14   Adding Python 3.x to PATH during installation.

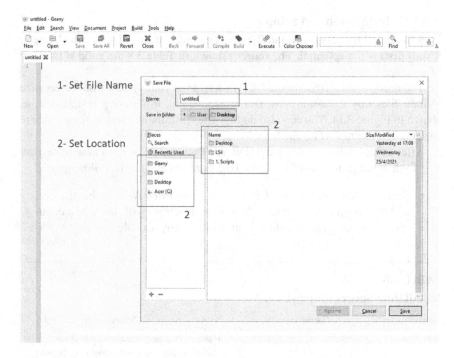

FIGURE 3.15 File naming and location setting in Geany IDE (Python).

- **Set as Python Program**: You need to tell Geany that your new document will be a Python program. Click *File > Save As*, or hit the *Ctrl* and *S*, and a new pop-up window will ask you to set the filename and location, as shown in Figure 3.15.
- **Filename and Location**: Convention suggests using names with small letters, no spaces, and descriptive words for program file names, so things like *myfirst* or *firstprogram* or *program1* are all OK. You need, however, to end your file name with **.py** to tell Geany that this is a Python program file. The location is entirely arbitrary; a good practice is to create an individual folder for each project.
- **Write Your Code**: Now that you have created the document and told Geany that it would be a Python program, you can now write your Python code.
- **Run Your Program**: *Compile*, then *Build*, then *Execute* your program.

For simplicity, we will begin with the good old *Hello World* program; write the simple code shown in Figure 3.16 in your new document. Remember, DO NOT indent your code, i.e. do not add any space or tab before the code, as shown in the figure (we will talk about this later).

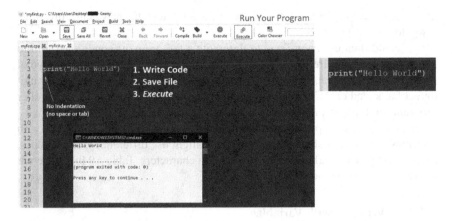

FIGURE 3.16 The *Hello World* program (Python) in Geany and its output.

Then, save and run your program, which in Python means you just need to hit *Execute*. If you recall from Table 2.6, Python uses an interpreter, so no need for *Compile* or *Build* like in C++. So, if everything went smoothly, you should see the output shown in Figure 3.16.

If you can see the output shown in Figure 3.16, you have successfully installed the Geany IDE and correctly added Python to PATH. This also means that you are now ready to proceed to following sections and hands-on programming exercises.

By now, you can already see the differences between C++ and Python; in C++, we needed about six lines to write the Hello World program; in Python, we needed just one line. This is an example of Python's simplicity and readability, and this is just the beginning.

If you could not see the output in Figure 3.16, that means something went wrong. So, we suggest you review your steps and ensure success before proceeding to the next section.

3.2.2 WORKING WITH DATA (VARIABLES AND COLLECTIONS)

As discussed before, the purpose of Electronic Systems, including all *Controller Programs*, is to manage *data*; controllers receive, process, and *produce* data (in the form of output data or commands based on output data). So, this section reviews the following concepts: *Program Variables* and *Data Collections (lists)* in Python (*Python 3.9.5 Documentation*, 2021).

3.2.2.1 Program Variables

In Python, a *variable* is a space holder where we can store a value temporarily. For example, let *roomTemp* be a variable that indicates the room temperature, and let us assign it a value of 24. Let us also assume the temperature room rose to

26.5°, so, in our program, we can update *roomTemp* with the new value, this time, it would be equal to 26.5.

We could then use *roomTemp* to *automate* a fan or an air conditioner unit to *control* the temperature in the room. For example, based on the current value of *roomTemp*, we could autonomously switch on or off the fan or air conditioner unit (or set fan speed or AC temperature). That was a simple example of a controller program used in *Automation*.

In the above example, the *value* assigned to *roomTemp* was a number with decimals. Other variables in other situations might use different *Types* of values, such as integers, logical operators, or even text characters; Table 3.9 lists different *Variable Types* in Python.

3.2.2.2 Working with Variables

In Python, data is assigned to *variables* which the program can then manipulate to produce the needed results. For example, suppose you want to write a program to convert room temperature from Celsius to Fahrenheit. In that case, your program must include two variables, *C* and *F*, the conversion formula, and the interface to input values and display results.

So, in your program, you would need to *Declare*, *Manipulate*, and *Display* variables to perform the temperature conversion. We will first focus on declaring and displaying variables; then, we will discuss data manipulation.

3.2.2.3 Declaring Variables in Python

Before you can work with a variable, you need to declare it. In Python, you can do so through the *declare variable* structure, which includes two elements: the variable's *name* and *value*, as shown in Figure 3.17.

TABLE 3.9
Variable Types in Python

Type	Details
Integer (int)	Integers, whole numbers without decimals
A floating point number (float)	Whole numbers with decimals (fractions), up to 15 decimal places (in Python, all floats are actually doubles, compared to C++)
Complex numbers	Numbers with real and imaginary components, e.g. $4+5j$ (in C++, complex numbers are available only through libraries)
Boolean (bool)	Logical values, either *True = 1, or False = 0*
String (str)	A string is a list of individual characters, so, the *Hello* String is an array of chars, ['H', 'e', 'l', 'l', 'o'] There is No *Char* variable type in Python (compared to C++), instead, a single character is considered a string with length = 1 The fact that strings are arrays is used extensively in *String Operations*

```
# Declaring Variables
# varibleName - Value

myAge = 27                    #   Integer
roomTemp = 26.4               #   Float (registered as 26.400000000)
clearance = 8.44395433        #   Float (registered as 8.443954330)
isCondition = True            #   Boolean (logical value)
firstLetter = "s"             #   String (length = 1)
welcomeMsg = "hello"          #   String (length = 5)

myComplex = 4 + 6j            #   Complex number
```

FIGURE 3.17 Declaring variables in Python.

As shown in the figure, you do not need to declare the variable type in Python, as the variable type is understood from the context or based on the value. For example, the value of *myAge* is 27, so that must be an *Integer*, the value of *welcomeMsg* is "Hello", so it must be a *String*, and so on. Also, in Python, you cannot *readily* set variable types or initiate variables (declare variables without values), like in C++, but there are always workarounds.

Other things to notice in the figure are the general syntax of Python (vs. C++). For example, the *Semicolon* is optional and used only if you want to run multiple commands on a single line. Finally, using the hash "#" to create the *Python Comments* is a powerful tool for any developer.

3.2.2.4 Manipulating Variables in Python

After variables have been declared, we can use *Operators* to manipulate their values to achieve the effects we intend with our program. Returning to the example above, after declaring two variables, *C* and *F*, we can now use operators to perform the conversion. Operators are divided into several types: *arithmetic*, *assignment*, *comparisons*, *logical*, and *custom* operators. We will see these operators in action in the next section.

3.2.2.5 Displaying Variables in Python

In Python, displaying variables could be part of a *system–human* interface to show the program's output to the end user. Using the same example, a user inputs a temperature in *C*; the program performs the conversion (manipulation), then displays the output, converted in *F*.

Furthermore, displaying variables could be an excellent troubleshooting tool for you to debug your program and verify the values it is producing against your algorithm, as we shall see later. In Python, we can display variables with the *print* module, as shown in Figure 3.18.

```
# Displaying Variables

myAge = 27;
roomTemp = 26.4

print(roomTemp)
print("The room temperature is: " + str(roomTemp))

msg = "My age is : " + str(myAge)

print(msg)
```

```
C:\WINDOWS\SYSTEM32\cmd.exe                      -    □    X
26.4
The room temperature is: 26.4
My age is : 27


--------------------
(program exited with code: 0)

Press any key to continue . . .
```

FIGURE 3.18 Displaying variables in Python using the *print* module.

As shown in the figure, we can also display the output in a constructed form by concatenating the variable's value to a sentence string and print the whole thing out. We could also treat the output construct (sentence + value) as a separate variable, construct it separately, and then pass it to the print module to display the output.

However, to do this, we need to *cast* the variable to a *String* before combining it with text. *Type Casting* allows us to re-declare a variable type to something else to enable features specific to the new type. For example, as we did here, we cast the variable to a String to enable *concatenation*, which is exclusive to Strings.

3.2.2.6   Variable (Data) Collections

In many situations, it is easier or more effective to work with data as a collection or a set of data points. In Python, there are four built-in types of data Collections: *Lists*, *Tuples*, *Sets*, and *Dictionaries*. For this book, we will focus only on *Lists* and *Dictionaries* when working on Python (and later Raspberry Pi). Figure 3.19 shows examples of lists in Python.

Lists are ordered, changeable, and allow duplicates. As shown in the figure, we can access, manipulate, and update items from lists. We can add items to lists, remove items from lists, and combine lists. *Dictionaries* are ordered, changeable, and do not allow duplicates. They store data sets in *key-value* pairs, where each item is defined through a key (index) and a value. An example of Python Dictionary is shown in Figure 3.20.

```
 1
 2   # Python Lists
 3   temps = [23.4, "John", 49, 25.3341]
 4   print("Second value in Array: " + temps[1])
 5
 6   temps[1] = "Tim"
 7   print("UPDATED Second value in Array: " + temps[1])
 8
 9
10
11
12
13
14
15
16
```

C:\WINDOWS\SYSTEM32\cmd.exe

Second value in Array: John
UPDATED Second value in Array: Tim

(program exited with code: 0)

Press any key to continue . . .

FIGURE 3.19 An example of *Lists* in Python.

```
 1
 2   # Python Dictionaries
 3
 4   SensorData = {
 5       "heatSensor": 23.5,
 6       "humidityS":  23.4,
 7       "ThingID":    "342A",
 8       "Thingtype":  23
 9   }
10
11   print("Remote Sensor Data: " + str(SensorData))
12
13
14
15
16
17
18
```

C:\WINDOWS\SYSTEM32\cmd.exe

Remote Sensor Data: {'heatSensor': 23.5, 'humidityS': 23.4, 'ThingID': '342A', 'Thingtype': 23}

(program exited with code: 0)

Press any key to continue . . .

FIGURE 3.20 An example of *dictionaries* in Python.

Dictionaries are vital when working with IoT data, as we use them to package raw data into web-friendly formats, such as JSON or MQTT, as we shall see in Chapter 5.

Few things to notice about Python Collections; as we can see in Figures 3.19 and 3.20, lists and dictionaries can take variables of different types, as discussed in Table 3.9. Also, there is no need to pre-define the size of lists (like in C++) because we can easily add/remove items from lists. Furthermore, Lists and

Dictionaries have several built-in functions, or methods, that could be powerful tools for data management and manipulation, as we shall see later.

3.2.3 Manipulating Data (Operators and Conditionals)

In Python, we can manipulate data with *Operators* and *Conditionals*. Operators are pre-defined commands that perform specific operations, while Conditionals are sub-routines that execute only when certain conditions are met. With Operators and Conditionals, we can translate our algorithms from ideas or diagrams into code.

3.2.3.1 Python Operators

As briefly discussed earlier, Python operators can be divided into several categories, depending on functionality: *arithmetic, assignment, comparisons, logical,* and *custom* operators. In the following few subsections, we discuss these operators with examples.

3.2.3.2 Python Operators: Arithmetic

Table 3.10 shows the arithmetic operators available in Python. These are the familiar operators we use in simple arithmetic operations, such as addition or subtraction.

The last two operators, *Exponentiation* and *Floor Division*, combine several operations in a single command, especially the floor division (division, then floor). This could prove to be very valuable when working with large volumes of data sets.

3.2.3.3 Python Operators: Assignment

Table 3.11 shows some of the assignment operators available in Python. As the name implies, these operators are used when assigning a value to a variable.

From an algebraic point of view, the operations shown in this table do not make sense; how can x be equal to $x+1$? But in Python, and indeed any other programming language, the equal sign is not as a comparison (x *equals to* 5) but rather as an *assignment* (*assign* 5 *to variable* x).

TABLE 3.10

Arithmetic Operators in Python

Operator	Name	Description	Example
+	Addition	Adds together two values	x+y
–	Subtraction	Subtracts one value from another	x−y
*	Multiplication	Multiplies two values	x * y
/	Division	Divides one value from another	x / y
%	Modulus	Returns the division remainder	x % y
**	Exponentiation	x to the power of y	x ** y
//	Floor division	x / y, then floor (*rounddown*) the result	x // y

---

TABLE 3.11

Assignment Operators in Python

Operator	Example	Equivalent to	Description
=	x = 5	x = 5	Assign 5 to variable x
+=	x += 3	x = x + 3	Update x; assign x its current value +3
-=	x -= 3	x = x - 3	Update x; assign x its current value -3
*=	x *= 3	x = x * 3	Update x; assign x its current value multiplied by 3
/=	x /= 3	x = x / 3	Update x; assign x its current value divided by 3

```python
roomTemp = 23.4

print("Original Value: " + str(roomTemp))

roomTemp += 3
print("Original Value: " + str(roomTemp))

roomTemp = roomTemp - 3
print("Original Value: " + str(roomTemp))
```

```
C:\WINDOWS\SYSTEM32\cmd.exe                    —    □    X
Original Value: 23.4
Original Value: 26.4
Original Value: 23.4

-------------------
(program exited with code: 0)

Press any key to continue . . . _
```

FIGURE 3.21 Assigning and updating variables in Python.

Furthermore, the equal sign is also used to *update* variables, as shown in the rest of the table, by first performing an arithmetic operation on the current value of the variable and then assigning the result to become the new value of the variable. An example of an update operation is also shown in Figure 3.21.

The figure shows two versions of the update commands, the extended operation (x = x + 3) and the *shorthand* (x += 3). There is no difference in performance between the two versions, so it is just personal preference and code readability.

3.2.3.4   Python Operators: Comparison, Logical, Identity, and Membership Operators

Table 3.12 shows the *Comparison, Logical, Identity, and Membership* operators in Python. These operators are presented here together because they are often used together.

As the names imply, comparison operators compare variables, while logical operators combine multiple comparisons. Identity operators compare objects, while membership operators check for inclusion within other objects and lists. These operators are often used in combinations with *Conditionals, Loops,* and *Functions.*

Hopefully by now, you can begin to see the *Readability* of Python code, especially when you consider how *Logical, Identity,* and *Membership* are taken directly from the English language, making code easier to read and comprehend.

3.2.3.5   Python Operators: Math

Table 3.13 shows some of the math operators available in the Math Module in Python. Math operators are advanced mathematical operations that can be used for data processing.

The operators listed in Table 3.13 are just samples: the Math Module is very extensive, and it also includes mathematical constants such as *Pi, g,* and much more. Therefore, the easiest way to find the command for an operation you need is to search for it online. For example, if you want to find the square root in Python, just search for *square root python 3*, and you will find plenty of online resources that include the original APIs, sample code, and tutorials.

TABLE 3.12

Comparison, Logical, Identity, and *Membership* **Operators in Python**

Type	Operator	Example	Description
Comparison	==	x == y	x equals to y
	!=	x != y	x not equals to y
	>	x > y	x greater than y
	<	x < y	x less than y
	>=	x >= y	x greater than or equal to y
	<=	x <= y	x less than or equal to y
Logical	and	Condition A **and** condition B	returns True if *all* are True
	or	Condition A **or** condition B	returns True if *any* is True
	not	**not** (Condition A)	return opposite of condition (inverse)
Identity	is	x is y	returns True if x, y are the **same object**
	is not	or	returns False if x, y are **not the same**
Membership	in	and	returns True if x is **in** object y
	not in	or	returns False if x is **not in** object y

TABLE 3.13

Math Operators (Samples) in the Math Module in Python

Function	Description
math.max(x,y)	Find the highest value between x and y
math.min(x,y)	Find the lowest value between x and y
math.sqrt(x)	Finds the square root of x
math.round(x)	Round x (rounding factor can be set).
math.ceil(x)	Returns the value of x rounded up to its nearest integer (RoundUp)
math.floor(x)	Returns the value of x rounded down to its nearest integer (RoundDown)
math.abs(x)	Returns the absolute value of x (removes negative sign, if any)
math.cos(x)	Returns the cosine of x, in radians
math.acos(x)	Returns the arccosine of x, in radians
math.cosh(x)	Returns the hyperbolic cosine of x, in radians
math.asin(x)	Returns the arcsine of x, in radians
math.atan(x)	Returns the arctangent, given (x=sin/cos), in radians
math.atan2(x,y)	Returns the arctangent, given (x=sin, y=cos), in radians

3.2.3.6 Python Conditionals

As discussed before, conditionals are programming constructs that allow you to execute parts of your codes based on specific conditions or situations. Conditionals could be purely logical or functional. For example, they could capture different conditions or ensure successful program operations (without errors). We can use several types of conditionals in Python; the most common ones are the *If Statements* and *Exceptions*.

3.2.3.7 Python Conditionals: If Statements

The structure of an *If Statement* in Python is shown in Figure 3.22. The *If Statement* is the most common Conditional in Python and any programming language, for that matter.

The figure also shows the *else if* and *else* statements, which we can use to capture multiple *related* conditions. For example, a person must be a registered student first (condition1=True) before checking their class attendance record (condition2).

Unlike C++, Python does not implement the *Switch Case* construct. Therefore, you could always use combinations or multiple *if* or *else if* statements to achieve the same effects, or you can create it yourself as a *Function* or a *Class*.

3.2.3.8 C++ Conditionals: Exceptions

Sometimes, the purpose of the conditional is operational. In some cases, we cannot fully predict what will happen when the program runs, so we tell the program first to *Try* certain things and *Catch* any possible errors if they occur, as shown in Figure 3.23.

```
# The If Statements

# Dependant Conditions
if condition1:
    # execute if Condition1 is True

elif condition2:
    # execute if Condition1 is False & Condition 2 is True

else:
    # execute if Both Conditions are False


# Independant Conditions
if condition1:
    # execute if Condition1 is True

if condition2:
    # execute if Conditions is True
```

FIGURE 3.22 The structure and syntax of the *If Statement* in Python.

There are many situations where *Exceptions* are helpful; a typical example is handling user input. The program might instruct the user to input an integer, but the user could ignore that and input something else, which, if unchecked, could cause failure and crash the program.

The program would ask the user to input an integer; then, it would *Try* to capture that input. If the user inputted an integer, that input is *accepted* (successful Try), and the program proceeds. However, if the user inputted something else, the *Try* fails, triggering the code in the *Catch*, which could print out an error message.

Furthermore, if we put the Try/Catch construct in a loop, then the program will never proceed till the user inputs the valid input, and this is the premise of *User Input Validation*.

The *Exception* construct shown in Figure 3.23 is the simplest form of this construct; we could have multiple catch blocks for different errors/situations. We could also insert more elaborate constructs, such as If statements, loops, and functions.

3.2.4 REUSING CODE (LOOPS, FUNCTIONS, AND LIBRARIES)

In many cases, we need to reuse parts of our code; perhaps we need to perform a specific task on every item in a list, or while a particular condition is true, or whenever we need it.

```
try:
    # A block of code (with possible problems) to try
except:
    # A block of code to run in case problems do happen
```

FIGURE 3.23 The exceptions construct in Python.

There are several constructs in Python for reusing code; these include *Loops*, *Collection Loops*, *Functions*, and on a bigger scale, *Libraries* and *Classes*. Also, Python Collections have unique loops called Collection Loops, which allow for very powerful tools to work with data sets and structures, as we shall see next.

3.2.4.1 Reusing Python Code: Loops

In general, there are two types of loops in Python, the *For* and the *While* loops. As the names imply, the For loops reuse code *for* every item in a list or within a range, and the While loops reuse code *while* a particular condition is true. Both types are shown in Figure 3.24.

As shown in the figure, the For loop is designed to reuse a block of the program for every item in a list (or array) or every item within a range of values. This could be useful when working with structured data, such as data stored in lists, arrays, and ranges.

On the other hand, the While loop is best suited to operate on data based on situations and scenarios, often combined with *Conditionals*. The if statement could be configured to check if a specific situation is true/false, which could be a combination of several conditions. As a real-life example, if tuition fees are paid, a student registration remains valid/active. So, while a student is active (true), they could receive service (education, use of facilities, etc.)

3.2.4.2 Reusing Python Code: Collection Loops

As discussed above, in Python, we also have *Collections Loops* which are a special type of loops that work on Collections. Figure 3.25 shows the List loop in action.

As shown in the figure, the *List* loop utilizes a very intuitive and easy-to-read construct; *for an item in a list, do something*; this is another example of Python's readability and simplicity.

Python also allows us to use indices, as shown in Figure 3.25. Both approaches are powerful and used today. Another example of Collection loops in Python is the *Dictionary Loop*, which is more elaborate as it contains pairs of *Keys* and *Values*, as shown in Figure 3.26.

As shown in the figure, we could access keys only, values only, or *Items* (objects containing keys and values) from Dictionaries. We could then manipulate these items; we could update their values or keys, add or remove items, combine Dictionaries, and more.

```
for (Range/List):
    # Execute block for every item in list/within range

while (condition):
    # Execute block while condition is true
```

FIGURE 3.24   The *For* and *While* loops in Python.

```
# Collection loops - Lists
items = [23.4, "John", 49, 25.3341]

print("")
print("Print items directly")

for item in items:
    print(item)

print("")
print("Print items using index")

for i in range(len(items)):
    print(items[i])
```

```
Print items directly
23.4
John
49
25.3341

Print items using index
23.4
John
49
25.3341
```

FIGURE 3.25   The *List* loop in Python.

```
# Dictionary Loops
SensorData = {
"heatSensor":    23.5,
"humidityS":     23.4,
"ThingID":       "342A",
"Thingtype":     23
}

print("\nPrint Keys only")
for key in SensorData:
    print(key)

print("\nPrint Values only")
for value in SensorData.values():
    print(value)

print("\nPrint Keys & Values")
for key,value in SensorData.items():
    print(key,value)
```

```
Print Keys only
heatSensor
humidityS
ThingID
Thingtype

Print Values only
23.5
23.4
342A
23

Print Keys & Values
heatSensor 23.5
humidityS 23.4
ThingID 342A
Thingtype 23
```

FIGURE 3.26   The *Dictionary* loop in Python.

3.2.4.3   Reusing Python Code: Functions

Sometimes, we need to reuse blocks of code only *when needed*; for that purpose, we use the *function* construct, as shown in Figure 3.27.

As seen in the figure, the function construct contains two main elements: the *declaration*, which defines the body of the function, or what it does, and the *call*, which is how we call the function to act from the main body of the program. Sometimes, we need functions to perform tasks (print a message, close a file, etc.), and sometimes we need functions to perform tasks *and* return a value. Figure 3.28 shows these two types of functions.

If you have already noticed, the structure of the function declaration in Python follows a similar structure to the variable declaration; *name and body* (instead

```python
# A function Declaration
def myfunction():
    # Body of Function
    # Block of code to execute when called


# A function call
myfunction()
```

FIGURE 3.27   The *Function* construct in Python.

```python
# Perform task only
def myfunction():
    # Body of Function
    # Block of code to execute when called

# Perform task & return value
def myfunction2():
    # Body of Function
    # Block of code to execute when called
    return True
```

FIGURE 3.28   Functions with or without a *Return value* in Python.

of value). In Python, and as discussed in Table 3.9, there is no need to declare a function type (like in C++).

The function's type would be determined, once again, from the context; if the function returns a Boolean, then it is a Boolean function, if it returns a String, then it is a String function, and if it does not return anything, then it is a *none* function (equivalent to *void* in C++).

3.2.4.4   Functions Arguments

Some functions need data to perform their tasks; the temperature conversion program discussed earlier is a good example. Figure 3.29 shows the complete version of this program.

The figure shows the function to convert from Celsius to Fahrenheit. As seen in the figure, the function takes input data (temperature in C), performs the conversion (data manipulation), then displays the output data (temperature in F). The input data is called the function *Arguments*.

As shown in the figure, argument definitions are part of the function declaration, where we declare how to implement them. For example, in the *convertCtoF* function, we declared that this function accepts a variable called *temperature_C*, which will then be processed in a mathematical formula, as shown in the function definition (function body).

As also seen in the figure, the variables *temperature_C* and *temperature_F* are available only inside the function. So if we attempt to print *temperature_C* instead of *tempC* we would get a "variable not defined" error. You should try and see it for yourself.

Furthermore, we could have changed *temperature_C* and *temperature_F* to *tempC* and *tempF* inside the function, and this program would still work, but this is not a good idea as we might encounter bugs and operational issues. Hence, it is a good practice to use different variable names within function bodies to avoid errors and bugs and improve program readability.

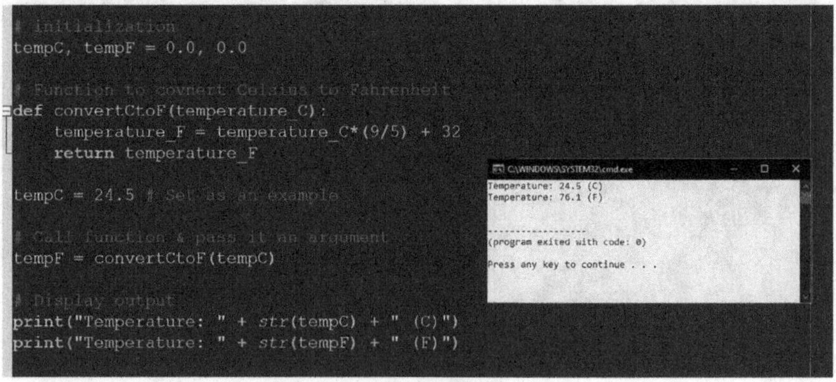

```python
# initialization
tempC, tempF = 0.0, 0.0

# Function to covnert Celsius to Fahrenheit
def convertCtoF(temperature_C):
    temperature_F = temperature_C*(9/5) + 32
    return temperature_F

tempC = 24.5 # Set as an example

# Call function & pass it an argument
tempF = convertCtoF(tempC)

# Display output
print("Temperature: " + str(tempC) + " (C)")
print("Temperature: " + str(tempF) + " (F)")
```

```
C:\WINDOWS\SYSTEM32\cmd.exe                    —   □   ×
Temperature: 24.5 (C)
Temperature: 76.1 (F)
--------------------
(program exited with code: 0)
Press any key to continue . . .
```

FIGURE 3.29   A function with *arguments* in Python.

3.2.4.5 The Syntax in Python vs. C++

If you have completed both the C++ and Python sections of this chapter, then you are in the unique position to compare the two languages. For example, you can compare C++ (Figures 3.2–3.13) and Python (Figures 3.16–3.29) and observe the following.

- **No End-of-Line Semicolons**: While a simple thing, forgetting a semicolon and struggling to find it is one of the most frustrating errors in C++, luckily it is optional in Python.
- **No Brackets for Code Blocks**: In C++, blocks of code (loops, functions, conditionals) are enclosed in brackets. The situation gets more complicated in nested blocks (loops within loops, nested if statements, multi-dimensional loops, etc.). Forgetting a bracket or figuring out where it goes is another frustrating problem in C++.
- **Indentation Is Significant in Python**: Instead, Python uses *Indentation*; each sub-block signifies the parent–child relationship, as shown in Figure 3.30.

As shown in the figure, there are four indentation levels. We start with level 0, with no indentation at all. Then each level is defined with a tab or four spaces (more on that later). Items on the same tab (or level) are considered siblings (or in the same block), while items in further tabs (or levels) are considered sub-blocks (or children) of current tabs.

```
     reset_sensor()

129  while True:
130      try:
131          # sensor control (open or close gate as per water level)
132          water_height = maximum_water_height - measure_distance()
133          if water_height > water_limit:
134              close_gate(motor_speed, motor_rate)
135          else:
136              open_gate(motor_speed, motor_rate)
137
138          # button control - open
139          if (GPIO.input(open_button)==0):
140              open_gate(motor_speed,motor_rate)
141              sleep(0.2)
142
143      except KeyboardInterrupt:
144          GPIO.cleanup()
145          exit()
146
     0   1   2   3    <---- Indentation Levels
```

FIGURE 3.30   The use of indentation to signify code blocks in Python.

For example, in line 129, we declare a *while loop*, and all lines after that (130 through 145) are indented. Therefore, all these lines are part of the while loop. Similarly, the contents of the *try* block are lines 131 through 142, and the contents of the *except* block are lines 144 and 145.

Since the try and except lines are on the same indentation levels, they are considered *siblings*, which is helpful to keep track of your program. Similarly, the *if*, *else*, and the second *if* statements are all siblings under the *Try* block. Finally, lines 134, 136, 140, and 141 are the contents of these conditionals.

With Indentation and the removal of semicolons and brackets, and the use of natural language (the human-like operators and commands), Python code becomes easy to read and even easier to maintain. That is one of the reasons behind its popularity.

However, the use of Indentation creates a problem unique to Python; the *Indentation error*, which arises from improperly applying indentation in Python. The following situations are few examples of how that could happen.

- Mixing spaces with tabs to make indentations (must use tabs only)
- Setting inappropriate IDE settings (tab settings)
- Using multiple IDEs with different indentation settings
- Copy-pasting code with mismatched indentation.
- Leaving extra lines with extra spaces

3.2.4.6   Python: We Are Done

At this point, we have covered all major areas of Python concepts. Of course, there is plenty to learn, and we encourage you to use online resources for more practice. But for this book, we covered enough material to begin working with IoT systems where Python is used, such as Raspberry Pi and Beaglebone systems.

3.3   THE LINUX OPERATING SYSTEM

When working with embedded systems, especially *Computer-boards* embedded systems, we will encounter a version of the Linux OS. For example, the Raspberry Pi uses *Raspbian*, while Beaglebone uses *Ubuntu*, two different versions of the Linux OS. This section reviews the Linux OS and essential concepts you will need to learn.

Linux (pronounced LEENUUKS) is a family of open-source OSs first released in 1991 by *Linus Torvalds*. Today, Linux systems and distributions are the largest installed general-purpose OSs in the world (*What Is Linux?*, 2021).

Two versions of Linux OS systems exist: *Linux Desktops* and *Linux Servers*. Linux Desktops are Operating Systems that also include graphical user interfaces (GUIs) for human users, while Linux Servers focus on Internet operations, i.e. serving data to the clients.

Although Linux Desktops cover only 2.3% of the world's personal computer market, they are widely used everywhere else. Through the Linux-based *Android*

FIGURE 3.31 The Linux OS and some of its distributions.

and *Chrome OS* systems, Linux systems are used today in mobile phones, netbooks, embedded systems, smart homes, smart TVs, IoT devices, routers, game consoles, wearables, smart cars, and much more.

As for Linux *Servers*, 96.4% of the world servers are Linux Servers, while 90% of Cloud infrastructure is powered by Linux, and 74% of all smartphones are Linux-based.

Linux Popularity comes from the fact that it is open source, entirely free, and is governed under the GNU General Public License. This means anyone with the right skills can copy, modify, and then *redistribute* Linux to others. As a result, there are many different versions, or *Distributions* of Linux Systems, sometimes simply referred to as *Distros,* as shown in Figure 3.31.

3.3.1 COMPONENTS OF A LINUX SYSTEM

Regardless of the distribution, every Linux system, be it a *Desktop* or a *Server*, must contain the components listed below (*Linux Kernel | Documentation*, 2021). One way to differentiate between distros is by comparing the features of their components. For example, *Ubuntu* might have a different graphical server compared to *Debian* or *Fedora*, and so on.

- **The Bootloader**: The software that manages the boot process (start) of the system.
- **The Kernel**: The core of the OS, it manages the CPU, memory, and peripherals.

- **The Init System**: A sub-system that *bootstraps the user space*, or allocates computer resources, to run the system and manage its *Daemons* (next).
- **Daemons**: Background services used by the system (printing, sound, scheduling, etc.).
- **The Graphical Server**: A sub-system that displays graphics on the monitor, often referred to as the *X server* or simply *X*.
- **The Desktop Environment**: For users to interact with, there are different environments to choose from. Each environment includes built-in applications, such as file managers, web browsers, configuration tools, and games.
- **The Applications**: Aside from the built-in applications, Linux offers thousands of third-party software for various uses and purposes. Most modern Linux distros include app store-like tools that centralize and simplify application testing and installation. For example, *Ubuntu* has the *Ubuntu Software Center*, shown in Figure 3.32.

As shown in the figure, one can view, review, and install any Linux App from the centre, just like any other App store currently available in mobile devices, which are also Linux based.

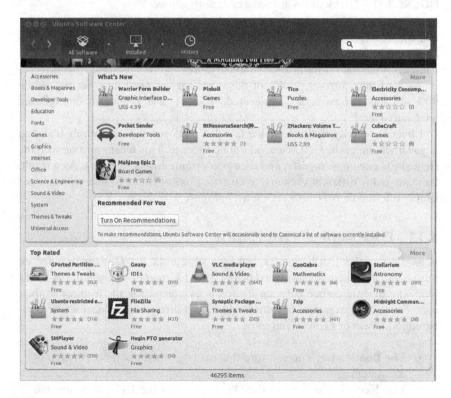

FIGURE 3.32   The Ubuntu software center. (*Ubuntu Software Center*, 2020.)

3.3.2   THE LINUX DISTRIBUTIONS (DISTROS)

Due to the open source and free nature of Linux, there are many different Distributions of Linux systems. Different *Distros* cater for different uses and user experience, as shown in Figure 3.33. Nearly every Linux distribution can be downloaded for free, burned onto disk or USB thumb drive, and installed on as many machines as you like. Popular Linux distributions include:

Linux *Desktop* Distributions
- Mint
- Manjaro
- Debian (the parent *Raspbian*, the Raspberry Pi OS)
- Ubuntu
- Antergos
- Fedora
- Zorin
- Elementary OS
- OpenSUSE

Linux *Server* Distributions
- Red Hat Enterprise Linux
- Ubuntu Server
- SUSE Enterprise Linux

Each distribution provides different features or focuses to Linux. Some distros opt for modern user interfaces, such as *Gnome* or Elementary OS's *Pantheon*, while

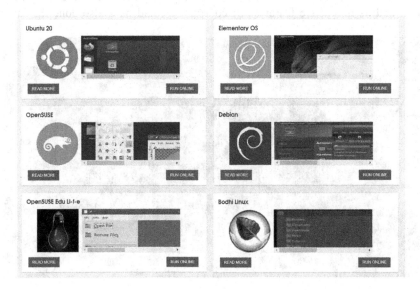

FIGURE 3.33   Online emulations of some Linux distributions.

others stick with the traditional environments. Some server distributions are free, such as *Ubuntu Server*, while others are priced, such as *Red Hat Enterprise Linux*, as they include user support.

3.3.3 THE LINUX COMMANDS (GENERAL, NETWORKING, APT-GET)

While some Linux distros offer a GUI-based user interface today, the use of *Command-Line* is still very extensive. For example, the command line is used in file/folder navigation, software management, maintenance, and environment setup (*Linux Command Line|Ubuntu*, 2021).

3.3.3.1 The Terminal

The first thing you would need is a *Terminal*, which is an application that provides a text-based interface for typing commands and reading the output of these commands, Figure 3.34.

We have already worked with the Terminal in our C++ and Python exercises, as shown in Figures 3.2 and 3.16. You could also run these programs directly from the Terminal. In fact, you can write and execute Python code directly in the Terminal; just type *Python* in the command prompt, which will start the *Python environment*. Figure 3.35 shows the same code from Figure 3.18, completely written and executed in the Terminal.

We could also use the Terminal to run pre-written Python programs; launch the Terminal, navigate where you saved your.py file (using file navigation commands), then run the program by typing *python filename.py*, and it will run just like it did with Geany.

This was the old way of writing and running programs before the days of the IDE and its interactive features. Of course, we could have also done the same

FIGURE 3.34 The *Terminal* in Ubuntu.

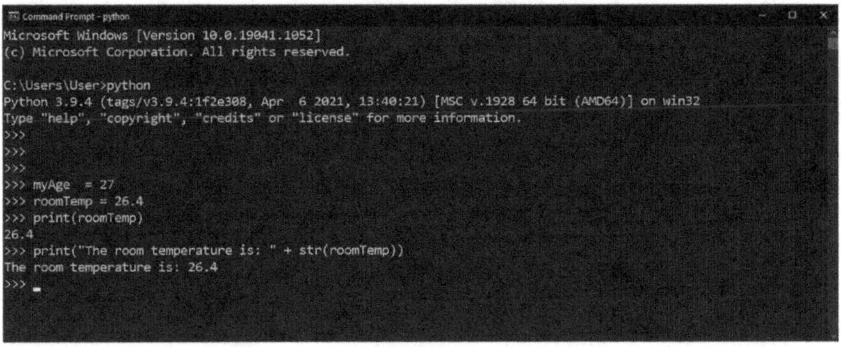

```
Command Prompt - python                                                    –  □  X
Microsoft Windows [Version 10.0.19041.1052]
(c) Microsoft Corporation. All rights reserved.

C:\Users\User>python
Python 3.9.4 (tags/v3.9.4:1f2e308, Apr  6 2021, 13:40:21) [MSC v.1928 64 bit (AMD64)] on win32
Type "help", "copyright", "credits" or "license" for more information.
>>>
>>>
>>>
>>> myAge  = 27
>>> roomTemp = 26.4
>>> print(roomTemp)
26.4
>>> print("The room temperature is: " + str(roomTemp))
The room temperature is: 26.4
>>>
```

FIGURE 3.35 The Python environment in the terminal.

thing in C++, but it would need more work as we would need to execute commands for *Compile*, *Build*, and *Execute*.

3.3.3.2 Linux Commands

Table 3.14 lists out several Linux commands that you will need to be familiar with. These commands are designed to prepare you for our work in Chapter 5 (Raspberry Pi IoT).

You can practice these commands if you have an available Linux system, or you can get one available. If not, then we recommend you use an online Linux *emulator*. These are web-based applications that simulate Linux and are perfect for learners and beginners. Just search for *Linux OS online*, and you will find plenty online, as also shown in Figure 3.33.

While you are at it, you might also search for *Linux commands beginners*, where you will find plenty of online sources and references about Linux commands and how to use them. We recommend you practice as many commands and distros as you can.

3.3.3.3 The apt-get Commands

The *Advanced Package Tool* (APT) is a library used for software management in several Linux distributions, such as *Ubuntu*, *Debian*, and related distros, such as *Raspbian*. It includes three main programs, *apt*, *apt-get*, and *apt-cache*. We will work mainly with *apt-get* to add, remove, and manage software on the Raspberry Pi or the Beaglebone boards.

The APT library also manages relations and dependencies of software packages. So, for example, if you install package X, APT would identify and install all its *dependencies*; all other packages it *depends* on, all behind the scenes and with minimal user interference.

Furthermore, the APT library keeps track of all the installed software packages and their *relationship tree*, the dependency relationship map of all installed packages. Table 3.15 lists out some of the major *apt-get* commands and their effects.

TABLE 3.14
Useful Linux Commands for Beginners (*Linux Command Line|Ubuntu*, 2021)

Command	Meaning	example	Effect (Result)
pwd	print working directory	pwd	Displays current working folder
cd	Change directory	cd	Changes to target directory (parent, child, home)
whoami	Who am I?	whoami	Displays current user information
mkdir	Make directory	mkdir (name)	Makes a new directory with the provided name
ls	List	ls	Lists out contents of current folder
mv	Move (file)	mv (file) (location)	Moves file to defined location
cp	Copy (file)	cp (file) (location)	Copies file to defined location
man	Manual	man (command)	Provides information about selected command
sudo	Superuser Do (pronounced *soodoo*)	sudo (command)	Performs command as superuser (admin rights)

TABLE 3.15
Apt-get Commands for Software Management (*AptGet/Howto|Ubuntu*, 2021)

Command	Example	Effect (Result)
install	sudo apt-get *install* package1 package2	Installs a package onto the system. Can install multiple packages
remove	sudo apt-get *remove* package1 package2	Removes a package from the system. Can remove multiple packages
autoremove	sudo apt-get *autoremove*	Removes packages auto-installed from other packages but no longer needed
update	sudo apt-get *update*	Updates dependency lists (refresh list)
upgrade	sudo apt-get *upgrade*	Upgrades all installed packages
check	sudo apt-get *check*	Checks for broken dependencies
autoclean	apt-get *autoclean*	Removes .deb files from packages no longer installed on system, saves significant disk space
clean	apt-get *clean*	Removes ALL packages from cache. Would require reinstalling ALL packages

Unfortunately, things could go wrong. For example, if you add/remove packages carelessly to your Linux system, you break dependencies and cause problems. Therefore, we recommend the following best practices in managing your Linux system:

• **Update *Before & After***: Make sure to *update* your system before and after you make any changes. For example, before and after you install or remove a package.

- **Upgrade Regularly**: Change is the only constant, especially in the world of open-source systems. Possibly the package you installed last month was updated today, or perhaps new dependencies were added to it or removed from it.
- **Only Reliable Sources**: Another feature of the open-source world; you need to be careful of the sources. Take some time to check and verify the source of the package you need before installing it and seek alternatives if you are unsure.
- **Read Error Codes and Act Accordingly**: Sometimes, apt-get commands (update, upgrade, and check) could report problems in your systems that require action. Luckily, the APT library provides us with the means to resolve these problems, as discussed below.

3.3.4 REFERENCE: SYSTEM MANAGEMENT COMMANDS

System management commands allow you to manage your Linux system and all installed software packages. Be it related to the APT library or general system diagnostics.

Table 3.16 lists out some of the possible issues and action you can take to remedy these situations. But, again, if you follow the guidelines discussed above,

---

TABLE 3.16 PART 1

Reference: Possible apt-get and General Issues and How to Handle Them

Apt-get error code	*The following packages have been kept back, package1, package2, package3*
Cause	A mismatch occurred between packages and their dependencies
Solution	Reinstall these packages (to upgrade their dependencies)
Action	Copy the name of the packages from the error message, then install them using:
	Apt-get install pacakge1 package2 package3
apt-get error code	*Failed to fetch {some package} Hash Sum mismatch*
Cause	You have an error in your package list
Solution	You need to reset your package list
Action	Run clean then update
	sudo apt-get clean
	sudo apt-get update
apt-get error code	**The following signatures couldn't be verified because the public key is not available NO_PUBKEY** *87C9C49AE9B24D7F*
Cause	Some repositories require a Key to access their software
Solution	You need to add the Key to your system
Action	Copy the Key given in the error message, paste it in the two commands below
	gpg --keyserver hkp://keyserver.ubuntu.com:80 --recv PasteKeyHere
	gpg --export --armor PasteKeyHere | sudo apt-key add -
	Then update
	sudo apt-get update

TABLE 3.16 PART 2

Reference: Possible apt-get and General Issues and How to Handle Them

apt-get error code	*The following packages were automatically installed and are no longer required*
Cause	You installed an older version of a package, then updated it
	Its dependencies changed, and some of the older dependencies are no required
Solution	You need to autoremove these older packages
Action	**sudo apt-get autoremove**
General error code	**(Ubuntu only)** *Failed to fetch {some package} error 404 package not found ,or error 403 Forbidden*
Cause	The repo (Repository) in question or its mirror site is down
Solution	You can either try again at a different time or try another server
Action	**System => software & Updates => download from: => other ... => Select best server => choose server = reset**
General error code	**(Ubuntu only)** *recurring "System error detected" pop-ups*
Cause	An old error flag that has already been corrected but not fully cleared for the system
Solution	Error logging needs to be refreshed
Action	**sudo rm/var/crash/***

your system should run smoothly, and you would not encounter any of the issues listed in the table.

Therefore, you need not memorize or note down any of the items in the table. Instead, consider Table 3.16 as *just in case* reference that you will use if you encounter any of the issues listed in the table, issues you can avoid if you follow the guidelines above.

With this, we can say we covered all essential issues related to the Linux OS. We will revisit Linux in Chapter 5 when we work with the Raspberry Pi system.

REFERENCES

Adding Python to PATH. (2019). Geek University. https://geek-university.com/python/add-python-to-the-windows-path/

AptGet/Howto|Ubuntu. (2021). Ubuntu Community. https://help.ubuntu.com/community/AptGet/Howto

C++ Documentation. (2021). Cplusplus. https://www.cplusplus.com/doc/tutorial/

Linux Command Line|Ubuntu. (2021). *Ubuntu.* https://ubuntu.com/tutorials/command-line-for-beginners#1-overview

Linux Kernel|Documentation. (2021). *Linux.* https://www.kernel.org/doc/html/v4.12/index.html

Python 3.9.5 Documentation. (2021). *Python.* https://docs.python.org/3/reference/index.html#reference-index

Ubuntu Software Center. (2020). *Wikipedia.* https://en.wikipedia.org/wiki/Ubuntu_Software_Center#/media/File:Ubuntu_Software_Center_13.10.png

What Is Linux? (2021). *Linux.* https://www.linux.com/what-is-linux/

4 Arduino-Based IoT Systems

4.1 THE ARDUINO BOARDS

As discussed in Chapter 2, the Arduino is a *Controller Board*; it consists of a microcontroller and additional components to facilitate operations. Consequently, there are various types of Arduino boards, depending on setup and desired functionality. The most common and widely used Arduino boards are *Arduino Uno*, *Arduino Nano*, and *Arduino Mega*. Other less common boards, such as the *Arduino Leonardo*, the Wi-Fi-equipped *Arduino Yun*, and the waterproof *LilyPad Arduino*, are typically used for highly specialized applications.

Furthermore, many Arduino-compatible boards have been developed for various uses with additional features for improved functionalities, such as the *NodeMCU*, *ESP32*, and the *WeMos D1* development boards. For the purposes of this book, we will refer to these boards as the *Arduino boards, Controller Boards, Controller-on-Chip* systems, or *Single-Board Controllers*. We will use these terms interchangeably, depending on the context.

4.1.1 THE ARDUINO UNO

The Arduino Uno is the most widely used and documented board of the whole Arduino family. Moreover, it is the best option for beginners to get started in tinkering with electronics and coding, as it is relatively cheap, easy to set up, and highly robust. Arduino Uno is a development board based on the Atmel ATmega328P microcontroller with a clock speed of 16 MHz, flash memory of 32 kb, and static random-access memory (SRAM) of 2 kb (Figure 4.1).

The ATmega328P microcontroller on the board comes pre-programmed with a bootloader that allows for uploading new code without an external hardware programmer. In addition, an ATmega16U2 microcontroller is programmed as a USB-to-serial converter (Aqeel, 2018).

The board consists of 14 digital input/output (IO) pins, of which six, namely pins 3, 5, 6, 9, 10, and 11, can be used as pulse-width modulation (PWM) outputs. PWM provides voltage control, which can control the brightness of LEDs and the speed of motors by varying the voltage. These digital pins operate at 5 V, can provide or receive 20 mA each, and have an internal pull-up resistor of 20–50 kΩ. Next, six analogue pins allow the board to read inputs from analogue sensors. These pins provide 10 bits of resolution, or 1,024 different values and measure up to 5 V. The Arduino Uno has convenient power management and built-in voltage regulation functionality (Aqeel, 2018).

DOI: 10.1201/9781003218395-6

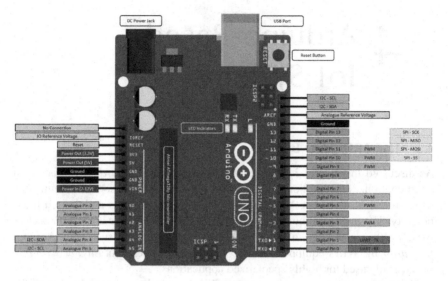

FIGURE 4.1   An Arduino Uno Rev. 3 development board.

With an operating voltage of 5 V, it can be powered directly through the USB-B port, an external power supply, in the form of a 7–12 V DC power source at the DC power jack, or by connecting a battery lead to the VIN and GND pins. The 5 V and 3V3 pins provide a regulated 5 and 3.3 V supply, respectively, from the onboard regulator, with a maximum current draw of 50 mA for powering external modules, sensors, and actuators (Aqeel, 2018).

In terms of communication protocols, the Arduino Uno can communicate via Universal Asynchronous Receiver/Transmitter (UART) serial protocol using digital pin 0 as the data receiver (RX) and digital pin 1 as the data transmitter (TX) (Aqeel, 2018).

The board also supports Serial Peripheral Interface (SPI) protocol; pin 11 as the *Master Out Slave In* (MOSI) line for sending data from the master to the peripherals, pin 12 as the *Master In Slave Out* (MISO) line for sending data from the slave to the master, pin 13 as the *Serial Clock* (SCK) pin for synchronizing data transmission (generated by the master), and pin 10 as the *Slave Select* (SS) pin which the master uses to enable and disable specific devices. Lastly, the board supports Inter-integrated Circuit (I2C) protocol with pin A4 as the data signal (SDA) and pin A5 as the clock signal (SCL).

Other elements added to the board include a RESET button for resetting the microcontroller, an LED mapped to pin 13 for debugging and testing purpose, an LED to indicate power, and two LEDs for RX and TX which blink when serial communication takes place. The dimensions of the board are 68.6 mm in length and 53.4 mm in width. The weight of the board is 25 g (Aqeel, 2018).

4.1.2 THE ARDUINO NANO

The Arduino Nano is a small board based on the Atmel ATmega328p microcontroller with a clock speed of 16 MHz, flash memory of 32 kb, and SRAM of 2 kb, as such, very similar to the Arduino Uno but packaged differently. With a length of 45 mm, width of 18 mm, and weight of 7 g, the Arduino Nano is less than half the size of the Arduino Uno, making it ideal for applications with limited or constrained space requirements (*Arduino Nano*, 2018) (Figure 4.2).

Another difference is the addition of two extra analogue pins, bringing the total to eight, while the digital pin count remains at 14. Similarly, pins 3, 5, 6, 9, 10, and 11 can be used as PWM outputs. The 5 V operating voltage and 7–12 V input voltage of the board are similar to the Arduino Uno. One limitation of the Arduino Nano is that it lacks a DC power jack and must be powered via the mini-USB port or VIN and GND pins exclusively (*Arduino Nano*, 2018).

In terms of communication protocols, the Arduino Nano matches the Arduino Uno once again. It supports UART, SPI, and I2C communication protocols, with pins 0 and 1 as RX and TX, pins 10, 11, 12, and 13 as SS, MOSI, MISO, and SCK lines, as well as pin A4 and A5 as SDA and SCL signals, respectively. In addition, the built-in LED is connected to pin 13.

4.1.3 THE ARDUINO MEGA

The Arduino Mega 2560 is a development board based on the Atmel ATmega2560 microcontroller. Resultingly, there is a considerable difference between the

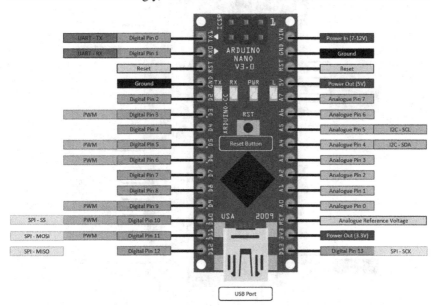

FIGURE 4.2 An Arduino Nano development board.

Arduino Uno and Nano and the Arduino Mega as the microcontroller itself is different. Like the Arduino Uno and Nano, the Arduino Mega has a clock speed of 16 MHz but with an increase in flash memory capacity of 256 kb and SRAM of 8 kb (*Arduino Mega*, 2017) (Figure 4.3).

The Arduino Mega is more powerful than the Arduino Uno and Nano in terms of speed and number of IO pins. It has 54 GPIO pins; of which 15 pins, namely pins 2 to 13 and pins 44 to 46, can be used as PWM outputs, and 16 analogue pins. With a length of 101.6 mm and width of 53.34 mm, the Arduino Mega is even larger than the Arduino Uno.

The 5 V operating voltage and 7–12 V input voltage of the board are similar to the Arduino Uno and Nano (*Arduino Mega*, 2017).

Arduino Mega boards are typically used for projects which require many IO pins and different communication protocols, such as 3D printing and computer numerical control (CNC) robotics.

Four UART serial ports are available, with pins 0, 19, 17, and 15 as RX and pins 1, 18, 16, and 14 as TX. As for SPI protocol, pins 50, 51, 52, and 53 function as the MISO, MOSI, SCK, and SS lines. Lastly, for I2C protocol, pins 20 and 21

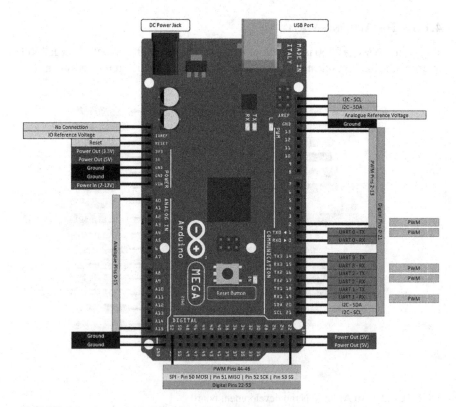

FIGURE 4.3   An Arduino Mega Rev. 3 development board.

represent the SDA and SCL signals, respectively. The built-in LED is connected to pin 13 (*Arduino Mega*, 2017).

4.1.4 THE NODEMCU

The NodeMCU is a small, low-cost, open-source Arduino-based development board specially targeted for IoT applications. It features an integrated ESP8266 microcontroller equipped with a 32-bit microprocessor, operating at 80 MHz clock frequency, along with 4 Mb of flash memory and 64 kb of SRAM (Figure 4.4).

The most significant difference between the NodeMCU and the Arduino boards is the inclusion of a built-in 2.4 GHz, 801.11 b/g/n standard compatible Wi-Fi module for seamless wireless network connectivity. The much higher processing power than the Arduino boards, coupled with the wireless network connectivity and deep-sleep operating features, makes the NodeMCU ideal for IoT projects (*ESP8266*, 2015).

With an operating voltage of 3.3 V, the NodeMCU can be powered directly through the micro-USB port, or via the VIN and GND pins, with an input voltage of 5–10 V. The NodeMCU board has three 3.3 V power output pins, labelled 3V3, along with three corresponding ground pins, labelled GND. The 3.3 V pins are the output of an onboard voltage regulator and can supply up to 600 mA of power to external components (*ESP8266*, 2015).

As such, only peripherals with a power rating of 3.3 V can be connected to the NodeMCU board, while 5 V rated components would not be compatible. In addition, the board has 16 digital IO pins, of which four pins, namely pins D2, D5, D6, and D8, can be used as PWM outputs, along with a single analogue pin, A0, which can be used to measure analogue voltage in the range of 0–3.3 V.

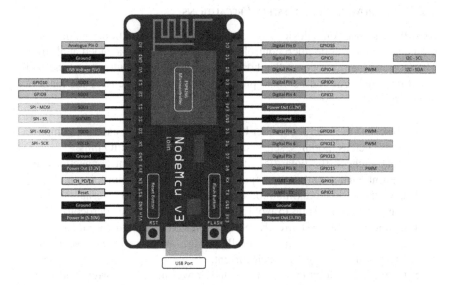

FIGURE 4.4 A NodeMCU development board.

Lastly, the NodeMCU supports communication protocols including UART, SPI, and single-bus I2C channel on pins D1 and D2, representing the SCL and SDA signals, respectively. The board includes a CH340G USB-to-UART controller, which converts USB signals to serial protocol and allows the host computer to communicate with the ESP8266 microcontroller. Additionally, the NodeMCU features two buttons, one labelled RST, to reset the ESP8266 microcontroller and another labelled FLASH, for downloading and upgrading firmware. The built-in LED is connected to pin D0 (*ESP8266*, 2015).

4.2 ARDUINO PERIPHERALS

For the Arduino boards, the additional onboard components are designed or added only to facilitate the operations of the onboard microcontroller. That includes input/output operations, power management, and special data management. However, these onboard components are not enough to run complex systems that may involve different types of input data, different types of output commands, and more; this is where and why we need *Peripherals*.

4.2.1 ARDUINO COMPATIBLE ADD-ONS

As discussed in Chapter 2, a wide variety of Peripherals can be combined with embedded systems to enhance operations. All Arduino boards discussed in this chapter are compatible with all the Peripherals listed in Section 2.4. We will use some of these peripherals in the hands-on projects and exercises in this chapter.

4.2.2 HARDWARE SETUP: SAFETY PRECAUTIONS

As with most electronic devices and components, specific actions can damage or even destroy the fragile microcontroller boards and must be avoided at all times. Therefore, these microcontroller boards must be handled with care, and additional tips are suggested below to prevent malfunction and ensure the longevity of the boards.

1. Power off the microcontroller board before connecting external components such as modules, sensors, and actuators to the GPIO pins.
2. Double-check the polarities of all external component connections to prevent wiring up the wrong pins, which can cause a short circuit.
3. Do not exceed a maximum of 40 mA power draw from external components on the GPIO pins to avoid permanent damage to the microcontroller.
4. Connecting an LED directly to output pins on the board without a resistor can damage the microcontroller board; as the resistor prevents the LED from drawing too much current.
5. Connecting output pins to the ground draws enormous current and kills the microcontroller board almost instantly.

6. Supplying more than the rated input voltage to the power input pin can burn out the microcontroller board.
7. Supplying more than the rated operating voltage to external components such as modules and sensors can also damage these devices.
8. Placing the microcontroller board on a conductive surface will short out the GPIO pins.

4.3 THE ARDUINO INTEGRATED DEVELOPMENT ENVIRONMENT (ARDUINO IDE)

The Arduino Integrated Development Environment (IDE) is an application used to write, compile, and upload controller programs to Arduino-compatible controller boards. It is free, open source, and cross-platform; it can run on Windows, macOS, and Linux OS (Aqeel, 2018).

The IDE consists of two parts: an editor used for preparing the necessary code and a compiler for compiling and uploading the program into the microcontroller. The code, called a sketch, is written in Arduino programming language using a combination of simplified C/C++ programming language. It follows the same basic rules and conventions of C/C++ but with some Arduino-specific functions and structure (Aqeel, 2018).

4.3.1 INSTALLATION & SETUP

In this section, we outline installation steps for Windows systems. Instructions for other OS are available online.

4.3.1.1 Arduino IDE Installation for Windows 10

1. Go to the Microsoft Store and search for Arduino IDE.
2. Click on Install/Get, and the program will be installed on the computer.
3. Once the installation is complete, the program will be launched automatically.
4. Basic Arduino board drivers are automatically installed when connected to a computer.

4.3.1.2 Arduino IDE Installation for Windows 8 and Below

1. Download the Arduino IDE Installer from the official Arduino site. https://www.arduino.cc/en/Main/Software.
2. Once the download is complete, proceed with the installation.
3. Choose all components to install to the default installation directory.
4. The process will extract and install the required files and components.
5. Once the installation is complete, the program will launch automatically.
6. Basic Arduino board drivers are automatically installed when connected to a computer.

4.3.2 ARDUINO IDE BASICS

The Arduino IDE has a minimalist design with only five headings on the menu bar, namely File, Edit, Sketch, Tools, and Help, which are context-sensitive, meaning only items relevant to the current work are available. In addition, a series of buttons in the toolbar underneath the menu bar provides various functionalities for writing, compiling, and uploading sketches to the boards. The functionality of these buttons is explained further, starting from left to right (Figure 4.5).

1. **Verify**: Checks the code for errors before compiling.
2. **Upload**: Compiles the code and uploads to board.
3. **New**: Creates a new sketch.
4. **Open**: Opens a previously saved sketch.
5. **Save**: Saves the current sketch.
6. **Serial Monitor**: Opens the serial monitor.

4.3.3 ARDUINO PROGRAMMING

Arduino programs can be divided into three main parts: structure, values, and functions. The IDE also includes a syntax highlighting feature, making it easier for beginners.

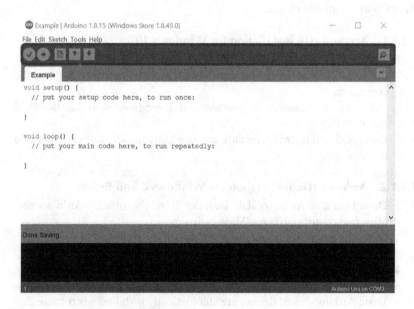

FIGURE 4.5 Arduino IDE interface and buttons.

4.3.3.1 The Structure of an Arduino Program

The basic Arduino language consists of two main structures, **setup()** and **loop()**. The *setup* function is used to initialize variables and pin modes. This function runs *once* when the microcontroller board is powered on or reset. The *loop* function is used to run the main logic of the code *repeatedly* and *continuously* (*Arduino References*, 2020).

When the whole program in the loop function has been completed, it goes back to the start of the loop and repeats the process. The loop function is used to control the microcontroller board actively. Control structures such as if, for, and while statements follow the usual C/C++ language conventions as detailed in Chapter 3. This is also the case for arithmetic, comparison, Boolean, and operators (*Arduino References*, 2020).

4.3.3.2 Variables

Arduino code mainly consists of two types of variables, namely *constants* and *data types*. Constants are pre-defined expressions in the Arduino language. They are used to make the programs easier to read and can be classified into groups. The first group is Boolean constants for defining logical levels. For example, a *true* value represents a non-zero value, though often defined as one, while a *false* value is set with a zero. The *true* and *false* constants are typed in lowercase, unlike HIGH, LOW, INPUT, and OUTPUT constants.

The second group, including HIGH and LOW values, is used for defining pin levels. When reading or writing to a digital pin, only these two possible values can be defined.

Lastly, the third group is used for defining digital pin modes, such as INPUT, INPUT_PULLUP, and OUTPUT. Meanwhile, data types such as *int*, *double*, *float*, and *Boolean* follow the usual C/C++ language conventions detailed in Chapter 3. In addition, the *void* keyword is used only in function declarations. It indicates that the function is expected to return no information to the function from which it was called (*Arduino References*, 2020).

4.3.3.3 The Arduino Functions

Arduino functions provide the main functionality of interacting with the Arduino board and any connected hardware components. Therefore, the Arduino functions can be divided based on the types of hardware we discussed earlier, namely *digital IO* (Input Output) functions, *analogue IO* functions, *time* functions, and *communication* functions.

There are three standard *digital IO* functions in basic Arduino systems. The **pinMode()** function configures the specified digital pin to behave either as an input or an output. Changing a pin with **pinMode()** changes the electrical behaviour of the pin. For example, digital pins configured as INPUT are said to be in a high-impedance state.

This makes them helpful in reading data from modules and sensors. Meanwhile, pins configured as OUTPUT are said to be in a low-impedance state. This means they can provide a substantial current to other components, up to 40 mA in the case of Arduino boards.

Next, the **digitalWrite()** function is used to set a HIGH or a LOW value to a digital pin. For example, if the pin was configured as an OUTPUT with **pin-Mode()**, its voltage would be set to the corresponding value, 5 or 3.3 V, based on board type. Thus, it can be used to power external components such as LEDs. On the other hand, if the pin was configured as an INPUT, **digitalWrite()** will enable (HIGH value) or disable (LOW value) the internal pull-up on the input pin (*Arduino References*, 2020).

The **digitalRead()** function reads the value from a specified digital pin, either HIGH or LOW. For example, when a pin is configured as an INPUT and used to read data with **digitalRead()**, the microcontroller will report HIGH if a voltage greater than 3 or 2 V is present at the pin 5 and 3.3 V boards. Correspondingly, the board will report LOW if a voltage of less than 1.5 or 1 V is present at the pin, for 5 and 3.3 V boards.

Next, for *analogue IO*, the **analogRead()** function reads the value from the specified analogue pin. Arduino boards contain a multichannel, 10-bit analogue to digital converter (ADC). This means that it will map input voltages between 0 V and the operating voltage, 5 or 3.3 V depending on the board type, into integer values between 0 and 1,023. For instance, on an Arduino Uno board with a 5 V operating voltage, this yields a resolution between readings of 5 V divided by 1,024 units, or 0.0049 V (4.9 mV) per unit.

The input range can be changed using **analogReference()**. On ATmega microcontroller-based Arduino boards such as the Uno, Nano, and Mega, it takes about 100 ms (0.0001 second) to read an analogue input, so the maximum reading rate is about 10,000 times a second (*Arduino References*, 2020).

Besides, the **analogWrite()** function writes an analogue value to a pin via PWM. With a duty cycle between 0 (always off) and 255 (always on), the PWM wave can be used to light up an LED at varying brightnesses or drive a motor at various speeds. After a call to **analogWrite()**, the pin will generate a steady rectangular wave of the specified duty cycle.

For the *Time* functions, the **delay()** function pauses the program for the specified amount of time in milliseconds. However, the use of **delay()** in a sketch has significant drawbacks, as no other reading of sensors, mathematical calculations, or pin manipulation can go on during the function. Next, the **millis()** function returns the number of milliseconds passed since the Arduino board began running the current program. This number will return to zero after approximately 50 days.

Lastly, the *Serial* function is used for communication between the Arduino board and a computer or other devices. All Arduino boards have at least one serial port, also known as a UART. The Arduino IDE serial monitor can be used to communicate with the board. For example, the **Serial.begin()** function sets the data rate in bits per second (baud) for serial data transmission. The **Serial.print()** function prints data to the serial port as human-readable text. It shows what is going on inside the Arduino board from the computer.

Numbers and floats are printed using an ASCII character for each digit. Bytes are sent as a single character. Characters and strings are sent as is, e.g. **Serial. print(78)** outputs 78, **Serial.print('N')** outputs N, and **Serial.print("Hello World")** outputs Hello World.

For floating-point numbers, an optional second parameter specifies the number of decimal places to use. For example, **Serial.print(1.23456, 0)** outputs 1, **Serial.print(1.23456, 2)** outputs 1.23, and so on. The **Serial.read()** function reads incoming serial data.

4.3.3.4   Uploading Arduino Sketches (Programs) to the Arduino Boards

Once the sketch has been prepared on the IDE, it can be easily uploaded to the microcontroller board via a USB connection. Before uploading a sketch, the correct microcontroller board must be selected from the Tools menu based on the current setup. Next, from the available options, select the correct serial port board connection (Figure 4.6).

Finally, click the upload button in the toolbar to compile and upload the sketch to the board. If there are any errors in the sketch, a warning message will appear, prompting the user to make the appropriate changes. Most new users often experience difficulty with compiling due to Arduino's stringent syntax requirements. If there are any mistakes in the syntax and punctuation, the code will not compile.

Once the sketch is successfully compiled, it is then uploaded to the board. The Arduino IDE uploads the script to the microcontroller via UART communication. UART supports bi-directional, asynchronous and serial data transmission.

It has two data lines, one to *transmit* (TX) and another to *receive* (RX). Once connected, data flows from TX to RX of the receiving UART. As UART is an asynchronous serial transmission, it has no clocks. Thus, UART adds start and stop bits that are being transferred. This helps the receiving UART know when to start reading bits as the bits represent the start and the end of the data packet.

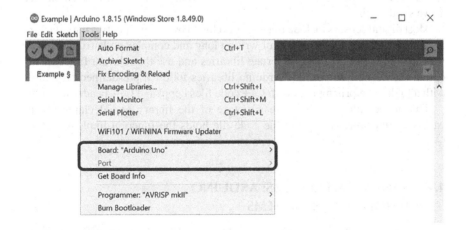

FIGURE 4.6   Selecting the board type and port in Arduino IDE.

When the receiving UART detects a start bit, it will read the bits at baud rate. Baud rate refers to the UART data transmission speed and is set to 9,600 by default. Baud rate is based on symbol transmission rate but is similar to bit rate. The RX and TX LEDs on the microcontroller board blink as the sketch is uploaded. Arduino IDE will display a message when the upload is complete.

The serial monitor is added to the Arduino IDE to transmit textual data to and from the microcontroller board. The serial monitor can be opened by clicking the corresponding button in the toolbar. The serial monitor is used mainly for interacting with the microcontroller board using the computer and is an excellent tool for real-time monitoring and debugging.

For example, the microcontroller transmits sensor data back to the host computer via UART communication to be displayed via the serial monitor. The baud rate on the serial monitor must be set to the corresponding value specified in the sketch using the **Serial.begin**() function.

4.3.3.5   The Arduino Libraries and Third-Party Resources

Thanks to the versatility and popularity of the Arduino ecosystem, the large and ever-growing Arduino community has developed a significant number of third-party software resources over the years. From sample code to Arduino libraries, these open-source resources are beneficial, not only for beginners but also for advanced users.

Arduino *libraries* are a collection of programs that take a complex task and boil it down to simple-to-use functions. These libraries are roughly divided into libraries that interact with a specific component or implement new functions to expand the Arduino board capabilities.

Some libraries are included in the Arduino IDE by default, while other libraries for third-party components such as modules, sensors, and actuators can be installed from external sources. Libraries can be downloaded through the Arduino IDE *Library Manager* or by installing libraries from *Zip files* downloaded online, as we shall see later.

Most digital sensors include libraries developed by their respective manufacturers for ease of use. Thus, instead of writing long and complex code from scratch, we can simply import the appropriate libraries and use the relevant functions to obtain the desired output. All Arduino libraries follow a pre-defined structure, with a folder comprising files with C++ code files (.cpp) and C++ header files (.h).

The header file describes the structure of the library and declares all its variables and functions, while the code file holds the function implementation (*Arduino Libraries*, 2020).

4.4   HANDS-ON PROJECTS: ARDUINO AUTONOMOUS SYSTEMS

This section will help beginners understand and familiarize themselves with electronic circuit assembly and programming. You will learn how to interact with basic components, including LEDs, pushbuttons, sensors, and actuators.

TABLE 4.1

Components Required for the Hands-On Work

No	Components	Quantity
1	Arduino Uno Rev. 3	1
2	LoLin NodeMCU V3	1
3	ESP8266 Wi-Fi module	1
4	GL55 light intensity sensor	1
5	HC-SR04 ultrasonic distance sensor	1
6	DHT11 temperature and humidity sensor	1
7	Pushbutton module	1
8	Active piezoelectric buzzer	1
9	SG90 micro servo motor	1
10	Red LED	5
11	Blue LED	5
12	Resistor (1 kΩ)	5
13	Resistor (10 kΩ)	5
14	Solderless breadboard	1
15	Jumper cables (male to male)	1 set (40 pcs)
16	Jumper cables (male to female)	1 set (40 pcs)

We will use *Arduino Uno* for these projects, but any other Arduino board or Arduino-compatible board can also be used. To maximize the learning experience, we recommend you procure the components shown in Table 4.1. This would allow you *learn by doing.*

Alternatively, and as discussed in the *IoMT Training Kit* section, all items listed in the table, with software pre-installed and configured, are included in the IoMT Training Kit, which you can purchase separately through us. Refer to the *IoMT Training Kit* section for details.

4.4.1 PROJECT 4.1: THE BLINKING LED

This project will demonstrate to beginners how to interface essential components such as an LED with the microcontroller board to produce an output. The microcontroller and corresponding Arduino sketch will automatically switch the LED on and off at 1-second intervals, resulting in a blinking effect.

The speed at which the LED switches on and off can be altered by increasing or decreasing the time delay, leading to a faster or slower blinking effect. This project is considered one of the most straightforward examples and is typically used to test microcontroller boards to ensure functionality.

In this project, a resistor is connected to the cathode of the LED and the ground pin on the board. This pull-down resistor ensures that the LED is always in a LOW state, unless set to HIGH by the program. Thus, the LED is switched off when LOW and switched on when HIGH.

Equipment
1. Arduino Uno
2. Red LED
3. 1 kΩ resistor
4. Breadboard
5. Jumper cables

Connections
1. Positive of LED (long leg) connects to pin **13** on the Arduino board.
2. Negative of LED (short leg) connects to either one leg of the resistor.
3. Second leg of resistor connects to pin **GND** on the Arduino board (Figures 4.7 and 4.8).

Circuit

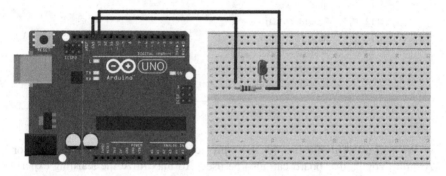

FIGURE 4.7 Circuit diagram connections for Project 4.1.

Sketch

```
void setup()
{
  pinMode(13, OUTPUT);          //set pin 13 as output
}

void loop()
{
  digitalWrite(13, HIGH);       //switch LED on
  delay(1000);                  //delay 1 second
  digitalWrite(13, LOW);        //switch LED off
  delay(1000);                  //delay 1 second
}
```

FIGURE 4.8 Arduino sketch for Project 4.1.

4.4.2 PROJECT 4.2: THE ALTERNATELY BLINKING LED

This next project will demonstrate on interfacing multiple components simultaneously, in this case, two LEDs, one red and one blue. Similar to the first project, the microcontroller and corresponding Arduino sketch will automatically switch the first LED on and off at 1-second intervals, followed by the second LED at alternate 1-second intervals. When the red LED is switched on, the blue LED will be switched off and vice versa.

Equipment
- Arduino Uno
- Red LED (LED 1)
- Blue LED (LED 2)
- 1 kΩ resistor ×2
- Breadboard
- Jumper cables

Connections
- Positive of LEDs (long leg) connects to pin **7** and pin **8** on the Arduino board.
- Negative of LEDs (short leg) connects to either one leg of the resistors.
- Second leg of resistors connects to pin **GND** on the Arduino board (Figures 4.9 and 4.10).

Circuit

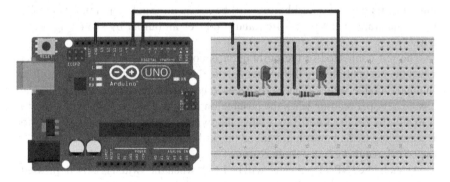

FIGURE 4.9 Circuit diagram connections for Project 4.2.

Sketch

```
void setup()
{
    pinMode(7, OUTPUT);          //set pin 7 as output
    pinMode(8, OUTPUT);          //set pin 8 as output
}

void loop()
{
    digitalWrite(7, HIGH);       //switch LED 1 on
    delay(1000);                 //delay 1 second
    digitalWrite(7, LOW);        //switch LED 1 off
    digitalWrite(8, HIGH);       //switch LED 2 on
    delay(1000);                 //delay 1 second
    digitalWrite(8, LOW);        //switch LED 2 off
}
```

FIGURE 4.10   Arduino sketch for Project 4.2.

4.4.3   PROJECT 4.3: BUTTON-CONTROLLED LED

This project demonstrates how to interface a pushbutton to switch on an LED. As such, beginners will learn how to configure components as inputs and outputs. In this case, the pushbutton will be set as an input. The microcontroller reads the state of the pushbutton and produces an output by switching on the LED.

The pin connected to the pushbutton is configured as an INPUT. However, when the pushbutton is in the open state, the INPUT pin will be floating, resulting in unpredictable values. Therefore, we must use a pull-up or pull-down resistor to ensure a proper reading when the pushbutton is open. The purpose of this resistor is to pull the pin to a known state when the switch is open. In this case, the resistor is connected to the power input pin on the pushbutton and the power output pin on the board, resulting in a pull-up resistor.

As such, the INPUT pin value will be LOW when the switch is closed (pressed) and HIGH when the switch is open (not pressed).

Equipment
- Arduino Uno
- Red LED
- Pushbutton
- 1 kΩ resistor ×2
- Breadboard
- Jumper cables

Connections

- Connect the **GND** leg of pushbutton to pin **GND** on the Arduino board.
- Connect the **OUT** leg of pushbutton to pin **7** on the Arduino board.
- Connect the **VCC** leg of pushbutton to either one leg of a resistor.
- Second leg of resistor connects to pin **5 V** on the Arduino board.
- Positive of LED (long leg) connects to pin **13** on the Arduino board.
- Negative of LED (short leg) connects to either one leg of a resistor.
- Second leg of resistor connects to pin **GND** on the Arduino board.
- Use common **5 V** and **GND** pins on the Arduino board (Figures 4.11 and 4.12).

Circuit

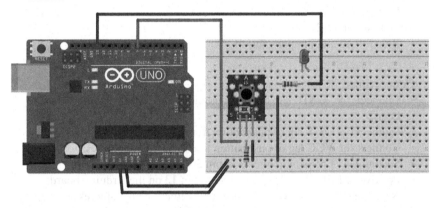

FIGURE 4.11   Circuit diagram connections for Project 4.3.

Sketch

```
int pushbutton = 7;                    //define variable pushbutton
int pinLED = 13;                       //define variable pinLED

void setup()
{
  pinMode(pushbutton, INPUT);          //set pushbutton as input
  digitalWrite(pushbutton, HIGH);      //input HIGH when open (pull-up resistor)
  pinMode(pinLED, OUTPUT);             //set pinLED as output
}

void loop()
{
  if(digitalRead(pushbutton) == LOW)   //input LOW when closed
  {
  digitalWrite(pinLED, HIGH);          //switch LED on
  }
  else
  {
  digitalWrite(pinLED, LOW);           //switch LED off
  }
}
```

FIGURE 4.12   Arduino sketch for Project 4.3.

4.4.4 PROJECT 4.4: BUTTON-CONTROLLED LED TOGGLE

Similar to the previous project, input from a pushbutton is used to toggle an LED on and off. However, instead of continuously holding the pushbutton to switch on the LED, for this project, simply pressing the pushbutton once (clicking on it) will switch on the LED. Likewise, pressing the pushbutton a second time would switch off the LED.

Equipment
- Arduino Uno
- Red LED
- Pushbutton
- 1 kΩ resistor ×2
- Breadboard and jumper cables

Connections
- Connect the **GND** leg of pushbutton to pin **GND** on the Arduino board.
- Connect the **OUT** leg of pushbutton to pin **7** on the Arduino board.
- Connect the **VCC** leg of pushbutton to either one leg of a resistor.
- Second leg of resistor connects to pin **5 V** on the Arduino board.
- Positive of LED (long leg) connects to pin **13** on the Arduino board.
- Negative of LED (short leg) connects to either one leg of a resistor.
- Second leg of resistor connects to pin **GND** on the Arduino board.
- Use common **5 V** and **GND** pins on the Arduino board (Figures 4.13 and 4.14).

Circuit

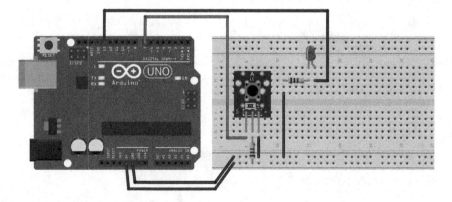

FIGURE 4.13   Circuit diagram connections for Project 4.4.

Sketch

```
int pushbutton = 7;                  //define variable pushbutton
int pinLED = 13;                     //define variable pinLED

void setup()
{
  pinMode(pushbutton, INPUT);        //set pushbutton as input
  digitalWrite(pushbutton, HIGH);    //input HIGH when open (pull-up resistor)
  pinMode(pinLED, OUTPUT);           //set pinLED as output
}

void loop()
{
  if(digitalRead(pushbutton) == LOW)  //input LOW when closed
  {
    digitalWrite(pinLED, !digitalRead(pinLED));
    delay(500);                      //time delay for click to take effect
  }
}
```

FIGURE 4.14   Arduino sketch for Project 4.4.

4.4.5   PROJECT 4.5: BUTTON-CONTROLLED LEDS

This project demonstrates a system with a single input and multiple outputs. Specifically, the input from one pushbutton will be used to control two LEDs at the same time. In this case, when the pushbutton is continuously pressed, the first LED is switched on while the second LED is switched off. Alternately, when the pushbutton is released, the first LED will be switched off, and the second LED will be switched on.

Equipment
- Arduino Uno
- Red LED (LED 1)
- Blue LED (LED 2)
- Pushbutton
- 1 kΩ resistor ×3
- Breadboard
- Jumper cables

Connections
- Connect the **GND** leg of pushbutton to pin **GND** on the Arduino board.
- Connect the **OUT** leg of pushbutton to pin **7** on the Arduino board.
- Connect the **VCC** leg of pushbutton to either one leg of a resistor.
- Connect the second leg of the resistor to pin **5 V** on the Arduino board.
- Positive of LED 1 (long leg) connects to pin **12** on the Arduino board.
- Negative of LED 1 (short leg) connects to either one leg of a resistor.
- Second leg of resistor connects to pin **GND** on the Arduino board.

- Positive of LED 2 (long leg) connects to pin **13** on the Arduino board.
- Negative of LED 2 (short leg) connects to either one leg of a resistor.
- Second leg of resistor connects to pin **GND** on the Arduino board.
- Use common **5 V** and **GND** pins on the Arduino board (Figures 4.15 and 4.16).

Circuit

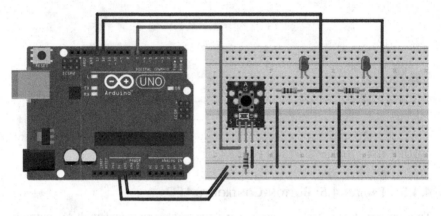

FIGURE 4.15   Circuit diagram connections for Project 4.5.

Sketch

```
int pushbutton = 7;                  //define variable pushbutton
int pinLED1 = 12;                    //define variable pinLED1
int pinLED2 = 13;                    //define variable pinLED2

void setup()
{
  pinMode(pushbutton, INPUT);        //set pushbutton as input
  digitalWrite(pushbutton, HIGH);    //input HIGH when open (pull-up resistor)
  pinMode(pinLED1, OUTPUT);          //set pinLED1 as output
  pinMode(pinLED2, OUTPUT);          //set pinLED2 as output
}

void loop()
{
  if(digitalRead(pushbutton) == LOW)  //input LOW when closed
  {
  digitalWrite(pinLED1, HIGH);        //switch LED 1 on
  digitalWrite(pinLED2, LOW);         //switch LED 2 off
  }
  else
  {
  digitalWrite(pinLED1, LOW);         //switch LED 1 off
  digitalWrite(pinLED2, HIGH);        //switch LED 2 on
  }
}
```

FIGURE 4.16   Arduino sketch for Project 4.5.

4.4.6 Exercise 4.1: Arduino LEDs and Pushbuttons

Exercises are unsolved projects that you would need to solve on your own, and by following along with the previous projects, you would develop the needed skills to do so. You now can configure microcontroller boards and interact with basic components, including pushbuttons and LEDs as inputs and outputs.

The use of pull-up and pull-down resistors and the corresponding digital states, HIGH and LOW, are better understood. As such, the exercise below is designed to test your understanding of developing electronic circuits by interfacing and connecting simple components with a microcontroller board and programming the board to receive an input and produce an output. For this exercise, you are to develop a system with the following requirements.

Hold the pushbutton to blink LED 1 while LED 2 is switched on. When the button is not held, LED 2 should blink while LED 1 is switched off. Using the components suggested below, develop the corresponding electronic circuit and sketch required for the proposed system.

Equipment
- Arduino Uno
- Red LED (LED 1)
- Blue LED (LED 2)
- Pushbutton
- 1 kΩ resistor ×3
- Breadboard
- Jumper cables

4.4.7 Project 4.6: The Light Intensity Sensor (Arduino)

This project demonstrates how to interface a light intensity sensor or photoresistor to a microcontroller board to measure light intensity in Lux, the SI unit for luminance.

Photoresistors have low resistance in bright light and high resistance in the dark. Since voltage is proportional to the resistance in an electric circuit, measuring this change in resistance and the corresponding change in voltage, the light intensity level is determined.

The photoresistor uses a voltage divider concept to measure light intensity level. The light intensity sensor used in this project is made up of a photoresistor mounted on a breakout board module with a built-in 10 kΩ resistor.

The photoresistor forms the upper part of the voltage divider, while the 10 kΩ resistor forms the lower part, as shown in Figure 4.17. Thus, the sensor has an analogue voltage range of 0–5 V when connected to the Arduino Uno.

By connecting the photoresistor to an analogue port on the microcontroller board and using the **analogRead()** function, we can obtain a reading between 0 and 1,023. We can also use the calculations shown below to convert analogue values into Lux (*Light Sensor*, 2016) (Figure 4.18).

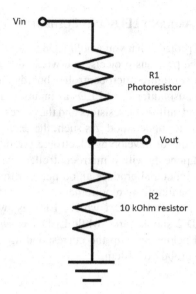

FIGURE 4.17   Voltage divider for measuring light intensity level.

Calculation

$Rldr = \frac{500}{Lux}$ ... Eq. 1

From voltage divider,

$Vout = \frac{Z2}{Z1 + Z2} * Vin$

$Vout = \frac{Rldr}{10\ kOhm + Rldr} * 5\ V$

$Rldr = \frac{10Vout}{5 - Vout}$

From Eq. 1,

$\frac{500}{Lux} = \frac{10Vout}{5 - Vout}$

$Lux = \frac{500\,(5 - Vout)}{10Vout}$

$Lux = \frac{50\,(5 - Vout)}{Vout}$

$Lux = \left(\frac{250}{Vout}\right) - 50$

Voltage per step unit,

$\frac{5V}{1024} = 0.0049\ V$

FIGURE 4.18   Light intensity level calculation.

Equipment
- Arduino Uno
- GL55 light intensity sensor
- Breadboard
- Jumper cables

Connections
- Connect the **VCC** leg of GL55 to pin **5 V** on the Arduino board.
- Connect the **A0** leg of GL55 to pin **A0** on the Arduino board.

- Connect the **GND** leg of GL55 to pin **GND** on the Arduino board (Figures 4.19 and 4.20).

Circuit

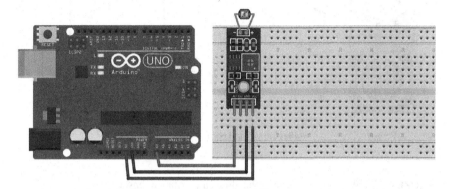

FIGURE 4.19 Circuit diagram connections for Project 4.6.

Sketch

```
double Light (int RawA0)                  //function to calculate luminance
{
  double Vout=RawA0*0.0049;
  int lux=(250/Vout)-50;
  return lux;
}

void setup()
{
  Serial.begin(9600);                     //display output in serial monitor
}

void loop()
{
  Serial.print("Light Intensity: ");      //display sensor values
  Serial.print(int(Light(analogRead(0))));
  Serial.println(" Lux");
  delay(1000);                            //refresh data every 1 second
}
```

FIGURE 4.20 Arduino sketch for Project 4.6.

4.4.8 PROJECT 4.7: THE ULTRASONIC DISTANCE SENSOR (ARDUINO)

This project demonstrates how to interface an ultrasonic sensor to a microcontroller board for measuring distance. The HC-SR04 ultrasonic sensor uses sonar to determine the distance to an object, as shown in Figure 4.21. The transmitter (trigger) sends a signal in the form of a high-frequency sound wave. When the sound wave hits an object, it is reflected towards the sensor.

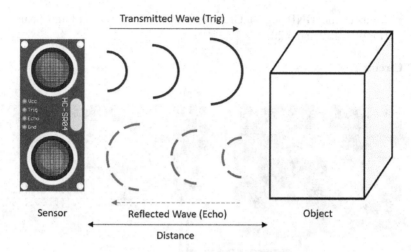

FIGURE 4.21 Working principle of the ultrasonic distance sensor.

The receiver (echo) receives this reflected sound wave. As such, the trigger pin is the output, while the echo pin is the input. The onboard IC measures the time interval between when the sound wave was transmitted and received (travel time), and since the speed of sound is a known constant, the distance between the object and sensor can be calculated (Figure 4.22).

Calculation

$$Distance = \frac{Travel\ Time}{2} * Speed\ of\ Sound$$

$$Speed\ of\ sound = 343\ m/s = 0.0343\ cm/uS$$

$$= 13503.9\ in/s = 0.0135\ in/uS$$

FIGURE 4.22 Distance measurement calculation.

Equipment
- Arduino Uno
- HC-SR04 ultrasonic distance sensor
- Breadboard and jumper cables

Connections
- Connect the **VCC** leg of HC-SR04 to pin **5 V** on the Arduino board.
- Connect the **TRIG** leg of HC-SR04 to pin **11** on the Arduino board.
- Connect the **ECHO** leg of HC-SR04 to pin **12** on the Arduino board.
- Connect the **GND** leg of HC-SR04 to pin **GND** on the Arduino board (Figures 4.23 and 4.24).

Circuit

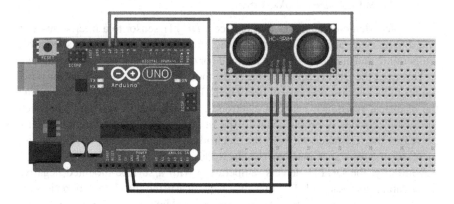

FIGURE 4.23 Circuit diagram connections for Project 4.7.

Sketch

```
int trigPin = 11;                    //define trigger pin
int echoPin = 12;                    //define echo pin
long duration, cm, inches;           //define variables

void setup()
{
  Serial.begin (9600);               //display output in serial monitor
  pinMode(trigPin, OUTPUT);          //set trigger pin as output
  pinMode(echoPin, INPUT);           //set echo pin as input
}

void loop()
{
  digitalWrite(trigPin, LOW);        //short low pulse to ensure clean high pulse
  delayMicroseconds(5);
  digitalWrite(trigPin, HIGH);       //short high pulse of 10 microseconds
  delayMicroseconds(10);
  digitalWrite(trigPin, LOW);

  pinMode(echoPin, INPUT);           //detect reflected high pulse at echo pin
  duration = pulseIn(echoPin, HIGH);
  cm = (duration/2) * 0.0343;        //convert travel time to distance
  inches = (duration/2) * 0.0135;

  Serial.print(inches);              //display distance values
  Serial.print("in, ");
  Serial.print(cm);
  Serial.print("cm");
  Serial.println();
  delay(2000);                       //refresh data every 2 seconds
}
```

FIGURE 4.24 Arduino sketch for Project 4.7.

4.4.9 PROJECT 4.8: THE DHT11 TEMPERATURE AND HUMIDITY SENSOR (ARDUINO)

This project demonstrates how to interface a DHT11 sensor to a microcontroller board to measure ambient temperature and humidity. Many Arduino-compatible temperature and humidity sensors, analogue or digital, are available on the market.

However, the DHT11 sensor is one of the most popular sensors for this purpose, thanks to its low cost and ease of use. The DHT11 detects humidity by measuring the electrical resistance between electrodes. The change in resistance between the two electrodes is proportional to the humidity. A higher relative humidity decreases the resistance between the electrodes, while a lower relative humidity increases the resistance between the electrodes.

Similarly, the DHT11 detects temperature with a surface-mounted negative temperature coefficient (NTC) thermistor by measuring the change in resistance due to a temperature change. An increase in ambient temperature results in a lower resistance. The built-in IC processes this information and converts the signals into a digital output.

Being a digital sensor, the DHT11 includes a library that significantly enhances ease of use as we can simply use the built-in functions to retrieve the required information. Therefore, the first step to using the DHT11 sensor library is importing and installing the relevant files.

Installing the DHT sensor library by Adafruit
- Select the Sketch tab.
- Select Include Library and choose Manage Libraries.
- Search for DHT in the Search Bar.
- Select DHT sensor library by Adafruit.
- Select the latest version and click *Install*.

Note: If downloading libraries from online sources, select Add. ZIP Library and select the downloaded Zip file. A message will be displayed at the bottom of the IDE stating that the library has been successfully installed. The library is now ready for use (Figure 4.25).

Equipment
- Arduino Uno
- DHT11 temperature and humidity sensor
- Breadboard
- Jumper cables

Connections
- Connect the + leg of DHT11 to pin **3.3 V** on the Arduino board.
- Connect the **OUT** leg of DHT11 to pin **4** on the Arduino board.
- Connect the − leg of DHT11 to pin **GND** on the Arduino board (Figures 4.26 and 4.27).

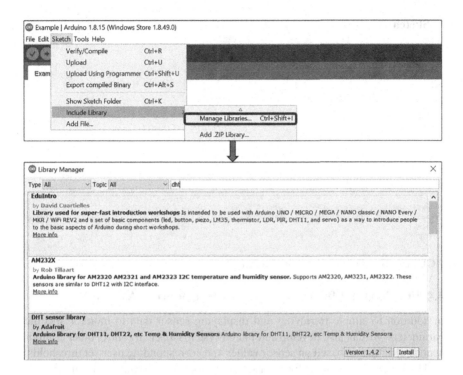

FIGURE 4.25 Installing Arduino libraries.

Circuit

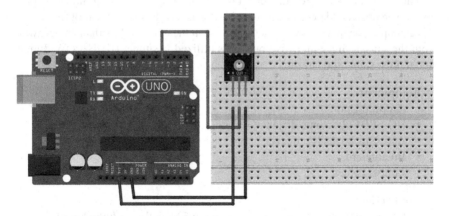

FIGURE 4.26 Circuit diagram connections for Project 4.8.

Sketch

```
#include <DHT.h>                              //import sensor library
#define DHTPIN 4                              //define signal pin
#define DHTTYPE DHT11                         //define sensor model
DHT dht(DHTPIN, DHTTYPE);

void setup()
{
  Serial.begin(9600);                         //display output in serial monitor
  dht.begin();                                //start DHT sensor
}

void loop()
{
  float t = dht.readTemperature();            //get sensor readings using library functions
  float h = dht.readHumidity();

  Serial.println("Temperature="+String(t)+" *C");   //display sensor values
  Serial.println("Humidity="+String(h)+" %");
  delay(1000);                                //refresh data every 1 second
}
```

FIGURE 4.27   Arduino sketch for Project 4.8.

4.4.10   PROJECT 4.9: SENSOR-ACTUATOR INTERACTIONS (ARDUINO)

In addition to simple retrieving and displaying sensor data to monitor specific parameters, we can also develop automated systems that can control other components and actuators based on sensor values and corresponding user-set thresholds.

This interactive system forms a feedback loop that continuously monitors a specific parameter and produces an automated output when the pre-set range is exceeded. As an extension to Project 4.7, this project will guide you in developing a system that monitors the distance to an object and sounds a buzzer when the object gets too close to the sensor.

This principle is utilized in a car reverse sensor system that monitors the distance to an object and beeps when the object gets too close to the rear of the car. In this example, the buzzer will be activated when the object is less than 15 cm away from the sensor. Since an active buzzer is utilized, a simple HIGH/LOW digital signal must sound the buzzer.

Equipment
- Arduino Uno
- HC-SR04 ultrasonic distance sensor
- Active piezoelectric buzzer
- Breadboard
- Jumper cables

Connections
- Connect the **VCC** leg of HC-SR04 to pin **5 V** on the Arduino board.
- Connect the **TRIG** leg of HC-SR04 to pin **11** on the Arduino board.
- Connect the **ECHO** leg of HC-SR04 to pin **12** on the Arduino board.
- Connect the **GND** leg of HC-SR04 to pin **GND** on the Arduino board.
- Connect the **VCC** leg of buzzer to pin **5 V** on the Arduino board.

- Connect the **I/O** leg of buzzer to pin **10** on the Arduino board.
- Connect the **GND** leg of buzzer to pin **GND** on the Arduino board (Figures 4.28 and 4.29).

Circuit

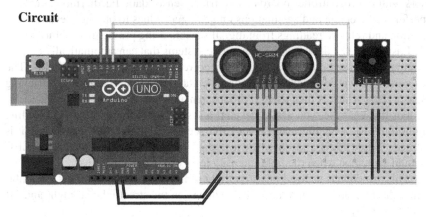

FIGURE 4.28 Circuit diagram connections for Project 4.9.

Sketch

```
int buzzPin = 10;              //define buzzer pin
int trigPin = 11;             //define trigger pin
int echoPin = 12;             //define echo pin
long duration, cm, inches;    //define variables

void setup()
{
  Serial.begin (9600);        //display output in serial monitor
  pinMode(trigPin, OUTPUT);   //set trigger pin as output
  pinMode(echoPin, INPUT);    //set echo pin as input
}

void loop()
{
  digitalWrite(trigPin, LOW); //short low pulse to ensure clean high pulse
  delayMicroseconds(5);
  digitalWrite(trigPin, HIGH); //short high pulse of 10 microseconds
  delayMicroseconds(10);
  digitalWrite(trigPin, LOW);

  pinMode(echoPin, INPUT);     //detect reflected high pulse at echo pin
  duration = pulseIn(echoPin, HIGH);
  cm = (duration/2) * 0.0343;  //convert travel time to distance
  inches = (duration/2) * 0.0135;

  Serial.print(inches);        //display distance values
  Serial.print("in, ");
  Serial.print(cm);
  Serial.print("cm");
  Serial.println();

  if (cm < 15)                 //beep buzzer if distance is less than 15 cm
  {
    digitalWrite(buzzPin, HIGH); //switch buzzer on
  }
  else
  {
    digitalWrite(buzzPin, LOW);  //switch buzzer off
  }
  delay(2000);                 //refresh data every 2 seconds
}
```

FIGURE 4.29 Arduino sketch for Project 4.9.

4.4.11   Exercise 4.2: Arduino Autonomous Systems

Based on the previous projects, you can now interface analogue and digital sensors with microcontroller boards and retrieve sensor data. Furthermore, you can perform conversion and calculations on analogue values to obtain relevant information and retrieve readings from digital sensors using pre-defined libraries.

Lastly, you can also develop interactive systems that can automatically control components based on sensor values and corresponding user-set thresholds. The exercise below is designed to test your understanding of interfacing and retrieving sensor data, which is then used to produce an automated output.

For this exercise, you are to develop a system that monitors the surrounding light intensity level and controls an LED accordingly; switches it off when it is already bright (day) and on when it is dark (nighttime). Specifically, the LED should switch on when the light intensity level drops below 50 Lux.

This principle is utilized in a streetlight sensor system that monitors the ambient light intensity and automatically switches on the streetlights at night and off during the day.

Equipment
- Arduino Uno
- GL55 light intensity sensor
- Red LED
- 1 kΩ resistor
- Breadboard
- Jumper cables

4.5   HANDS-ON PROJECTS: ARDUINO-BASED IOT SYSTEMS

As discussed in the earlier chapters, we can develop IoT systems for *Remote Monitoring* and *Remotely Monitored/Controlled Autonomous Systems*. In this section, we introduce Arduino-based implementations of these systems, using Arduino boards, compatible hardware, and Arduino-supported frameworks and technologies.

4.5.1   Project 4.10: IoT Remote Monitoring Systems (Arduino)

As an extension to Project 4.8, this project will guide readers in developing an IoT remote monitoring system that retrieves temperature and humidity information from a DHT11 sensor and uploads the data to a cloud server via a Wi-Fi network.

You will learn to interface wireless network modules to extend connectivity functionality to microcontroller boards that do not have this capability, such as the Arduino Uno, Nano, and Mega. You will also learn to set up IoT clients to broadcast sensor data to cloud servers and view this information via a dashboard.

4.5.1.1 Setting Up an IoT Client to View Information

ThingSpeak is a secure and straightforward IoT client enabling users to upload sensor data to the cloud server, implement data analytics using MATLAB, and utilize the stored data values to initiate specific commands. Although there is an abundance of free, open-source clients in the IoT ecosystem, ThingSpeak is renowned as an IoT client service pioneer and is highly popular thanks to its ease of use and reliability.

4.5.1.2 Configuring the ThingSpeak IoT Client

1. Create a free ThingSpeak user account at http://thingspeak.com.
2. Create a new channel.
3. Enable two fields for Temperature and Humidity and save the channel.
4. Click on the API Keys tab and note the Write API Key (Figure 4.30).

4.5.1.3 Interfacing with Wireless Network Module

Since most Arduino boards do not include wireless network connection functionality, an external network module must be connected to the board. In this section, you will learn to interface the *ESP8266* Wi-Fi module with an Arduino Uno board to upload sensor data to the cloud server via a Wi-Fi network.

The IoT client then retrieves this information from the cloud server and displays the information on a dashboard. The ESP8266 module has eight pins and a rated power input of 3.3 V. However, the Arduino Uno has a power output of 5 V. Thus, a voltage divider is required to step down the voltage from the Arduino Uno to avoid damaging the ESP8266 module.

The voltage divider setup utilizes three 1 kΩ resistors and one 10 kΩ resistor. Next, as shown in Table 4.2, AT commands are used to set up a Transmission Control Protocol (TCP) connection to the ThingSpeak application programming interface (API). The ESP8266 module is also set as a Wi-Fi client via the corresponding AT commands.

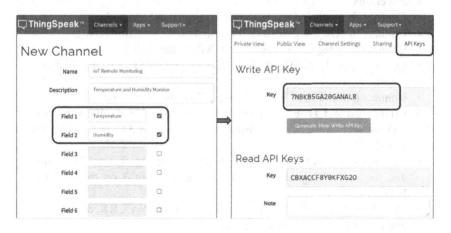

FIGURE 4.30 Configuring the ThingSpeak IoT Client.

TABLE 4.2
List of AT Commands for ESP8266
Wi-Fi Module

Commands	Description
AT+RST	Restart module
AT+CWMODE	Wi-Fi mode
AT+CWJAP	Join AP
AT+CWLAP	List AP
AT+CWQAP	Quit AP
AT+CIPSTATUS	Get status
AT+CIPSTART	Set up TCP or UDP
AT+CIPSEND	Send data
AT+CIPCLOSE	Close TCP or UDP
AT+CIFSR	Get IP
AT+CIPMUX	Set multiple connections
AT+CIPSERVER	Set as server

Equipment
- Arduino Uno
- ESP8266 Wi-Fi module
- DHT11 temperature and humidity sensor
- 1 kΩ resistor ×3
- 10 kΩ resistor
- Breadboard
- Jumper cables

Connections
- Connect the **+**leg of DHT11 to pin **3.3 V** on the Arduino board.
- Connect the **OUT** leg of DHT11 to pin **4** on the Arduino board.
- Connect the **−**leg of DHT11 to pin **GND** on the Arduino board.
- Connect pin 1, **GND**, of ESP8266 to pin **GND** on the Arduino board.
- Connect pin 2, **TX**, of ESP8266 to pin **2** on the Arduino board.
- Connect pin 4, **CH_EN**, of ESP8266 to either one leg of a 10 kΩ resistor and the second leg of the resistor connect to pin **3.3 V** on the Arduino board.
- Connect pin 7, **RX**, of ESP8266 to either one leg of a 1 kΩ resistor and the second leg of the resistor connect to pin **3** on the Arduino board.
- Connect either one leg of a second 1 kΩ resistor to pin 7, **RX**, of ESP8266 and the first leg of the first 1 kΩ resistor.

- Connect either one leg of a third 1 kΩ resistor to the second leg of the second 1 kΩ resistor and the second leg of the resistor third connect to pin **GND** on the Arduino board.
- Connect pin 8, **VCC**, of ESP8266 to pin **3.3 V** on the Arduino board (Figure 4.31).

Circuit

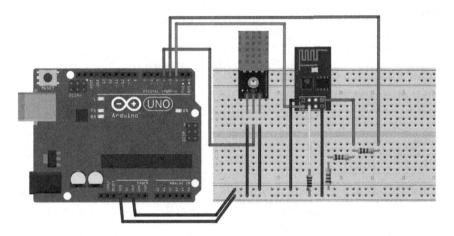

FIGURE 4.31   Circuit diagram connections for Project 4.10.

Sketch

Part 1: Set up the ESP8266 Wi-Fi module by setting the baud rate at 9,600 (Figure 4.32).

```
#include <SoftwareSerial.h>                    //import serial library (built-in to Arduino IDE)
SoftwareSerial espSerial = SoftwareSerial(2,3);  //set pin 2 as RX and pin 3 as TX

void setup()
{
    Serial.begin(115200);                      //start communication with host computer
    ESPserial.begin(115200);                   //enable serial library for communication with ESP8266
    Serial.println("Set Both NL & CR in the serial monitor.");
    Serial.println("Ready");
}

void loop()
{
    if (ESPserial.available())    {Serial.write(ESPserial.read());}
    if (Serial.available())       {ESPserial.write(Serial.read());}
}

// Copy and paste in serial monitor to change baud rate to 9600
// AT+UART_CUR=9600,8,1,0,0
```

FIGURE 4.32   Arduino sketch for Project 4.10 (Part 1).

- Upload the Arduino sketch to the board.
- Open the serial monitor (set baud rate to 115,200 and select Both NL & CR).
- Copy and paste the AT command in the sketch at the serial monitor text box.
- An OK message will be displayed upon success.

Part 2: Retrieve sensor data and upload information to IoT Client (Figure 4.33a and b).

```
#include <SoftwareSerial.h>                        //import serial library (built-in to Arduino IDE)
SoftwareSerial espSerial = SoftwareSerial(2,3);    //set pin 2 as RX and pin 3 as TX

#include <DHT.h>                                    //import sensor library
#define DHTPIN 4                                    //define signal pin
#define DHTTYPE DHT11                               //define sensor model
DHT dht(DHTPIN, DHTTYPE);

String apiKey = "input here";                       //ThingSpeak WRITE API key
String ssid = "input here";                         //Wi-Fi network SSID
String pass = "input here";                         //Wi-Fi network password

boolean DEBUG=true;

void showResponse(int waitTime)                     //set up communication with ESP8266
{
    long t=millis();
    char c;
    while (t+waitTime>millis()){
      if (espSerial.available()){
        c=espSerial.read();
        if (DEBUG) Serial.print(c);
      }
    }
}

boolean thingSpeakWrite(float value1, float value2) //set up communication with ThingSpeak server
{
    String cmd = "AT+CIPSTART=\"TCP\",\"";          //AT command to start TCP connection
    cmd += "184.106.153.149";                       //api.thingspeak.com
    cmd += "\",80";                                 //connection port
    espSerial.println(cmd);
    if (DEBUG) Serial.println(cmd);
    if(espSerial.find((char*)"Error")){
      if (DEBUG) Serial.println("AT+CIPSTART error");
      return false;
    }

    String getStr = "GET /update?api_key=";         //Prepare GET string to upload sensor data
    getStr += apiKey;
    getStr +="&field1=";                            //update field 1 value (temperature)
    getStr += String(value1);
    getStr +="&field2=";                            //update field 2 value (humidity)
    getStr += String(value2);
    getStr += "\r\n\r\n";
```

FIGURE 4.33A   Arduino sketch for Project 4.10 (Part 2a).

```
cmd = "AT+CIPSEND=";                           //AT command to upload sensor data
cmd += String(getStr.length());
espSerial.println(cmd);
if (DEBUG)  Serial.println(cmd);
delay(100);
if(espSerial.find((char*)">")){
  espSerial.print(getStr);
  if (DEBUG)  Serial.print(getStr);
}
else{
  espSerial.println("AT+CIPCLOSE");
  if (DEBUG) Serial.println("AT+CIPCLOSE");
  return false;
}
return true;
}

void setup()
{
  DEBUG=true;
  Serial.begin(9600);                          //display output in serial monitor
  espSerial.begin(9600);                       //enable serial library for communication with ESP8266
  dht.begin();                                 //start DHT sensor

  espSerial.println("AT+CWMODE=1");            //AT command to set ESP8266 as client
  showResponse(1000);
  espSerial.println("AT+CWJAP=\""+ssid+"\",\""+pass+"\"");
  showResponse(5000);
  if (DEBUG) Serial.println("Setup completed");
}

void loop()
{
  float t = dht.readTemperature();             //get sensor readings using library functions
  float h = dht.readHumidity();

  Serial.println("Temperature="+String(t)+" *C"); //display sensor values
  Serial.println("Humidity="+String(h)+" %");
  thingSpeakWrite(t,h);                        //upload sensor data to ThingSpeak server
  delay(20000);                                //minimum 15 s delay between updates (free ThingSpeak account)
}
```

FIGURE 4.33B   Arduino sketch for Project 4.10 (Part 2b).

Note: Change the baud rate back to 9,600 in the serial monitor (Figure 4.34).

Output

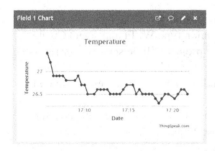 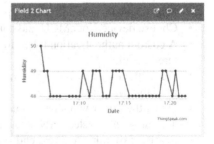

FIGURE 4.34   System output viewed via ThingSpeak IoT Client.

4.5.2 PROJECT 4.11: IoT REMOTELY OPERATED AUTONOMOUS SYSTEMS (ARDUINO)

This project will guide readers in developing an IoT remote control system that rotates a servo motor based on user inputs from the IoT client.

The IoT client, accessed via a mobile application, receives user input from a slider widget, converts the input into command values, and transmits this information over a Wi-Fi network to a wireless network-ready microcontroller.

From these commands, the microcontroller will rotate the servo from 0° to 180° based on the corresponding slider values. In this example, the low-power servo motor can be powered directly from the microcontroller and does not require an external power supply.

4.5.2.1 Setting Up IoT Client for Remote Control Systems

Blynk is a free, open-source, and user-friendly IoT client that provides an easy-to-use interface to monitor and control hardware projects from any iOS and Android smart device.

Upon downloading the Blynk mobile application, a graphic interface can be developed using the digital dashboard by simply dragging, dropping, and arranging widgets such as buttons, sliders, text displays, and graphs. These widgets can be used to visualize sensor data, control equipment remotely, set notifications and alerts, and manage multiple devices.

In addition, the dashboard is highly customizable, with interface elements that can be snapped together to build a functional user interface for any system.

4.5.2.2 Configuring the Blynk IoT Client

- Download the Blynk application from the Apple App Store or Google Play Store.
- Launch the application and create a new user account with your email and password.
- Select New Project and add the project name.
- Choose device NodeMCU and connection type Wi-Fi and select Create.
- A custom authentication token for the project will be sent to your registered email.
- Select the+icon in the top right-hand corner of the screen to view all available widgets.
- Select the Slider widget and hold down on it to resize or set the position.
- Tap the widget, select PIN, and choose Virtual V1.
- Set the start value to 0 and end value to 180.
- Tap the back button, then select the play icon in the top right-hand corner of the screen (Figure 4.35).

4.5.2.3 Interacting with Arduino-Compatible Boards: The NodeMCU

For this project, the NodeMCU microcontroller board is utilized instead to demonstrate to you how to work with other types of microcontroller boards. Since

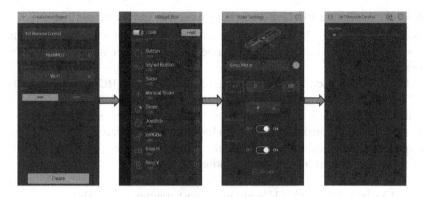

FIGURE 4.35 Configuring the Blynk IoT Client.

the NodeMCU is a third-party Arduino-compatible board, it is not included by default in the Arduino IDE. Thus, to program and interact with the NodeMCU, we first set up the board in the IDE.

4.5.2.4   Installing the ESP8266 Core on Arduino IDE

- Select the File tab and select Preferences.
- In the Additional Boards Manager URLs textbox, add the ESP8266 Core package.
  http://arduino.esp8266.com/stable/package_esp8266com_index.json.
- Next, select the Tools tab, followed by Board and Boards Manager.
- In the Boards Manager, search for esp8266 and install the package.
- Upon successful installation, ESP8266-based boards such as the NodeMCU 1.0 (ESP-12E Module) can be found in the Arduino IDE boards list.

Note: Installation of the ESP8266 Core requires Arduino IDE version 1.6.4 or higher (Figure 4.36).

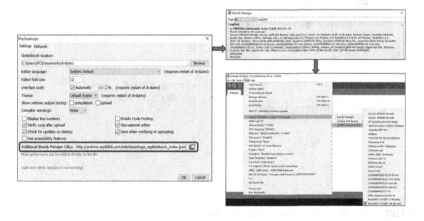

FIGURE 4.36 Configuring the NodeMCU microcontroller board.

4.5.2.5 Installing the USB-to-Serial Converter Driver (CH340G)

NodeMCU boards include a USB-to-Serial converter for communication with the host computer. The official design is based on the CP2102 chipset and offers the best compatibility.

Officially licensed modules such as the *Amica NodeMCU* boards use the CP2102 chipset. Low-cost *LoLin NodeMCU* boards meanwhile use the CH340G USB-to-Serial converter. Depending on the NodeMCU board, the appropriate driver must be installed. Generally, Windows immediately recognizes the CP2102 chipset and automatically downloads the required drivers, while the CH340G chipset requires separate driver installation.

- Connect the NodeMCU board to the host computer via USB.
- Download the Zip file of the CH340G driver from the *NodeMCU Developer Kit* webpage. The file is labelled *CH341SER*. Download the Windows version. https://github.com/nodemcu/nodemcu-devkit/tree/master/Drivers.
- Unzip the file and double click on the installer icon to run it.
- Select install and a notification message will appear upon successful driver installation (Figure 4.37).

Equipment
- LoLin NodeMCU
- SG90 micro servo motor
- Jumper cables

Connections
- Connect **Power** pin of servo motor to pin **3V3** on the NodeMCU board.
- Connect **Ground** pin of servo motor to pin **GND** on the NodeMCU board.

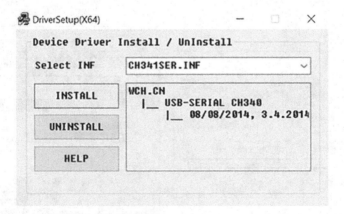

FIGURE 4.37 Installing the NodeMCU drivers.

- Connect **Command** pin of servo motor to pin **D8** on the NodeMCU board (Figures 4.38 and 4.39).

Circuit

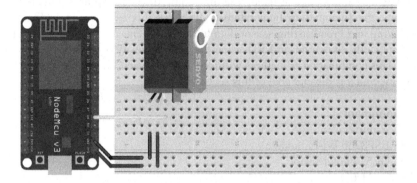

FIGURE 4.38 Circuit diagram connections for Project 4.11.

Sketch

```
#include <Servo.h>                    //servo library (built-in to Arduino IDE)
#include <ESP8266WiFi.h>             //ESP8266 library (built-in to Arduino IDE)
#include <BlynkSimpleEsp8266.h>      //Blynk IoT client library
#define BLYNK_PRINT Serial           //upload data to Blynk virtual pins

char auth[] = "input here";          //Blynk authentication key
char ssid[] = "input here";          //Wi-Fi network SSID
char pass[] = "input here";          //Wi-Fi network password


Servo servo;
BLYNK_WRITE(V1){                     //send data from slider widget to servo
servo.write(param.asInt());
}

void setup()
{
Blynk.begin(auth, ssid, pass);       //initialize Blynk IoT client
servo.attach(15);                    //define signal pin (D8 = GPIO15)
}

void loop()
{
Blynk.run();                         //run blynk IoT client service
}
```

FIGURE 4.39 Arduino sketch for Project 4.11.

Note: Download the Blynk library from the Library Manager. Ensure that you have selected the correct board, NodeMCU 1.0 (ESP-12E Module), and port settings in the Tools tab before uploading the sketch.

4.5.3 Exercise 4.3: Arduino-Based IoT Systems

By following along with the previous projects, you are now able to retrieve information via sensors, utilize these sensor readings to automate control of specific outputs, and broadcast the sensor data to IoT clients for remote monitoring.

With this knowledge at hand, you are required to develop an IoT system to monitor the surrounding light intensity level for this exercise. In addition to retrieving and broadcasting sensor data to the IoT client, the system should also automatically switch on an LED when the light intensity level drops below 50 Lux. This combination of features will form an automated IoT remote monitoring system, which is the end goal of this section.

Equipment
- Arduino Uno
- ESP8266 Wi-Fi module
- GL55 photoresistor
- Red LED
- 1 kΩ resistor ×4
- 10 kΩ resistor
- Breadboard
- Jumper cables

REFERENCES

Aqeel, A. (2018). *Introduction to Arduino IDE – The Engineering Projects*. The Engineering Projects. https://www.theengineeringprojects.com/2018/10/introduction-to-arduino-ide.html

Arduino Libraries. (2020). *The Arduino Platform*. https://www.arduino.cc/en/guide/libraries

Arduino Mega. (2017). *The Arduino Platform*. https://www.arduino.cc/en/pmwiki.php?n=Main/arduinoBoardMega2560

Arduino Nano. (2018). *The Arduino Platform*. https://www.arduino.cc/en/pmwiki.php?n=Main/ArduinoBoardNano

Arduino References. (2020). *The Arduino Platform*. https://www.arduino.cc/reference/en/

ESP8266. (2015). MakeIt. https://www.make-it.ca/nodemcu-arduino/nodemcu-details-specifications/

Light Sensor. (2016). Circuits4you.Com. https://circuits4you.com/2016/05/13/arduino-light-sensor/

5 Raspberry Pi-Based IoT Systems

5.1 THE RASPBERRY PI BOARDS

As discussed in Chapter 2, the Raspberry Pi is *Computer Board*; it consists of a Central Processing Unit (CPU) and added components that make up a full-fledged computer system on a single board. Today, the Raspberry Pi is one of the best-selling computers of all time and is widely used in many areas, thanks to its low cost, modularity, and open-source features.

Consequently, there are various types of Raspberry Pi boards, depending on setup and desired functionality. Several generations of *Pi* boards have been released, all featuring a Broadcom System-on-a-Chip (SoC) with an integrated Advanced RISC (Reduced Instruction Set Computing) Machines (ARM)-compatible CPU and on-chip Graphics Processing Unit (GPU). For the purposes of this book, we will refer to these boards as the *Raspberry Pi boards*, *Computer Boards*, *Computer-on-Chip* systems, or *Single-Board Computers (SBCs)*. We will use these terms interchangeably, depending on the context.

5.1.1 THE RASPBERRY PI MODEL B

The first-generation Raspberry Pi Model B was released in February 2012. In 2014, the Raspberry Pi Model B+ was released featuring an improved design, representing the standard mainline form-factor we are familiar with today (Figure 5.1).

While both boards featured Broadcom BCM2835 SoCs and single-core ARM11 processors running at 700 MHz, the RAM capacity was increased from 256 Mb to 512 Mb, along with the addition of two more USB 2.0 ports, for a total of four. Both boards featured HDMI connectivity, an Ethernet port, a 3.5 mm jack for audio and composite video out, and a micro-USB port for the power supply (Piltch, 2020).

The Raspberry Pi 2 Model B was released in February 2015 and featured an improved Broadcom BCM2836 SoC with a 900 MHz 32-bit quad-core ARM Cortex-A7 processor and 1 Gb RAM. The upgrade to a quad-core instead of a single-core processor provided a massive speed boost for the Operating System (OS) and multi-threaded applications. The Raspberry Pi 3 Model B was released a year later with an upgraded Broadcom BCM2837 SoC featuring a 1.2 GHz 64-bit quad-core ARM Cortex-A53 processor and 1 Gb RAM. This was the first board in the series to feature built-in 2.4 GHz 802.11b/g/n Wi-Fi and Bluetooth 4.1 connectivity.

DOI: 10.1201/9781003218395-7

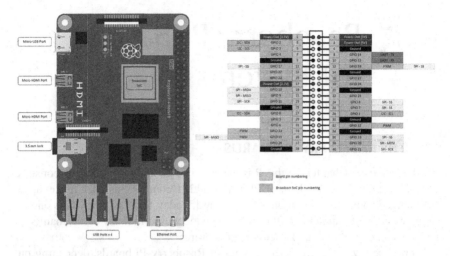

FIGURE 5.1   A Raspberry Pi 4 Model B board.

The Raspberry Pi 3 Model B+ was launched in 2018 with a faster 1.4 GHz processor, a three times faster gigabit Ethernet connection, 2.4/5 GHz dual-band 802.11b/g/n/ac Wi-Fi support, and upgraded Bluetooth 4.2 connectivity. The Raspberry Pi 4 Model B, released in June 2019, is the latest and most powerful version of the highly popular series.

It features a Broadcom BCM2711 SoC with a 1.5 GHz 64-bit quad-core ARM Cortex-A72 processor, up to 8 Gb of RAM, Bluetooth 5.0, full gigabit Ethernet, two USB 2.0 ports and two USB 3.0 ports, replacing the four USB 2.0 ports previously, and dual-monitor support via a pair of micro-HDMI ports for up to 4K resolution. The Pi 4 is also powered via a USB-C port.

All Raspberry Pi Model B boards have similar dimensions to simplify installation and mounting, with a length of 85.6 mm and a width of 56.5 mm. Additionally, apart from the first-generation Raspberry Pi Model B board comprising a shorter 26-pin GPIO header, all subsequent boards come with a standard 40-pin GPIO header with support for Universal Asynchronous Receiver/Transmitter (UART), Serial Peripheral Interface (SPI), and Inter-integrated Circuit (I2C) communication protocol.

Secure Digital (SD) cards, in micro-SD form-factor (standard SD on Raspberry Pi Model B), are used to store the OS, applications, and files. Since the SD card functions as the primary storage, a minimum memory capacity of 16 Gb is advised. Furthermore, a high-speed Class 10 SD card is recommended to ensure snappy performance. The recommended power supply rating for these boards is 5 V and 2.5–3 A (Piltch, 2020).

5.1.2   THE RASPBERRY PI MODEL A

While the Model B is the more popular and standard form-factor, the Model A boards have a more compact design that ditches most of the bulky Ethernet and

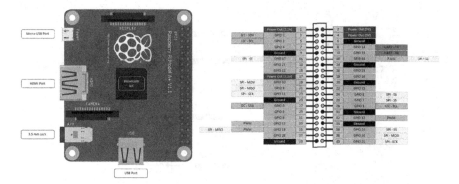

FIGURE 5.2 A Raspberry Pi 3 Model A+ board.

full-size USB ports, resulting in a smaller footprint while still offering the same processor and capabilities (Figure 5.2).

The first-generation Raspberry Pi Model A was launched 1 year after the Raspberry Pi Model B, featuring the same Broadcom BCM2835 SoC and single-core ARM11 processor running at 700 MHz with 256 Mb RAM. The board included one HDMI port, one USB 2.0 port, a 3.5mm jack for audio and composite video out, and a 26-pin GPIO header (Heath, 2018).

An improved Raspberry Pi Model A+ board released a year later bumped the RAM up to 512 Mb and added a 40-pin GPIO header instead. Skipping a generation and following a long absence of 4 years, the Raspberry Pi 3 Model A+ was introduced in 2018 as the successor for the respective form-factor. This board brought about a whole host of changes to bring it in line with the corresponding Raspberry Pi 3 Model B+ board. It featured the same Broadcom BCM2837 SoC with a 1.4 GHz processor quad-core ARM Cortex-A53 processor, though RAM was slashed by half to 512 Mb (Heath, 2018).

Most notable, however, was the addition of 2.4/5 GHz dual-band 802.11b/g/n/ac Wi-Fi and Bluetooth 4.2 wireless network connectivity, which was severely lacking in the previous boards. A micro-SD card slot (standard SD on Raspberry Pi Model A) for system storage and micro-USB port for power supply are standard across all Model A boards. The Model A form-factor has slightly smaller dimensions with a length of 65 mm and a width of 56.5 mm.

5.1.3 THE RASPBERRY PI ZERO

For applications where the size of the electronic components is of great concern, the smaller Raspberry Pi Zero with a lower price and reduced capabilities was released in November 2015. At roughly a third of the size of the standard Model B boards, with a length of 65 mm and width of 30 mm, it offers some, but not all, of the same functionality. The Pi Zero models lack the 3.5 mm jack, Ethernet, full-size USB 2.0, and HDMI ports. These components are replaced with a micro-USB data port and a mini-HDMI port in their respective places (Figure 5.3).

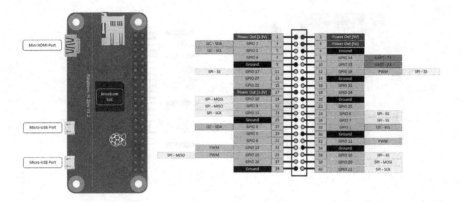

FIGURE 5.3   A Raspberry Pi Zero W board.

In February 2017, the Raspberry Pi Zero W, a version with single band 2.4 GHz 802.11b/g/n Wi-Fi and Bluetooth 4.1 capabilities, was launched. The Raspberry Pi Zero and Zero W use the same Broadcom BCM2835 SoC as the first-generation Raspberry Pi Model B, although now running at 1 GHz CPU clock speed with 512 Mb RAM (Brodkin, 2017).

A micro-SD card slot for system storage and micro-USB port for power supply are present across all Zero boards. Unlike all other Pi models, the 40-pin GPIO header is omitted on the Pi Zero and Zero W, with solderable through-holes in the pin locations. In January 2018, the Raspberry Pi Zero WH was launched, a version of the Zero W with pre-soldered GPIO headers (Brodkin, 2017).

5.2   THE RASPBERRY Pi PERIPHERALS

The Raspberry Pi boards can be connected to a wide range of hardware components, modules, sensors, and actuators. In fact, one of the most significant advantages of Raspberry Pi boards is the compatibility with almost all of the Peripherals listed in Chapter 2, with a few minor exceptions that will be discussed below.

5.2.1   Official Raspberry Pi Accessories

In order to expand their capabilities and functionality, most Raspberry Pi boards are equipped with high-speed Camera Serial Interface (CSI) and Display Serial Interface (DSI) connectors that support official first-party accessories developed by the Raspberry Pi Foundation. The CSI connector is included on all Model B, Model A, and Zero boards, while the DSI connector is also available on all boards, with the exception of the Raspberry Pi Zero.

The official accessories include a Raspberry Pi Touch Display and Camera Module. The Touch Display is a 7-inch full-colour liquid crystal display (LCD) with a resolution of 800×480 and 10-finger capacitive touch support. The Touch Display converts the Pi into a stand-alone device that can be utilized as a custom tablet or an all-in-one interactive device.

For instance, Raspberry Pi boards equipped with the Touch Display can be used as a vehicle infotainment system or a smart home hub. It requires two connections to the Pi, power from the GPIO header and a ribbon cable that connects to the DSI port (*RPi Touch Display*, 2021).

Meanwhile, the Camera Module can be used to take high-definition video and still photographs. The original 5-megapixel model was released in 2013, and an 8-megapixel model was introduced in 2016. For both iterations, there are visible light and infrared (IR) versions. In addition, a 12-megapixel High-Quality Camera Module was released in 2020.

While there is no IR version of this module, the IR filter can be removed if required. The Camera Module connects to the CSI port on the Pi via a ribbon cable. It is commonly used for home security applications and wildlife camera traps (*RPI Camera Module*, 2021) (Figure 5.4).

5.2.2 THIRD-PARTY ACCESSORIES

One thing to bear in mind is that by default, the Raspberry Pi is just a bare SBC. By connecting third-party accessories such as a monitor via the HDMI port as well as a mouse and keyboard via the USB ports, the Raspberry Pi can be converted into a full-fledged desktop computer.

Additional components such as speakers can also be connected to the 3.5 mm jack to enhance the desktop experience. Furthermore, wireless accessories such as Bluetooth headsets and video game controllers can also be connected to the Raspberry Pi boards (Figure 5.5).

Touch Display

Camera Module

FIGURE 5.4 Raspberry Pi touch display and camera module.

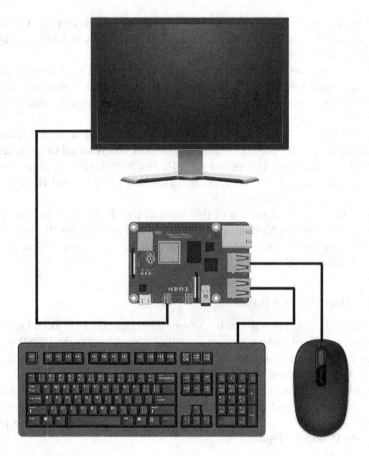

FIGURE 5.5 Using the Raspberry Pi as a desktop computer.

Additionally, the included USB ports and underlying Linux-based OS on the Raspberry Pi enables connection with many USB-compatible adapters similar to Windows-based computers, which was simply not possible with Arduino boards. For example, a USB SIM card adapter can be connected to the Raspberry Pi to provide cellular network connectivity to the board.

Next, a USB Global Positioning System (GPS) adapter enables location monitoring with the Pi, while a USB Wi-Fi or Ethernet adapter provides network connection capability for boards that lack this feature, such as the early-generation Model B and Model A boards, as well as the Pi Zero (Figure 5.6).

However, the crowning feature of the Raspberry Pi boards, in any iteration, is the 40-pin GPIO header. These pins provide direct access for connecting almost all Arduino-compatible external hardware components, including modules,

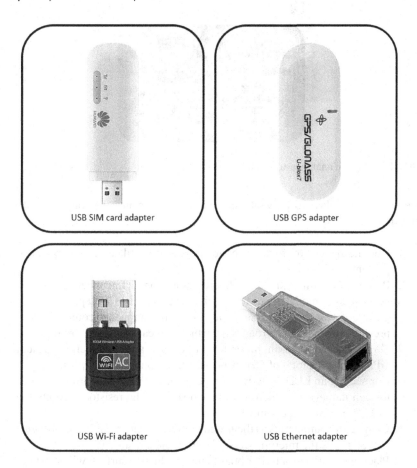

USB SIM card adapter

USB GPS adapter

USB Wi-Fi adapter

USB Ethernet adapter

FIGURE 5.6 Raspberry Pi USB-compatible adapters.

sensors, and actuators. However, one limitation of the Raspberry Pi GPIO header is the lack of analogue pins.

As such, analogue sensors cannot be interfaced directly with the board. Instead, these sensors must first be connected to an external analogue-to-digital converter (ADC) which is then connected to the Pi. The ADC must convert the analogue input to digital signals to be read by the Pi (Gus, 2016) (Figure 5.7).

5.2.3 HARDWARE SETUP: SAFETY PRECAUTIONS

As with most electronic devices and components, specific actions can damage or even destroy the fragile microprocessor boards and must be avoided at all times. Therefore, these boards must be handled with care, and additional tips

FIGURE 5.7   An analogue-to-digital converter.

are suggested below to prevent malfunction and ensure the longevity of the boards.

1. Operate the microprocessor board in a well-ventilated environment to prevent overheating.
2. Power off the microprocessor board before connecting external components such as modules, sensors, and actuators to the GPIO pins.
3. Double-check the polarities of all external component connections to prevent wiring up the wrong pins, which can cause a short circuit.
4. Do not exceed a maximum of 16 mA power draw from each individual GPIO pin and a total of 50 mA power draw from all GPIO pins.
5. Connecting an LED directly to output pins on the board without a resistor can damage the microprocessor board; as the resistor prevents the LED from drawing too much current.
6. Connecting output pins to the ground draws an enormous amount of current and kills the microprocessor board almost instantly.
7. Placing the microcontroller board on a conductive surface will short out the GPIO pins.
8. When powering off the Raspberry Pi, select the shutdown option from the start menu, wait for the green **ACT** LED light to flash several times before switching off, and only then switch off the power supply to avoid SD card corruption.

Additionally, all Raspberry Pi models, including the Model B, Model A, and Zero boards, feature two built-in red and green notification LEDs. These LEDs labelled **PWR** and **ACT,** respectively, can alert users on different conditions of the board as follows (Table 5.1).

5.3   THE RASPBERRY Pi OPERATING SYSTEM

Raspberry Pi OS, formerly known as Raspbian, is the primary and official OS for the Raspberry Pi family provided by the Raspberry Pi Foundation. It is a highly optimized Linux-based OS that can run on every Raspberry Pi board (Watson, 2020).

TABLE 5.1

Raspberry Pi LED Notifications

Item	LED Light	Description
PWR LED	Off	Power off
	Steady red	Power on
	Blinking red	Low voltage (below 4.63 V)
ACT LED	Steady green	Cannot read SD card
	Steady flashing green	SD card is corrupt
	Intensive flashing green during boot	Boot success
	Intensive flashing green during use	Write/read in progress

The OS uses a modified version of the Lightweight X11 Desktop Environment (LXDE) as its desktop environment. LXDE is specifically designed for single-chip computers and those with low resources. It uses an Openbox stacking window manager together with its own theme to bring a cohesive and unique user experience (Watson, 2020).

The Raspberry Pi OS has some unique features that set it apart from others, as well as familiar components that will make it easier for beginners to get accustomed to. The user interface looks similar to many standard desktops, such as Windows and macOS.

There is a menu bar at the top of the screen, containing an application menu as well as set shortcuts to the Terminal, Chromium web browser, and a File Manager. The right side has Bluetooth, Wi-Fi, and volume controls alongside a digital clock (Figure 5.8).

The OS features three different installation options. Firstly, Raspberry Pi OS Lite is the smallest and most bare-bones version of the Raspberry Pi OS. It does not even come with a Desktop Environment. This minimalist version of the OS is operated via Command Line Interface (CLI) only and does not have a graphical user interface (GUI).

It includes the basic OS, command interpreters, and various server utilities. It can serve as a good starting point for building a headless server or as a base to build some other custom system. The downloaded image is less than 500 MB, and the installed image is less than 2 GB.

Next, Raspberry Pi OS with desktop is the basic GUI version of the OS. It includes basic software, utilities, and applications expected with a Linux system, such as a web browser, media player, terminal emulator, text editor, PDF viewer, calculator, and more, but with none of the Raspberry Pi-specific educational and programming utilities.

However, upon installation, you may use the Recommended Software utility to install only the additional utilities and applications that you need. The downloaded image is about 1.2 GB, and the installed image is about 4 GB. Lastly, Raspberry Pi OS with desktop and recommended software is the full version of

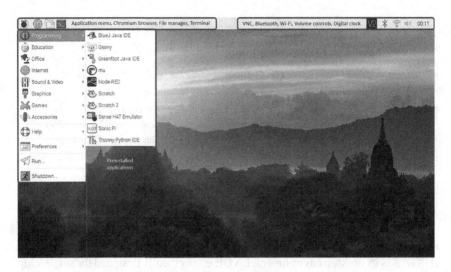

FIGURE 5.8   Raspberry Pi OS (Raspbian) desktop interface.

the OS. It has all the basic desktop version features and includes everything from the Recommended Software list.

This includes productivity tools such as the LibreOffice suite, games such as Minecraft Pi, and a plethora of educational applications and IDE software for teaching coding and developing custom projects, such as Wolfram Mathematica, NodeRed, Scratch, Sonic Pi, SmartSim, and the Sense HAT emulator.

The idea here is the reverse of the basic desktop; you may use the Recommended Software utility to remove the packages that you do not need. The downloaded image is nearly 3 GB, and the installed image is more than 8 GB.

5.3.1 Installation and Setup

In this section, we outline installation steps for the Raspberry Pi OS. A computer with an SD card reader or an external USB SD card adapter is required for this process.

1. Download the latest version of the Raspberry Pi Imager and install it. https://www.raspberrypi.org/software/.
2. Insert an SD card into the computer.
3. Open the Raspberry Pi Imager, click *Choose OS > Raspberry Pi OS (32-bit)*.
4. Click *Choose SD card* to select the connected SD card.
5. Click *Write* to install the operating system on the SD card.
6. Once complete, the program will automatically unmount the SD card.
7. Insert the SD card into the Raspberry Pi and power it up.
8. Connect to an external monitor (HDMI), keyboard, and mouse (Figure 5.9).

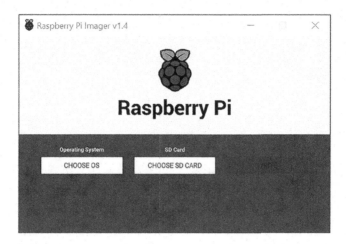

FIGURE 5.9   Raspberry Pi Imager software.

5.3.2   Virtual Network Computing (VNC), the Setup

Virtual Network Computing (VNC) is a graphical desktop sharing system that provides remote control of the desktop interface of one device, running the VNC Server, from another device, running the VNC Viewer. VNC Viewer transmits the keyboard and mouse events to VNC Server and receives updates to the screen in return.

The VNC can be used to remotely access and configure Raspberry Pi boards from a host computer for users that prefer this method rather than connecting an external monitor, keyboard, and mouse. By default, VNC Connect from RealVNC is included in Raspberry Pi OS (Ashwin, 2019).

Enabling VNC Server at the Raspberry Pi command line
1. Open the Terminal and enter command **sudo raspi-config**.
2. Select Interfacing Options > VNC > Yes.
3. Reboot the Raspberry Pi by entering command **sudo reboot**.
4. Open the Terminal, type command **ifconfig**, and note the private IP address of the Pi.

Connecting to the Raspberry Pi with VNC Viewer on the host computer
1. Download the VNC Viewer from RealVNC. https://www.realvnc.com/en/connect/download/viewer/
2. Enter the private IP address of the Pi into the VNC Viewer (Figure 5.10).

5.3.3   Geany IDE Basics (For Raspberry Pi)

Introduced briefly in Chapter 2, Geany is a robust, stable, and lightweight IDE, making it ideal for low resource devices such as Raspberry Pi boards. It is designed to have short load times, with limited dependency on separate packages

FIGURE 5.10 VNC viewer on the host computer.

or external libraries. In addition, it is cross-platform and runs on Linux, Windows, and macOS and has built-in support for more than 50 popular programming languages such as Python, C, Java, PHP, HTML, and many more.

Geany includes many useful features such as auto-completion, syntax highlighting, code folding, embedded terminal emulator, and function mapping. The IDE interface has two tree-style left-side panes, with one tab for symbols and one for documents. The large right-side pane is the editor with line numbers. This pane has a tab bar at the top, which you can use to switch from one document to another.

There is a menu bar at the top of the screen and a toolbar with commonly used features right below it. The File menu includes the usual options to create, open, and save documents. Meanwhile, the Edit menu lets you perform various functions, including inserting comments, tags, or dates. The preferences section in the Edit menu also has options for tweaking the interface. Next, you can use the *find in files* option from the Search menu to search for text in all documents in a folder at the same time.

Another strong point of Geany is that it is highly customizable. There are a ton of themes that can be enabled from the View settings. The View menu also includes options to disable the sidebar, message bar, menu bar, toolbar, or line numbers for a clean and distraction-free experience. This menu also houses options to change the font, colour, and more.

Additionally, the Document menu has various formatting tools from line breaking, wrapping, indentation, programming file type for language selection, and encoding, among other options. Finally, you can manage your Projects from the Project toolbar and find all files of a project listed by the editor so that you

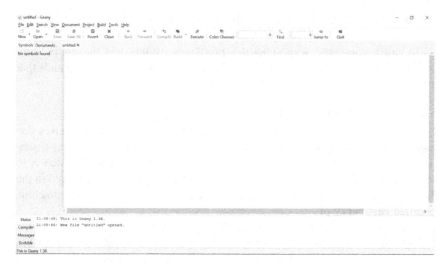

FIGURE 5.11 The Geany IDE (in the Raspberry Pi).

may select them when the need arises. As for the toolbar, apart from the standard options to create a new document or open a previously saved one, there is also a revert button for reloading the current document. You can compile the code right from the application and click on the build and execute buttons to run it. This obviously requires the coding platform to be installed; for instance, Python must be installed on the local machine to execute a Python script. There is also a text finder and an option to jump to a specific line in the code within the toolbar.

Furthermore, there is an interesting panel at the bottom of the screen. A status tab shows the activity log, a compiler tab that displays whether your code is fine, a messages tab for notifications from the IDE, and a scribble tab for notes. Geany also features a plugin system, wherein users can add more features such as a spell-check plugin into the IDE (Figure 5.11).

5.3.4 Raspberry Pi Programming

As the Raspberry Pi OS is a Linux-based OS, it follows the same terminal commands as any other Linux machine. This is especially beneficial for beginners since they do not have to memorize or make a note of different commands for the Raspberry Pi OS.

However, it can be challenging to keep track of all the Raspberry Pi commands. Therefore, a list of the most useful and essential Linux commands for interacting with Raspberry Pi boards is provided below. It should also be noted that Linux commands are case-sensitive. Another point to note on using Linux commands with the Raspberry Pi is user privileges. There are two user modes you can work with in Linux. One is a user mode with basic access privileges, and the other is a mode with administrator access privileges, also known as superuser or root. Some advanced tasks cannot be performed with basic privileges, so you will need the superuser privileges to perform them.

To run a command with superuser privileges, simply add the prefix **sudo** before the respective commands. This allows you to enter all the commands that are available within Linux without any restrictions.

5.3.4.1   Basic Linux Commands

Like all Linux distributions, Raspberry Pi OS has a powerful CLI that gives you more control over the device than you can get using the GUI. In fact, many essential tasks are either easier or only possible via commands. The first step is to open a *Terminal* window. A **pi@raspberrypi:~ $** prompt will be displayed in the Terminal, indicating that we are logged in as a user called **pi** and that our machine is called **raspberry pi**.

The $ refers to our permissions; in that, we have permission to edit any file or folder in our home directory, which in this case is **/home/pi/**. Forward slashes are always used to indicate folders and files within other folders. In this case, the current working directory is **pi**, which is inside **home**, which is inside the root of the file system.

One handy shortcut that can be used in the Terminal is pressing the up-arrow key to print the last entered command. This is a quick way to repeat previous commands or make corrections to commands (Cambell, 2021) (Figure 5.12).

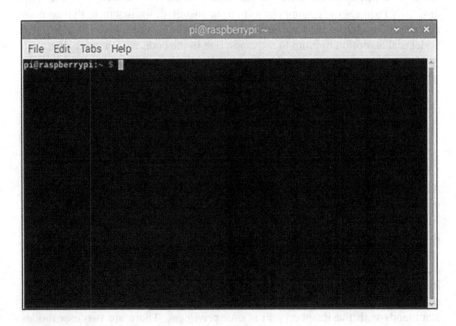

FIGURE 5.12   Raspberry Pi OS terminal window.

5.3.4.2   General Commands

As the name implies, general commands are general-purpose commands used for general management of the Raspberry Pi system (Table 5.2).

5.3.4.3   File and Directory Commands

Navigating around the file system is something we take for granted in a GUI environment with a built-in File Manager. However, with the appropriate commands, we can also navigate between directories, folders, and files from the CLI with great speed and precision. You may need to use the **sudo** command for certain actions on particular directories and files that require additional permissions (Taylor & Blom, 2021) (Table 5.3).

5.3.4.4   System Updates and Software Installation Commands

The Advanced Packaging Tool (APT) is a free software user interface that works with core libraries to handle the installation and removal of software on Linux distributions. APT simplifies the process of managing software on Linux machines by automating the retrieval, configuration, and installation of software packages. On Raspberry Pi OS, and generally on all Linux distributions, there is a package for each firmware, software program, and application installed. A list of all available packages is called a repository.

This repository and all installed packages must be updated regularly to keep your system safe and up to date. To use apt-get commands, we will need to use **sudo** as changes will be made to the OS. You also need to be connected to the Internet for these commands to work (Table 5.4).

5.3.4.5   Networking and Internet Commands

Networking commands allow you to perform networking operations, such as conducting connection testing, and other related networking diagnostic operations (Table 5.5).

5.3.4.6   System Information Commands

The Linux commands below allow us to check the hardware and software information of the Raspberry Pi board for troubleshooting and debugging (Table 5.6).

TABLE 5.2
Raspberry Pi General Commands

Command	Description
raspi-config	Opens the Raspberry Pi software configuration tool to alter board settings
poweroff	To shut down the Raspberry Pi
reboot	To reboot/restart the Raspberry Pi
clear	To clear/remove previously run commands and output text from the terminal screen

TABLE 5.3

Raspberry Pi File and Directory Commands

Command	Description
pwd	Shows the full path to the current directory
ls	Lists all contents of the current directory
ls -l	Lists all contents of the current directory, with more details
ls [directory]	Lists all contents of the specified directory
ls [filetype]	Lists all files of a certain type, for instance, .py Python files
cd	Returns to the root directory
cd ~	Returns to the home directory
cd -	Returns to the previous directory
cd [folder]	Switches to the specified folder in the current directory
cd [directory]	Switches to the specified directory on the system
mkdir [directory]	Creates a new directory with the specified name
mkdir [file] [directory]	Creates a new [file] in new [directory]
cp [file] [directory]	Copies [file] to another [directory]
cp -r [directory1] [directory2]	Copies [directory1] to [directory2]
mv [file] [directory]	Moves [file] to another [directory]
mv [directory1] [directory2]	Moves [directory1] to [directory2]
mv [oldfile] [newfile]	Renames an [oldfile] name to [newfile] name
rm [file]	Deletes [file]
rm -rf [directory]	Deletes [directory]
cat [file]	Display contents of [file]
nano [file]	Opens/Creates [file] in the *nano* text editor
python [file.py]	Runs [file.py] (executes Python program from Terminal)

TABLE 5.4

Raspberry Pi Software Management Commands

Command	Description
apt-get update	To download the latest package versions on your system and update the list of available packages in the repository. However, this does not install or upgrade any packages. Use it before installing new packages to make sure you are installing the latest version
apt-get upgrade	To upgrade and install the latest version of all installed packages from the repository. For this reason, you should always run an update before the upgrade
apt-get install [package]	Installs the specified package from the repository
apt-get remove [package]	Removes the specified package from the repository. However, this command leaves behind files related to the software, such as configuration files and logs
apt-get purge [package]	Completely deletes all data, configuration files, and logs from the application that was previously removed

TABLE 5.5

Raspberry Pi Networking Commands

Command	Description
ifconfig	Displays the current network configuration and IP address
iwconfig	Displays the wireless network adapter connection
iwlist wlan0 scan	List all currently available wireless networks
ping	Sends a *ping* to a remote address to test the connection
wget [URL]	Downloads the file from [URL], saves in current directory

TABLE 5.6

Raspberry Pi System Information Commands

Command	Description
cat /proc/cpuinfo	Displays the processor information
cat /proc/meminfo	Displays the memory information
cat /proc/partitions	Displays the size and number of partitions on the SD card
cat /proc/version	Displays the Raspberry Pi version
vcgencmd measure_temp	Displays the CPU temperature
htop	Displays the current CPU load, RAM usage, etc.
df –h	Displays the amount of free disk space
uptime	Displays the total runtime of the Raspberry Pi.
lsusb	Lists all USB hardware connected to the Raspberry Pi

5.3.4.7   Python Raspberry Pi Functions

As discussed in Chapter 3, Raspberry Pi programs are written in Python programming language. In addition to variables, data types, operations, and conditions detailed previously, Python code can also be organized or grouped into modules. A module is a separate file containing Python code that can be used by other Python programs through the use of the **import** keyword. For example, the **Rpi.GPIO** module is a Python library that handles interfacing with GPIO pins on the Raspberry Pi board.

This module is pre-installed on the latest versions of the Raspberry Pi OS. To manually install the module, open a terminal and enter the command **sudo apt-get install python-rpi.gpio python3-rpi.gpio** to add it to the Python and Python3 interpreter. Next, the module must be added to the Python script; **import Rpi. GPIO as GPIO**. Lastly, we have to declare the type of numbering system used for the GPIO pins. **GPIO.setmode(GPIO.BOARD)** uses the pins exactly as in the Raspberry Pi board, while **GPIO.setmode(GPIO.BCM)** uses the Broadcom SoC numbering instead.

It is also possible to import individual objects, or code segments, from a module rather than importing the whole module. For example, in the following projects, the sleep object is imported from the time module using the command **from time import sleep**. This allows us to add delays to the Python script by simply using the **sleep()** function instead of **time.sleep()** if we were to import the time module wholly.

Python code specific to Raspberry Pi boards mainly consists of constants used to interface with the GPIO pins. Constants are pre-defined expressions and can be classified into groups. The first group is Boolean constants for defining logical levels. For example, a true value represents a non-zero value, though often defined as one, while false is defined as zero. The second group, including high and low values, are used for defining pin levels. When reading or writing to a digital pin, only these two possible values can be defined. Lastly, the third group is used for defining digital pin modes, such as input and output.

Python functions provide the ability to interact with the Raspberry Pi boards and any connected hardware components. The **GPIO.setup** function configures the specified digital pin to behave either as an *input* or an *output*. For example, an input pin set using the function GPIO.IN is able to read data from modules and sensors, while an output pin set using the function GPIO.OUT can provide an electrical signal to activate other components.

Next, the **GPIO.output** function is used to set a *high* or a *low* value to a digital pin. For Raspberry Pi boards, a high output value would provide a voltage of 3.3 V, which can power external components such as LEDs. Meanwhile, the **GPIO.input** function reads the value from a specified digital pin, either high or low. For example, when a pin is configured as an input, the board will report high for a voltage between 1.8 and 3.3 V, while anything lower than 1.8 V will be read as low.

5.3.4.8   Running Python Programs on the Raspberry Pi Board

Unlike Arduino boards that require a host computer to code and upload sketches to the board, all Python programs are developed and run directly from the Raspberry Pi board. Once a Python script has been prepared on the Geany IDE, we can easily run the program from the IDE itself. Take note of the directory in which you are saving the file, e.g. **/home/pi**.

Alternatively, you can open a terminal window and navigate to the directory. The Python program was saved earlier, for instance, **cd /home/pi**, and run it directly from the CLI using the **python [*filename.py*]** command.

5.4   HANDS-ON PROJECTS: RASPBERRY Pi AUTONOMOUS SYSTEMS

Similar to Section 4.4, this section will help beginners understand and familiarize themselves with electronic circuit assembly and programming but for Computer-on-Chip systems instead. Readers will learn how to interact with basic components, including LEDs, pushbuttons, sensors, and actuators. In addition, you will learn to interface sensors to retrieve and process raw data from the environment to obtain useful information.

The microprocessor board selected for these projects is the *Raspberry Pi 4 Model B*. However, the examples from this section can be applied to other recent Raspberry Pi boards as well, namely the Raspberry Pi 3 (Model A+, B, B+) and Raspberry Pi Zero WH.

First-generation Raspberry Pi (Model A, A+, B, B+), Raspberry Pi 2 (Model B), as well as Raspberry Pi Zero and Zero W models are not recommended as software support for these boards may be lacking due to their age and limited processing power, resulting in the inability to run certain programs or install specific packages. As for the Raspberry Pi Zero and Zero W boards, the lack of onboard GPIO headers makes it difficult to connect external components.

All following projects and exercises are mirrored to Chapter 4 so that you can better understand the differences between *Controller Boards* and *Computer Boards* systems and how to use these different systems to produce the same output. To maximize the learning experience, we recommend you procure the components shown in Table 5.7. This would allow you to follow along and develop your system as you read the remainder of this chapter.

Alternatively, and as discussed in the *Internet of Mobile Things (IoMT) Training Kit* section, all items listed in Table 5.7 are included in the IoMT Training Kit, with all software pre-installed and configured, which you can purchase separately through us. Refer to the *IoMT Training Kit* section for details.

5.4.1 PROJECT 5.1: THE BLINKING LED

This project will demonstrate to beginners how to interface essential components such as an LED with the microprocessor board to produce an output. The Raspberry Pi and corresponding Python program will automatically switch the

---

TABLE 5.7

Components Required for the Hands-On Work

No	Components	Quantity
1	Raspberry Pi 4 Model B	1
2	Raspberry Pi 3 Model B	1
3	GL55 light intensity sensor	1
4	HC-SR04 ultrasonic distance sensor	1
5	DHT11 temperature and humidity sensor	1
6	Pushbutton module	1
7	Active piezoelectric buzzer	1
8	SG90 micro servo motor	1
9	Red LED	2
10	Blue LED	2
11	Resistor (1 kΩ)	5
12	Solderless breadboard	1
13	Jumper cables (male to female)	1 set (40 pcs)

LED on and off at 1-second intervals, resulting in a blinking effect. The speed at which the LED switches on and off can be altered by increasing or decreasing the time delay, leading to a faster or slower blinking effect.

In this project, a resistor is connected to the cathode of the LED and the ground pin on the board. This pull-down resistor ensures that the LED is always in a low state, unless set to high by the program. Thus, the LED is switched off when low and switched on when high. The board pin numbering is used for this example.

Equipment
1. Raspberry Pi 4 Model B
2. Red LED
3. 1 kΩ resistor
4. Breadboard
5. Jumper cables

Connections
1. Positive of LED (long leg) connects to pin **16** on the Raspberry Pi board.
2. Negative of LED (short leg) connects to either one leg of the resistor.
3. Second leg of resistor connects to pin **GND** on the Raspberry Pi board (Figures 5.13 and 5.14).

Circuit

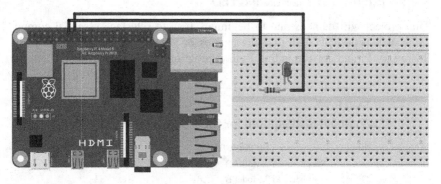

FIGURE 5.13   Circuit diagram connections for Project 5.1.

Script

```
import RPi.GPIO as GPIO                              #import Raspberry Pi GPIO module
from time import sleep                               #import sleep function from time module

GPIO.setmode(GPIO.BOARD)                             #board pin numbering
GPIO.setup(16, GPIO.OUT, initial=GPIO.LOW)           #set pin 8 as output and initial value low (off)

while True:                                          #loop function
    GPIO.output(16, GPIO.HIGH)                       #switch LED on
    sleep(1)                                         #delay 1 second
    GPIO.output(16, GPIO.LOW)                        #switch LED off
    sleep(1)                                         #delay 1 second
```

FIGURE 5.14   Python script for Project 5.1.

5.4.2 PROJECT 5.2: THE ALTERNATELY BLINKING LED

This next project will demonstrate on interfacing multiple components simultaneously, in this case, two LEDs, one red and one blue. Similar to the first project, the Raspberry Pi and corresponding Python program will automatically switch the first LED on and off at 1-second intervals, followed by the second LED at alternate 1-second intervals. When the red LED is switched on, the blue LED will be switched off and vice versa. The Broadcom SoC pin numbering is used for this example.

Equipment
- Raspberry Pi 4 Model B
- Red LED (LED 1)
- Blue LED (LED 2)
- 1 kΩ resistor ×2
- Breadboard
- Jumper cables

Connections
- Positive of LEDs (long leg) connects to pin **16** and pin **18** on the Raspberry Pi board.
- Negative of LEDs (short leg) connects to either one leg of the resistors.
- Second leg of resistors connects to pin **GND** on the Raspberry Pi board (Figures 5.15 and 5.16).

Circuit

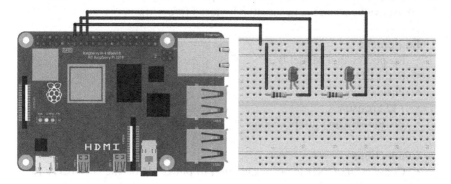

FIGURE 5.15 Circuit diagram connections for Project 5.2.

Script

```
import RPi.GPIO as GPIO          #import Raspberry Pi GPIO module
from time import sleep           #import sleep function from time module

GPIO.setmode(GPIO.BCM)           #Broadcom SoC pin numbering
GPIO.setup(23, GPIO.OUT, initial=GPIO.LOW) #set pin 23 as output and initial value low (off)
GPIO.setup(24, GPIO.OUT, initial=GPIO.LOW) #set pin 24 as output and initial value low (off)

while True:                      #loop function
    GPIO.output(23, GPIO.HIGH)   #switch LED 1 on
    sleep(1)                     #delay 1 second
    GPIO.output(23, GPIO.LOW)    #switch LED 1 off
    GPIO.output(24, GPIO.HIGH)   #switch LED 2 on
    sleep(1)                     #delay 1 second
    GPIO.output(24, GPIO.LOW)    #switch LED 2 off
```

FIGURE 5.16   Python script for Project 5.2.

5.4.3   PROJECT 5.3: BUTTON-CONTROLLED LED

This project demonstrates how to interface with a pushbutton to switch on an LED. As such, beginners will learn how to configure components as inputs and outputs. In this case, the pushbutton will be set as an input. The microprocessor reads the state of the pushbutton and produces an output by switching on the LED.

The pin connected to the button is configured as an input. However, when the pushbutton is in the open state, the input pin will be floating, resulting in unpredictable values. Therefore, we use the onboard Raspberry Pi pull-up resistor to ensure a clean reading. The purpose of this internal resistor is to pull the pin to a known state when the switch is open. In this case, the pull-up resistor provides a high (true) value at the input pin when the pushbutton is open (not pressed) and a low (false) value when the pushbutton is closed (pressed).

Equipment
- Raspberry Pi 4 Model B
- Red LED
- Pushbutton
- 1 kΩ resistor
- Breadboard and jumper cables

Connections
- Connect the **GND** leg of pushbutton to pin **GND** on the Raspberry Pi board.
- Connect the **OUT** leg of pushbutton to pin **18** on the Raspberry Pi board.
- Connect the **VCC** leg of pushbutton to pin **5 V** on the Raspberry Pi board.
- Positive of LED (long leg) connects to pin **16** on the Raspberry Pi board.
- Negative of LED (short leg) connects to either one leg of a resistor.
- Second leg of resistor connects to pin **GND** on the Raspberry Pi board.
- Use common **5 V** and **GND** pins on the Raspberry Pi board (Figures 5.17 and 5.18).

Circuit

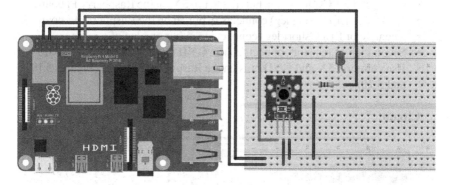

FIGURE 5.17   Circuit diagram connections for Project 5.3.

Script

```
import RPi.GPIO as GPIO                              #import Raspberry Pi GPIO module
from time import sleep                               #import sleep function from time module

GPIO.setmode(GPIO.BOARD)                             #board pin numbering
GPIO.setup(16, GPIO.OUT, initial=GPIO.LOW)           #set pin 16 as output and initial value low (off)
GPIO.setup(18, GPIO.IN, pull_up_down=GPIO.PUD_UP)    #set pin 18 as input and enable internal pull-up resistor

try:
    while True:                                      #loop function
        if GPIO.input(18) == False:                  #input false when closed
            GPIO.output(16, GPIO.HIGH)               #switch LED on
        else:
            GPIO.output(16, GPIO.LOW)                #switch LED off
except:
    GPIO.cleanup()
```

FIGURE 5.18   Python script for Project 5.3.

5.4.4   PROJECT 5.4: BUTTON-CONTROLLED LED TOGGLE

Similar to the previous project, input from a pushbutton is used to toggle an LED on and off. However, instead of continuously holding the pushbutton to switch on the LED, for this project, simply pressing the pushbutton once (clicking on it) will switch on the LED. Likewise, pressing the pushbutton a second time would switch off the LED.

Equipment
- Raspberry Pi 4 Model B
- Red LED
- Pushbutton
- 1 kΩ resistor
- Breadboard
- Jumper cables

Connections
- Connect the **GND** leg of pushbutton to pin **GND** on the Raspberry Pi board.

- Connect the **OUT** leg of pushbutton to pin **18** on the Raspberry Pi board.
- Connect the **VCC** leg of pushbutton to pin **5 V** on the Raspberry Pi board.
- Positive of LED (long leg) connects to pin **16** on the Raspberry Pi board.
- Negative of LED (short leg) connects to either one leg of a resistor.
- Second leg of resistor connects to pin **GND** on the Raspberry Pi board.
- Use common **5 V** and **GND** pins on the Raspberry Pi board (Figures 5.19 and 5.20).

Circuit

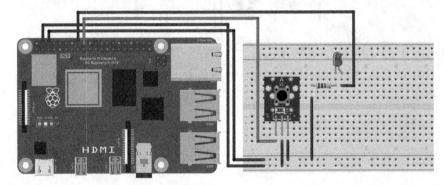

FIGURE 5.19   Circuit diagram connections for Project 5.4.

Script

```
import RPi.GPIO as GPIO                            #import Raspberry Pi GPIO module
from time import sleep                             #import sleep function from time module

GPIO.setmode(GPIO.BOARD)                           #board pin numbering
GPIO.setup(16, GPIO.OUT, initial=GPIO.LOW)         #set pin 16 as output and initial value low (off)
GPIO.setup(18, GPIO.IN, pull_up_down=GPIO.PUD_UP)  #set pin 18 as input and enable internal pull-up resistor

try:
    while True:                                    #loop function
        if GPIO.input(18) == False:                #input false when closed
            GPIO.output(16, not GPIO.input(18))    #switch LED on
            sleep(0.5)                             #time delay for click to take effect
except:
    GPIO.cleanup()
```

FIGURE 5.20   Python script for Project 5.4.

5.4.5   PROJECT 5.5: BUTTON-CONTROLLED LEDs

This project demonstrates a system with a single input and multiple outputs. Specifically, the input from one pushbutton will be used to control two LEDs at the same time. In this case, when the pushbutton is continuously pressed, the first LED is switched on while the second LED is switched off. Alternately, when the pushbutton is released, the first LED will be switched off, and the second LED will be switched on.

Equipment
- Raspberry Pi 4 Model B
- Red LED (LED 1)
- Blue LED (LED 2)
- Pushbutton
- 1 kΩ resistor ×2
- Breadboard
- Jumper cables

Connections
- Connect the **GND** leg of pushbutton to pin **GND** on the Raspberry Pi board.
- Connect the **OUT** leg of pushbutton to pin **22** on the Raspberry Pi board.
- Connect the **VCC** leg of pushbutton to pin **5 V** on the Raspberry Pi board.
- Positive of LED 1 (long leg) connects to pin **16** on the Raspberry Pi board.
- Negative of LED 1 (short leg) connects to either one leg of a resistor.
- Second leg of resistor connects to pin **GND** on the Raspberry Pi board.
- Positive of LED 2 (long leg) connects to pin **18** on the Raspberry Pi board.
- Negative of LED 2 (short leg) connects to either one leg of a resistor.
- Second leg of resistor connects to pin **GND** on the Raspberry Pi board.
- Use common **5 V** and **GND** pins on the Raspberry Pi board (Figures 5.21 and 5.22).

Circuit

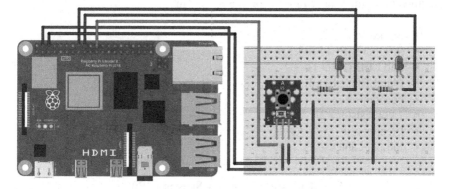

FIGURE 5.21   Circuit diagram connections for Project 5.5.

Script

```
import RPi.GPIO as GPIO                              #import Raspberry Pi GPIO module
from time import sleep                               #import sleep function from time module

GPIO.setmode(GPIO.BOARD)                             #board pin numbering
GPIO.setup(16, GPIO.OUT, initial=GPIO.LOW)           #set pin 16 (LED 1) as output and initial value low (off)
GPIO.setup(18, GPIO.OUT, initial=GPIO.LOW)           #set pin 18 (LED 2) as output and initial value low (off)
GPIO.setup(22, GPIO.IN, pull_up_down=GPIO.PUD_UP)    #set pin 22 as input and enable internal pull-up resistor

try:
    while True:
        if GPIO.input(22) == False:
            GPIO.output(16, GPIO.HIGH)               #switch LED 1 on
            GPIO.output(18, GPIO.LOW)                #switch LED 2 off
        else:
            GPIO.output(16, GPIO.LOW)                #switch LED 1 off
            GPIO.output(18, GPIO.HIGH)               #switch LED 2 on
except:
    GPIO.cleanup()
```

FIGURE 5.22   Python script for Project 5.5.

5.4.6   EXERCISE 5.1: THE RASPBERRY PI LEDS & BUTTONS

You can now configure microprocessor boards and interact with basic components, including pushbuttons and LEDs as inputs and outputs. In addition, the use of pull-up and pull-down resistors and the corresponding digital states, high and low, are better understood. As such, the exercise below is designed to test your understanding of developing electronic circuits by interfacing and connecting simple components with a microprocessor board and programming the board to receive and input and produce an output. For this exercise, you are to develop a system with the following requirements.

Hold the pushbutton to blink LED 1 while LED 2 is switched on. When the button is released, LED 2 should blink while LED 1 is switched off. Using the components suggested below, develop the corresponding electronic circuit and Python program required for the proposed system.

Equipment
- Raspberry Pi 4 Model B
- Red LED (LED 1)
- Blue LED (LED 2)
- Pushbutton
- 1 kΩ resistor ×2
- Breadboard
- Jumper cables

5.4.7   PROJECT 5.6: THE LIGHT INTENSITY SENSOR (RPI)

This project demonstrates how to interface a light intensity sensor or photoresistor to a microprocessor board to measure light intensity. However, since the Raspberry Pi board does not include an analogue port, unlike the Arduino board, it cannot measure light intensity in terms of Lux. This can only be done by reading the analogue values and converting them to Lux readings using the corresponding calculation.

Fortunately, the GL55 light intensity sensor includes a digital output that can be connected to the GPIO pins on the Raspberry Pi board. However, using this method, the light intensity measurement is limited to bright and dark readings as digital signals only have two conditions. The sensitivity of the photoresistor for digital output can be adjusted using the built-in potentiometer on the circuit board.

Equipment
- Raspberry Pi 4 Model B
- GL55 light intensity sensor
- Breadboard
- Jumper cables

Connections
- Connect the **VCC** leg of GL55 to pin **5 V** on the Raspberry Pi board.
- Connect the **D0** leg of GL55 to pin **16** on the Raspberry Pi board.
- Connect the **GND** leg of GL55 to pin **GND** on the Raspberry Pi board (Figures 5.23 and 5.24).

Circuit

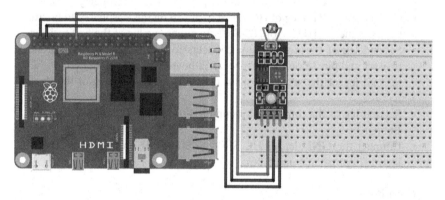

FIGURE 5.23   Circuit diagram connections for Project 5.6.

Script

```
import RPi.GPIO as GPIO                              #import Raspberry Pi GPIO module
from time import sleep                               #import sleep function from time module

GPIO.setmode(GPIO.BOARD)                             #board pin numbering
GPIO.setup(16, GPIO.IN, pull_up_down=GPIO.PUD_UP)    #set pin 16 as input and enable internal pull-up resistor

try:
    while True:                                      #loop function
        if GPIO.input(16) == False:
            print ('Bright')
        else:
            print ('Dark')
        sleep(0.2)
except:
    GPIO.cleanup()
```

FIGURE 5.24   Python script for Project 5.6.

5.4.8 PROJECT 5.7: THE ULTRASONIC DISTANCE SENSOR (RPi)

This project demonstrates how to interface an ultrasonic sensor to a microprocessor board for measuring distance. The output signal (echo) from the HC-SR04 ultrasonic sensor is rated at 5 V. However, the GPIO pins on the Raspberry Pi board are rated at 3.3 V. Sending a 5 V signal into the unprotected 3.3 V pin could damage the GPIO pins. Thus, the signal output of the HC-SR04 ultrasonic sensor needs to be converted from 5 to 3.3 V so as not to damage the Raspberry Pi board. As such, a voltage divider circuit, consisting of three resistors, to lower the HC-SR04 ultrasonic sensor output signal voltage is required.

Equipment
- Raspberry Pi 4 Model B
- HC-SR04 ultrasonic distance sensor
- 1 kΩ resistor ×3
- Breadboard
- Jumper cables

Connections
- Connect the **VCC** leg of HC-SR04 to pin **5 V** on the Raspberry Pi board.
- Connect the **TRIG** leg of HC-SR04 to pin **16** on the Raspberry Pi board.
- Connect the **ECHO** leg of HC-SR04 to either one leg of the first resistor.
- Second leg of the first resistor connects to the first leg of the second resistor and pin **18** on the Raspberry Pi board.
- Second leg of the second resistor connects to the first leg of the third resistor.
- Second leg of the third resistor connects to pin **GND** on the Raspberry Pi board.
- Connect the **GND** leg of HC-SR04 to pin **GND** on the Raspberry Pi board (Figures 5.25 and 5.26).

Circuit

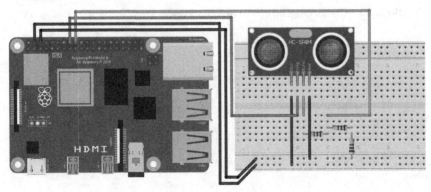

FIGURE 5.25 Circuit diagram connections for Project 5.7.

Script

```
import RPi.GPIO as GPIO                          #import Raspberry Pi GPIO module
import time                                       #import time module

GPIO.setmode(GPIO.BOARD)                         #board pin numbering
TRIG = 16
ECHO = 18
GPIO.setup(TRIG, GPIO.OUT)                       #set TRIG as output
GPIO.setup(ECHO, GPIO.IN)                        #set ECHO as input

while True:
    GPIO.output(TRIG, False)                     #short low pulse to ensure clean high pulse
    time.sleep(1)
    GPIO.output(TRIG, True)                      #short high pulse of 10 microseconds
    time.sleep(0.00001)
    GPIO.output(TRIG, False)

    while GPIO.input(ECHO) == 0:                 #save start time
        StartTime = time.time()
    while GPIO.input(ECHO) == 1:                 #save end time
        StopTime = time.time()

    TimeElapsed = StopTime-StartTime             #time difference between start and end
    distance = (TimeElapsed/2)*34300             #convert travel time to distance
    distance = round(distance,2)

    print ('Distance = '), distance, (' cm')     #display distance values
    time.sleep(1)                                #refresh data every 1 second

GPIO.cleanup()
```

FIGURE 5.26 Python script for Project 5.7.

5.4.9 PROJECT 5.8: THE DHT11 TEMPERATURE AND HUMIDITY SENSOR (RPi)

This project demonstrates how to interface a DHT11 sensor to a microprocessor board to measure ambient temperature and humidity. The DHT11 requires the Adafruit DHT library to retrieve the required information.

Installing the DHT sensor library by Adafruit
- First, update the package lists and install a few Python libraries.
    sudo apt-get update
    sudo apt-get install build-essential python-dev
- Then clone the Adafruit DHT library from the repository.
    git clone https://github.com/adafruit/Adafruit_Python_DHT.git
    cd Adafruit_Python_DHT
- Then install the library for Python and Python 3.
    sudo python setup.py install
    sudo python3 setup.py install

Equipment
- Raspberry Pi 4 Model B
- DHT11 temperature and humidity sensor
- Breadboard
- Jumper cables

Connections
- Connect the + leg of DHT11 to pin **5 V** on the Raspberry Pi board.
- Connect the **OUT** leg of DHT11 to pin **16** on the Raspberry Pi board.
- Connect the − leg of DHT11 to pin **GND** on the Raspberry Pi board (Figures 5.27 and 5.28).

Circuit

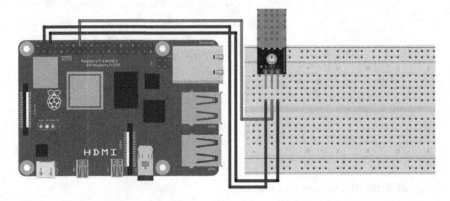

FIGURE 5.27   Circuit diagram connections for Project 5.8.

Script

```
import Adafruit_DHT                                              #import DHT sensor module
from time import sleep                                          #import sleep function from time module

sensor_type=Adafruit_DHT.DHT11                                  #define sensor type
sensor_gpio=23                                                  #define sensor gpio (Broadcom SoC pin numbering)

while True:
    humidity, temperature = Adafruit_DHT.read_retry(sensor_type, sensor_gpio)   #get sensor readings using module functions
    print('Temp={0:0.1f}*C  Humidity={1:0.1f}%'.format(temperature, humidity))  #display sensor values
    sleep(2)                                                    #refresh data every 2 seconds
```

FIGURE 5.28   Python script for Project 5.8.

5.4.10 PROJECT 5.9: SENSOR–ACTUATOR INTERACTIONS (RPI)

In addition to simple retrieving and displaying sensor data to monitor specific parameters, we can also develop automated systems that can control other components and actuators based on sensor values and corresponding user-set thresholds.

This interactive system forms a feedback loop that continuously monitors a specific parameter and produces an automated output when the pre-set range is exceeded. As an extension to Project 5.7, this project will guide you in developing a system that monitors the distance to an object and sounds a buzzer when the object gets too close to the sensor.

This principle is utilized in a car reverse sensor system that monitors the distance to an object and beeps when the object gets too close to the rear of the car.

In this example, the buzzer will be activated when the object is less than 15 cm away from the sensor. Since an active buzzer is utilized, a simple high/low digital signal will sound the buzzer.

Equipment
- Raspberry Pi 4 Model B
- HC-SR04 ultrasonic distance sensor
- Active piezoelectric buzzer
- Breadboard
- Jumper cable

Connections
- Connect the **VCC** leg of HC-SR04 to pin **5 V** on the Raspberry Pi board.
- Connect the **TRIG** leg of HC-SR04 to pin **16** on the Raspberry Pi board.
- Connect the **ECHO** leg of HC-SR04 to either one leg of the first resistor.
- Second leg of the first resistor connects to the first leg of the second resistor and pin **18** on the Raspberry Pi board.
- Second leg of the second resistor connects to the first leg of the third resistor.
- Second leg of the third resistor connects to pin **GND** on the Raspberry Pi board.
- Connect the **GND** leg of HC-SR04 to pin **GND** on the Raspberry Pi board.
- Connect the **VCC** leg of buzzer to pin **5 V** on the Raspberry Pi board.
- Connect the **I/O** leg of buzzer to pin **22** on the Raspberry Pi board.
- Connect the **GND** leg of buzzer to pin **GND** on the Raspberry Pi board.
- Use common **5 V** and **GND** pins on the Raspberry Pi board (Figures 5.29 and 5.30).

Circuit

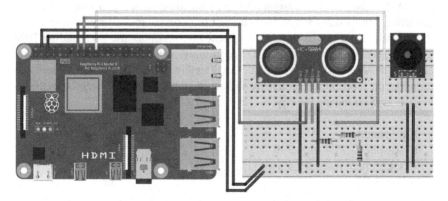

FIGURE 5.29   Circuit diagram connections for Project 5.9.

Script

```
import RPi.GPIO as GPIO                              #import Raspberry Pi GPIO module
import time                                          #import time module

GPIO.setmode(GPIO.BOARD)                             #board pin numbering
TRIG = 16
ECHO = 18
BUZZ = 22
GPIO.setup(TRIG, GPIO.OUT)                           #set TRIG as output
GPIO.setup(ECHO, GPIO.IN)                            #set ECHO as input
GPIO.setup(BUZZ, GPIO.OUT, initial=GPIO.LOW)         #set buzzer as output and initial value low (off)

while True:
    GPIO.output(TRIG, False)                         #short low pulse to ensure clean high pulse
    time.sleep(1)
    GPIO.output(TRIG, True)                          #short high pulse of 10 microseconds
    time.sleep(0.00001)
    GPIO.output(TRIG, False)

    while GPIO.input(ECHO) == 0:                      #save start time
        StartTime = time.time()
    while GPIO.input(ECHO) == 1:                      #save end time
        StopTime = time.time()

    TimeElapsed = StopTime-StartTime                 #time difference between start and end
    distance = (TimeElapsed/2)*34300                 #convert travel time to distance
    distance = round(distance,2)

    print('Distance = '), distance, (' cm')          #display distance values
    time.sleep(1)                                    #refresh data every 1 second

    if distance < 15:
        GPIO.output(BUZZ, GPIO.HIGH)                 #switch buzzer on
    else:
        GPIO.output(BUZZ, GPIO.LOW)                  #switch buzzer off
GPIO.cleanup()
```

FIGURE 5.30   Python script for Project 5.9.

5.4.11   EXERCISE 5.2: THE RASPBERRY PI AUTONOMOUS SYSTEMS

Based on the previous projects, you can now interface digital sensors with microprocessor boards and retrieve sensor data either directly or using pre-defined libraries. In addition, you are also able to develop interactive systems that can automatically control components based on sensor values and corresponding user-set thresholds.

The exercise below is designed to test your understanding of interfacing and retrieving sensor data, which is then used to produce an automated output. For this exercise, you are to develop a system that monitors the surrounding light intensity level and controls an LED accordingly, switches it off when it is bright and on when it is dark. This principle is utilized in a streetlight sensor system that monitors the ambient light intensity and automatically switches on the streetlights at night and off during the day.

Equipment
- Raspberry Pi 4 Model B
- GL55 light intensity sensor
- Red LED
- 1 kΩ resistor
- Breadboard
- Jumper cables

5.5 HANDS-ON PROJECTS: RASPBERRY PI-BASED IoT SYSTEMS

As discussed in the earlier chapters, we can develop IoT systems for *Remote Monitoring* and *Remotely Monitored/Controlled Autonomous Systems*. In this section, we introduce Raspberry Pi-based implementations of these systems, using Raspberry Pi boards, compatible hardware, and Linux-supported frameworks and technologies.

5.5.1 PROJECT 5.10: IoT REMOTE MONITORING SYSTEMS (RPI)

As an extension to Project 5.7, this project will guide you in developing an IoT remote monitoring system that retrieves temperature and humidity information from a DHT11 sensor and uploads the data to a cloud server via a Wi-Fi network.

Readers will learn to configure the IoT platform and corresponding application programming interface (API) to broadcast sensor data to cloud servers as well as set up an IoT client to view this information via a dashboard (Gibbs, 2016).

5.5.1.1 Configuring the Dweet.io IoT Platform

Dweet.io is a simple publishing and subscription service, also known as a *cloud server*, for machines, sensors, robots, and devices, collectively known as *things*. By using the Dweet.io IoT platform, messages are published as dweets, synonymous with tweets on Twitter. Each thing is assigned a unique thing name, and a thing may be subscribed to, which is analogous to following someone on Twitter.

Dweet.io enables the machine and sensor data to become publicly accessible through the Internet, allowing for simple data sharing. Dweet.io supports sending data in JavaScript Object Notation (JSON) format, so our dweets will contain a JSON object with a few attributes, which in this case is our sensor data. The Python module for Dweet.io is Dweepy, which can be installed using the command **sudo pip install dweepy**.

Based on Figure 5.31, the first step to publishing sensor data using the Dweet. io IoT platform is to import the Dweepy module. Next, the sensor data, in this case, temperature and humidity information, are packaged into an array, namely *iot_data*. The custom thing name, for instance, *iot_dht11*, allows the IoT client to accurately determine and retrieve the specific information once it is published to the cloud server. Dweet.io creates a JSON format that can be easily parsed by the IoT client to display the required information.

Equipment
- Raspberry Pi 4 Model B
- DHT11 temperature and humidity sensor
- Breadboard
- Jumper cables

Connections
- Connect the + leg of DHT11 to pin **5V** on the Raspberry Pi board.
- Connect the **OUT** leg of DHT11 to pin **16** on the Raspberry Pi board.
- Connect the − leg of DHT11 to pin **GND** on the Raspberry Pi board (Figure 5.32).

Circuit

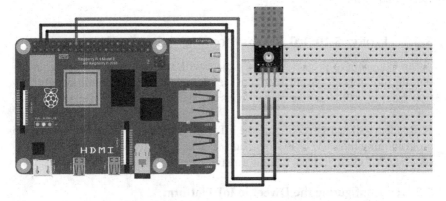

FIGURE 5.31   Circuit diagram connections for Project 5.10.

Script

```
import Adafruit_DHT                                    #import DHT sensor module
from time import sleep                                 #import sleep function from time module
import dweepy                                          #import Dweet.io module for Python

sensor_type=Adafruit_DHT.DHT11                         #define sensor type
sensor_gpio=23                                         #define sensor gpio (Broadcom SoC pin numbering)

while True:
    humidity, temperature = Adafruit_DHT.read_retry(sensor_type, sensor_gpio)  #get sensor readings using module functions
    print('Temp={0:0.1f}*C  Humidity={1:0.1f}%'.format(temperature, humidity)) #display sensor values
    iot_data = {'Temperature': temperature, 'Humidity': humidity}              #package sensor data in array
    dweepy.dweet_for('iot_dht11', iot_data)                                    #publish sensor data
    sleep(2)                                                                   #refresh data every 2 seconds
```

FIGURE 5.32   Python script for Project 5.10.

5.5.1.2   Configuring the Freeboard.io IoT Client

Freeboard.io is an open-source, cloud-based IoT client that converts dweet data streams into real-time, interactive visualizations and dashboards. Freeboard.io allows us to build a dashboard by selecting data sources and dragging and dropping customizable widgets to visualize the IoT data. It is a subscription-based paid service with a free 30-day trial period.

Setting up the Freeboard.io dashboard
1. Create a free account at Freeboard.io. https://freeboard.io/.
2. On the My Dashboards page, create a new dashboard.

3. Select Add under Datasources and add the required information.
4. Select Add Pane and select+in the pane.
5. Select Gauge widget type and add the required information.
6. In the Value column, select +Datasource.
7. Select Temperature and Humidity Monitor and select Temperature.
8. Select save, and the dashboard will display the temperature gauge widget.
9. Repeat steps 4–8 to add a second widget for displaying humidity information.

Note: The Thing Name under Datasources must correspond with the Python script (iot_dht11) (Figures 5.33 and 5.34).

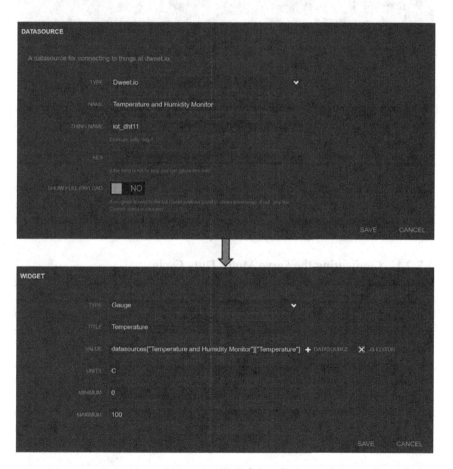

FIGURE 5.33 Configuring the Freeboard.io IoT Client.

Output

FIGURE 5.34   System output viewed via Freeboard.io IoT Client.

5.5.2 PROJECT 5.11: IoT REMOTELY OPERATED AUTONOMOUS SYSTEMS (RPI)

This project will guide you in developing an IoT remote control system that rotates a servo motor based on user inputs from the IoT client.

The IoT client, accessed via a mobile application, receives user input from a button widget, converts the input into command values, and transmits this information over a Wi-Fi network to the Raspberry Pi board.

From these commands, the Raspberry Pi will rotate the servo between two positions (0°/180°) based on the corresponding button state (on/off). The low-power servo motor can be powered directly from the board and does not require an external power supply.

5.5.2.1 Configuring the Servo Motor Duty Cycle

As discussed in Chapter 4, we understand that a conventional servo motor expects to receive a pulse roughly every 20 ms, or 50 Hz, and the length of the pulse determines the position of the servo motor. Thus, pulses ranging between 0.5 and 2.5 ms will move the servo shaft through the entire 180° of travel, though this may sometimes vary with different brands.

If the pulse is high for 0.5 ms, then the servo angle will be zero. If the pulse is high for 1.5 ms, then the servo will be at its centre position, or 90°. If the pulse is high for 2.5 ms, then the servo will be at 180°. This translates to about 2.5%–12.5% duty in a 50 Hz PWM cycle. We start with a 2.5% duty cycle so that the servo rotates to 0° startup. When the button is off, the duty cycle is set to 2.5%. When the button is toggled on, the duty cycle is set to 12.5% so that the servo rotates to 180°.

5.5.2.2 Configuring the Blynk IoT Client

At the moment, Blynk does not support newer Raspberry Pi hardware. Thus, we will be using a Raspberry Pi 3 Model B board for this example. To connect the

Raspberry Pi to the Blynk Cloud, the Blynk Python Library package must first be installed using the command **sudo pip install blynklib**.

- Download the Blynk application from the Apple App Store or Google Play Store.
- Launch the application and create a new user account with your email and password.
- Select New Project and add the project name.
- Choose device Raspberry Pi 3 B and connection type Wi-Fi and select Create.
- A custom authentication token for the project will be sent to your registered email.
- Select the+icon in the top right-hand corner of the screen to view all available widgets.
- Select the Button widget and hold down on it to resize or set the position.
- Tap the widget, select Output, choose Virtual V1, and set Mode to Switch.
- Tap the back button, then select the play icon in the top right-hand corner of the screen.

Note: The Push mode requires users to hold down on the button to turn on, while the Switch mode works like a toggle, press once to turn on and press once to turn off (Figure 5.35).

Equipment
- Raspberry Pi 3 Model B
- SG90 micro servo motor
- Jumper cables

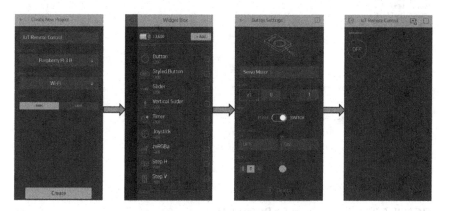

FIGURE 5.35 Configuring the Blynk IoT Client.

Connections
- Connect **Power** pin of servo motor to pin **5 V** on the Raspberry Pi board.
- Connect **Ground** pin of servo motor to pin **GND** on the Raspberry Pi board.
- Connect **Command** pin of servo motor to pin **16** on the Raspberry Pi board (Figures 5.36 and 5.37).

Circuit

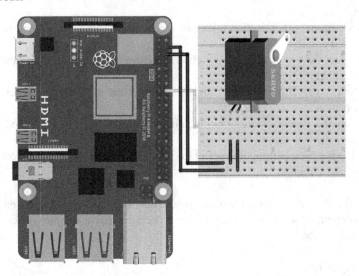

FIGURE 5.36   Circuit diagram connections for Project 5.11.

Script

```
import RPi.GPIO as GPIO                      #import Raspberry Pi GPIO module
import time                                  #import time module
import blynklib                              #import Blynk Python Library module

GPIO.setwarnings(False)
GPIO.setmode(GPIO.BCM)                       #Broadcom SoC pin numbering
GPIO.setup(23, GPIO.OUT)                     #set pin 23 as output

pwm=GPIO.PWM(23,50)                          #define variable pwm pin 23 and frequency 50 Hz
pwm.start(2.5)                               #define variable pwm start point 2.5 duty cycle (0 degrees)

auth_key = 'input here'                      #Blynk authentication key
blynk = blynklib.Blynk(auth_key)            #initialize Blynk IoT client

@blynk.handle_event('write V1')              #send data from button widget to servo
def write_handler_pin_handler(pin, value):
    button_state = (format(value[0]))
    if button_state == "0":
        pwm.ChangeDutyCycle(2.5)             #button open (not pressed), 0 degrees
    elif button_state == "1":
        pwm.ChangeDutyCycle(12.5)            #button close (pressed), 180 degrees
try:
    while True:
        blynk.run()                          #run Blynk IoT client service

GPIO.cleanup()
```

FIGURE 5.37   Python script for Project 5.11.

5.5.3 EXERCISE 5.3: THE RASPBERRY PI-BASED IOT SYSTEMS

By following along with the previous projects, you are now able to retrieve information via sensors, utilize these sensor readings to automate control of specific outputs, and broadcast the sensor data to IoT clients for remote monitoring.

With this knowledge at hand, for the next exercise, you are required to develop an IoT system to monitor the surrounding light intensity level. In addition to retrieving and broadcasting sensor data to the IoT client, the system should also automatically switch on an LED when it is dark. This combination of features will form an autonomous IoT remote monitoring system, which is the end goal of this section.

Equipment
- Raspberry Pi 4 Model B
- GL55 photoresistor
- Red LED
- 1 kΩ resistor
- Breadboard
- Jumper cables

REFERENCES

Ashwin. (2019). *Geany Is a Programmer Friendly Open Source Text Editor for Windows, Linux, macOS – gHacks* Tech News. GHacks. https://www.ghacks.net/2019/10/31/geany-is-a-programmer-friendly-open-source-text-editor-for-windows-linux-macos/

Brodkin, J. (2017). *New $10 Raspberry Pi Zero Comes with Wi-Fi and Bluetooth.* ArsTechnica. https://arstechnica.com/information-technology/2017/02/new-10-raspberry-pi-zero-comes-with-wi-fi-and-bluetooth/

Cambell, S. (2021). *42 of the Most Useful Raspberry Pi Commands.* Circuit Basics. https://www.circuitbasics.com/useful-raspberry-pi-commands/

Gibbs, M. (2016). *dweet.io: A Simple, Effective Messaging Service for the Internet of Things.* Network World. https://www.networkworld.com/article/3133738/dweetio-a-simple-effective-messaging-service-for-the-internet-of-things.html

Gus. (2016). *Raspberry Pi ADC (Analog to Digital Converter) – Pi My Life Up.* Pi My Life Up. https://pimylifeup.com/raspberry-pi-adc/

Heath, N. (2018). *Raspberry Pi 3 Model A+ Review: A $25 Computer with a Lot of Promise.* Tech Republic. https://www.techrepublic.com/article/raspberry-pi-3-model-a-review-a-25-computer-with-a-lot-of-promise/

Piltch, A. (2020). *Raspberry Pi 4: Review, Buying Guide and How to Use.* Tom's Hardware. https://www.tomshardware.com/reviews/raspberry-pi-4

RPI Camera Module. (2021). *Raspberry Pi Documentation.* https://www.raspberrypi.org/documentation/hardware/camera/

RPi Touch Display. (2021). *Raspberry Pi Documentation.* https://www.raspberrypi.org/documentation/hardware/display/

Taylor, M., & Blom, J. (2021). *Raspberry gPIo – learn.sparkfun.com.* SparkFun. https://learn.sparkfun.com/tutorials/raspberry-gpio/python-rpigpio-api

Watson, J. A. (2020). *Hands on with the New Raspberry Pi OS Release: Here's What You Need to Know.* ZD Net. https://www.zdnet.com/article/hands-on-with-the-new-raspberry-pi-os-release-heres-what-you-need-to-know/

Closing Remarks

Now that you have covered all chapters of this book, you are ready to embark on your Internet of Things (IoT) journey. You can begin by looking inwards at your organization, your institution, your home, your research, your country, and start from there.

Ask yourself, how can IoT benefit my organization? How can I improve efficiency? Better utilize data? Or even generate a new source of income? What kind of data would I need? Before you know it, you will find yourself implementing the step-by-step IoT processes discussed in Chapter 1.

You can also continue to learn IoT; perhaps you can re-implement the hands-on work using your hardware, perhaps your own controllers or different sensors, or your own system or machine. Perhaps you can work on Advanced Data Analytics algorithms and apply different languages, techniques, online libraries, and much more. The possibilities are endless.

We hope that this book contributes to your growth and that you never stop learning and tinkering. In the end, we hope this book helps you achieve success in IoT and related technologies.

We wish you all the best,
The authors

Index

Printed in the United States
by Baker & Taylor Publisher Services